THE
DUBLIN
DOCKER

THE
DUBLIN
DOCKER

Working Lives of Dublin's Deep-Sea Port

AILEEN O'CARROLL & DON BENNETT

IRISH ACADEMIC PRESS

First published in 2017 by
Irish Academic Press
10 George's Street
Newbridge
Co. Kildare
Ireland
www.iap.ie

9781911024842 (Paper)
9781911024866 (Kindle)
9781911024873 (Epub)
9781911024835 (PDF)

British Library Cataloguing in Publication Data
An entry can be found on request

Library of Congress Cataloging in Publication Data
An entry can be found on request

Interior design by www.jminfotechindia.com
Typeset in Adobe Garamond Pro 11/15

Cover design by edit+ www.stuartcoughlan.com

Front cover: Dockers standing between the No. 9 and the No. 10 sheds, c. 1960s. Left to right: Gabriel Downey, William 'Lonnie' Donovan, Thomas 'Tucker' Murphy, Gilmoro Redmond and Paddy Downey. (Donated by Aisling Murphy from Brian Murphy's collection to the Dublin Dock Workers' Preservation Society)

Back cover: Dockers unloading a cargo of Kellog's Cornflakes at the North Wall, Dublin, 4 June 1954. (© Irish Photo Archive; http://www.irishphotoarchive.ie)

Back flap: On a timber boat. Front from left: Paddy Daly, 'Gandhi' Savage and Strannie Fitzsimons. (Donated by Christy Fitzsimons to the Dublin Dock Workers Preservation Society)

Comhairle Cathrach
Bhaile Átha Cliath
Dublin City Council

This publication has been supported by Dublin City Council Heritage Office.

CONTENTS

ACKNOWLEDGEMENTS

We would like to thank Mr Liam Mc Ginn and the Association of Dublin Stevedores who commissioned the initial study. Their support allowed researcher Anne Stakelum to expertly conduct rich and descriptive interviews that captured the experiences of the last generation of traditional dockers. We would like to thank her for her important and necessary contribution to the project and Claire Kenny for research assistance. The members of The Dublin Dockworkers Preservation Society have been consistently welcome and open. In particular we would like to thank Alan Martin for allowing us to reprint many of the photographs from their collection and Declan P. Byrne for his support and insightful comments on our early drafts. This publication has been supported by Dublin City Council Heritage Office. The Dublin Port Company and Maynooth University are also thanked for their support, which enabled us to include these photographs.

Aileen O'Carroll would like to give particular thanks to Don's wife, Valerie McCarthy, and daughter, Aoife Bennett-Curry, for their support and encouragement. All books depend on the kindness of readers, so I would like to thank Harriet O'Carroll, Dermot Sreenan, Andrew Flood and Jane Gray for reviewing chapters as they progressed. I would like to thank Conor Graham and Fiona Dunne of Irish Academic Press, it has been a pleasure working with them.

In memory of my father, Gerry O'Carroll, 26/3/1941–22/11/2015.

INTRODUCTION

THE DUBLIN DOCKER

Aileen O'Carroll and Don Bennett

This book is a social and occupational history of the Dublin docker from the mid-nineteenth century to the 1970s. Drawing from ethnographic interviews with dock workers, minutes and documents produced by docker and stevedore organisations, folklore archives and secondary sources, our aim is to create a rich description of a working life and culture which was central to the life of Dublin city.

In 2008, Fintan Lane, editor of the *Irish Journal of Labour History* argued that 'the history of the Irish working class, like many facets of Irish social history, remains under-researched'.[1] There is surprisingly little written on occupational practices, work culture or casual labour in Ireland. The *Irish Journal of Labour History* is significant in focusing on labour issues, though the emphasis slants towards strike and political activity in the late nineteenth and early twentieth century with less on occupational culture.[2] From within the trade union movement a number of institutional histories have been produced.[3] The linen industry in the eighteenth century is the focus of an innovative study by Jane Gray and in the early twentieth century by Betty Messenger.[4] Miriam Nyhan has written on the experience of industrial workers in a Ford factory and a number of very valuable oral histories focusing on women's work have been produced in recent years documenting women's working experiences in Belfast, Dublin and in the home.[5] The interplay of class and community in small-town Ireland are given in

Marilyn Silverman's study on Thomastown in Co. Kilkenny and in the sadly out of print *The ruling trinity: a community study of church, state and business in Ireland* by Chris Eipper which describes life in Bantry, Co. Cork.[6]

Yet these studies are rare. There is a notable absence of a more sustained scholarship on work and the part it plays in Irish society. This is strange, as work not only takes much of our days, weeks and years but our work shapes our experience of life and our relationship with others. Is it because Ireland with little heavy industry and few mines, had few of the occupations that drew attention from researchers in other countries? Dock work has been extensively studied in other countries, yet not in Ireland.[7] Indeed Irish dockers feature strongly in research on international ports.[8] Is it that here the story of low-skilled casual work on the margins of respectable society does not appeal as a research subject? Is it the persistent influence of a nationalist myth that emphasises an idealistic rural society and hides urban and class divisions? Lane suggests class, within elite political culture, is 'wishfully dismissed as irrelevant in the Irish contract' and calls for a vision of labour history which breaks from the narrow bounds of solely trade unions activity, arguing instead that it is necessary to 'embrace the entire history of the working class, from politics to leisure, from workplace behaviour to family relations, from socio-economic conditions to socio-cultural values'.[9] We have endeavoured to be true to this vision in this book.

Overview of Dock Work in Dublin

Dockers in Dublin tended to specialise in one of two areas of work, the cross-channel dockers and the deep-sea. The cross-channel men worked the ships trading regularly between Dublin and London, Bristol, Liverpool, Glasgow and other British ports. The deep sea docker handled ships at the end of the Liffey, at Alexandra Basin, the North Wall Extension and Ocean Pier. Also working on the port were the cargo checkers, storemen, crane operators, timber and coal workers, warehousemen and boatmen.[10] Dublin Port was primarily an import

port, which as we will see in Chapter 2, meant that dockers were mostly charged with unloading ships.[11]

In the early years of the twentieth century, dockers were better paid than other labourers, if they managed to obtain a full week's work. However, as this book will illustrate, dockers were hired on a daily basis.[12] The Second World War was followed by an increase in direct trade in countries other than the United Kingdom. Interviewees suggested that at this point dockers in Dublin began to specialise in either cross-channel work or deep-sea work. This specialisation was probably linked to the introduction of two voluntary registers of dock workers in 1947, one for cross-channel and coal-trade dockers, the other for those in the deep-sea section. As we will see in Chapter 1, those whose names were on the registers were known as buttonmen and were given priority of employment. The second major change to dock work was decasualisation, that is, the permanent hiring of dock workers with a guaranteed weekly age. This was first introduced in 1961 for cross-channel dockers and in 1971 for the deep-sea section. In return for its introduction the dockers agreed to an end of a ban on the use of containers and a reduction in numbers employed through early retirement and redundancies.[13] The book ends in 1971 as the introduction of containers fundamentally changed dock work. It marked the beginning of the end of the traditional docker, his occupational culture and the docks as a significant Dublin employer.[14]

One of the most frequent questions asked of us is how many people worked on the docks. For many reasons this is a difficult question to answer, more than any other trade or industry. The numbers employed varied on 'a day-to-day, week-to-week, season-to-season and year-to-year' basis.[15] For example, if we look at the average figures for 1947, we find that the lowest number employed in a week was 235 and the highest 811.[16] The peak and trough months varied according to the cargos and was not consistent year on year.[17] Additionally, while it was possible at certain phases to know how many dockers were in receipt of a button, there was no complete registration of all who worked on the docks.

Employment figures can be found by looking at newspaper reports. These figures can best be considered as very broad estimations, as we have no sense of where the journalist writing the article obtained them. In terms of strike reports, did they ask the union how many would be affected by the strike? Did they ask all the various stevedores how much labour they would require for the duration of the strike period? Keeping these caveats in mind we find that in 1922 *The Irish Times* reported that 5,000 dockers and coal workers were likely to be affected by a proposed strike.[18] A Labour Court report on dock employment, using a different metric, suggested that there were 1,933 dockers in 1947, and 2,696 in 1948. Of those, 1,250 were registered dockers 420 deep sea, 280 chiefly coal dockers and 550 in the cross-channel.[19] In 1957 *The Irish Times* reported that 'in normal times there are approximately 2,000 dockers at work each day in the various parts of the port'.[20] A report commissioned by Dublin Port indicated that in 1961 there were 2,000 dockers equally split between both sides. By 1973 this had dropped to 750 (200 cross-channel, 550 deep-sea).[21] The impact of containers on employment figures was dramatic.

Over the twentieth century, though the tonnage of goods handled by the ports increased, the numbers employed decreased. However, until the introduction of containers, Dublin Port provided work for a significant proportion of the male working-class population of Dublin. The loss of such a significant employer was to have a devastating impact on the dockland communities.[22] Although it was clear that jobs would be lost as new technologies were adopted, no provisions or plans were put in place to provide alternative employment or support. We are in a similar place today, as again we are warned that technological advances will bring with them the threat of mass unemployment, yet as in the past, there is a sense that government and policymakers are absolving themselves of the problem.

Methodology

The core of this book is based on interviews conducted by Anne Stakelum with dockers, dockers' wives, stevedores and union representatives between 1995 and 1998.[23] The work was commissioned by the Association of Dublin Stevedores. Our starting point were interviews with Willie Murphy and Martin Mitten, both Ringsend dockers, and they introduced us to others dockers and their wives.

Many of the interviews took place in docker pubs, some in the interviewee's home and one as part of a walk along the south quays. The oldest interviewer began work on the docks in 1922 and a number had fathers who also worked as dockers and so recalled their memories of their father's experience. Most of the dockers interviewed by us were deep-sea dockers who were on the dockers register. Ringsend men had family connections to draw on. They were the most secure and best paid, in their own words the 'top dockers'.[24] Their relatively elite position within the occupational culture should be borne in mind. Don Bennett regularly attended the meetings of the *Dublin Dock Workers Preservation Society* for a number of years until his death in 2014. There he met with Brendan Dempsey, Mick Tierney and other retired dockers. Our own research was supplemented by fifty-six interviews drawn from other sources. The excellent archive of interviews collected by the North Inner City Folklore Project under the stewardship of Terry Fagan was particularly important as it contains many who were cross-channel dockers as well as dockers' wives and children. The oral histories conducted by Kevin C. Kearns were another invaluable source. Additionally we referred to interviews with ex-dockers which were conducted by UCD students Audrey Mac Cready, Josephine O'Connor, Anita Ní Nualláin, Louise Tobin, Neasa McHale and Ann Wade as part of their group thesis for the MLIS in 2013, the Bridge-IT project based in Trinity College Dublin, the National Folklore Archive at UCD, as well as an extensive interview with Des Brannigan conducted by Conor McCabe.

The 1901 census and 1911 census were also consulted for information pertaining to the earliest years of the twentieth century, as were historical accounts and newspaper reports of various union struggles. We also drew on the business records of the Association of Dublin Stevedores, which are in the UCD Archives, government reports in the National Archives, and the Irish Military Archives.

Economic information was obtained from reports of the Dublin Port and Docks Board, the Central Statistics Office and Thoms directories.

Overview

Chapter 1 focuses on the tradition of hiring daily labour at the 'read'. It discusses the location of the reads and the various strategies employed by the dockers in their pursuit of a day's work, including the importance of gang membership and family affinity. The uncertainty and stressful nature of this form of job hire is vividly described in cited oral history interviews. The chapter shows how in some instances, the inequities of this system was further exacerbated by an expectation of 'kickbacks', captured in dockers' lore by the tradition of leaving the drink. The transition, post-World War Two, to the 'button man' system is described. Although some long-time dock labourers were left out of the system, the button system provided job security to the core of dockers, and was less vulnerable to corruption.

Chapter 2 moves the focus from the windy quayside to the dark and crowded hold of the ship. It describes the skilled nature of dock work from the perspective of the commodities that were unloaded at Dublin docks and the tools used by the Dublin docker. The chapter begins with a description of the work done by 'coalies', dock workers who, wearing special boots called 'stingos', specialised in unloading coal. It describes the docker's tools of the trade such as the number seven shovel and the bag hook. Commodities imported through Dublin included timber, iron and copper ore, bricks, tea, coffee, cattle, the more pungent guano, and toys for Hector Grey's discount store. Each commodity was associated with a particular type of work and division of labour. 'Outside men' operated cranes, bogies, winches, and worked on gangplanks. 'Inside men' shovelled. Dockers required special skills, such as the creation of slings and hosts. Other roles, including tierer, tipper, toppers, checker, and singer-out are described. The dangerous aspects of dock work are illustrated by the often tragic events that dockers experienced.

In Chapter 3 we locate the Dublin docker within the history of Dublin as port city. It relates the changing shape and role of Dublin Port from medieval times to the 1970s. Silting of the Liffey made discharge at the quayside difficult, as ships could not negotiate the shallow channel. Dockers or fishermen rowed out to ships in the bay to unload or negotiate for unloading. From this work the occupation of hobbler was born. The emergence of the stevedore from hobbling is narrated. In the Irish context, the stevedore is the middleman who hires the labour and negotiates with the ship owner. The key Dublin stevedore families are introduced. The development of hobbling and stevedoring in Dublin is highly distinct in comparable occupational history. The chapter paints a vivid picture of the changing landscape of the docks.

Dockside labour relations and the long story of the dockers' trade union history, from their participation in the 1913 Dublin Lockout to the introduction of decasualisation and permanency are addressed in Chapter 4. The gang system, tight occupational communities and ship owners dependency on labour gave dockers leverage to influence the conditions and terms of employment. Trade union militancy, along with the daily experience of dock work and docklands community life, contribute to the rich dockers' tradition.

Our focus moves from the dockside to the home in Chapter 5, which considers the childhood and social life of those growing up with docker fathers. Dockers had large families and uncertain incomes. The strategies women used to manage household finances and avoid the ever-present threat of poverty are remembered. The work done by women, both in the home and in paid employment is highlighted as is how dockers met their wives and their families spent their leisure time.

In Chapter 6 we investigate the myth of the Dublin docker. In the wider society dockers had a reputation, virtually a status as hard-drinking men, and a source of potential trouble. The chapter explores how daily occupational life, language and lore were central to creating a sense of pride in their occupation and heritage. The rivalry between northside and southside dockers resulted in dark stories of riot, murder and the Animal Gang. Stories of gambling, dockside theft and pilfering, scams, and the ever-present pub, support the perception of the dockers as outside respectable society. On the other hand, there are lighter tales of rivalry expressed in quayside singing and docker's pride in participation on local football teams and boxing clubs.

Finally, in Chapter 7 we consider the essence of the tradition of the Dublin docker. What is it that makes the docker important in Dublin and unique in occupational culture?

In remembering the lives of generations of dock workers we hope to shed light both on the past but also on the present. With the demise of the Dublin docker, traditions established by generations of dock work were lost. Social history is important, as what we are today is partially shaped by those who came before us. Writing of his own working-class upbringing, academic Andy Medhurst reminds us that 'class is never simply a category of the present tense, it is a matter of history, a relationship with tradition, a discourse of roots'.[25] Dublin was formed in part on the docks. Arguably today's generation do not need to know how to lift a shovel containing stones of coal for hours on end, but they could benefit by relearning traditions of resistance, solidarity and community. Casual work, insecure housing and inequality is prevalent in today's Dublin, as is the damage these cause to mental and physical health. We can learn from the lives of Dublin dockers as they struggled, often with great wit and good humour, and in their resistance lies inspiration.

ONE

THE BUTTONMEN AND THE READ

> We were what you might call marathon runners;
> we could have qualified for marathons.[1]

The Read

Above, on an outdoor platform, a single figure stands, the sun not yet having risen over the harbour behind him. He is about to select the men who will be employed to work a cargo ship. A hundred or more men press round for the selection, or 'read'.[2] Other platforms are scattered throughout the Dublin waterfront at places with names like Crown Wall, Point Depot and 'Willies'. Troops of dockers are gathered at each site. The goal of the assembled, restless men is to be chosen for work. In the early morning light, the throng has gathered and swollen as men have arrived on foot from City Quay, from across the greater Sheriff Street area, and from Ringsend and similar neighbourhoods of central Dublin. Others have travelled from further away, from the Crumlin or Cabra districts of the city, on foot, by bike, bus or on the tram. Many have crossed in the half dark on the little wooden Liffey Ferry. The year is 1897, 1927, 1947 or 1967 – the employment system essentially the same through all that time span. The first read will start between twenty past and half past seven, though the crowd has been collecting since sometime earlier. By seven fifteen, thousands of dockers

Phil Carrick, Michael Carrick and Butch McDermott, opposite the Point Depot, 1950s. The Carricks were a prominent stevedore family. Here Butch McDermott is working as a checker, though he started life as a docker. (Donated by Dublin Stevedores to the Dublin Dock Workers Preservation Society)

will be on the Dublin wharfs, with hundreds around certain of the platforms.

Coal importers might have held their reads outside their offices all around the south quays: Tedcastles, MacLennons, Donnellys, Heitons and Dohertys were among the coal merchants of Dublin, all dependent on dockers' labour. Most often the selections for the colliers or coal ships were held at the gasometer, a high, round, prominent southside structure that stood behind Sir John Rodgerson's Quay until its demolition in 1993–94. At times, some of the dockers pushed for the collier reads to be transferred elsewhere, because, in the words of the port workers' own newspaper,

> the big gasometer causes strong freak winds to concentrate in the Cardiff Lane area, and a howling wind can make a line-up of employment anything but pleasant. We are sure this simple request will be attended to by the responsible people. Only a short distance is involved; and there is another winter coming![3]

That was in 1961. The gasometer continued to be a principal site for reads, however. The imposing stone warehouse known as Point Depot, 'the Point Store', or simply 'the Point', with its surrounding sett paving,

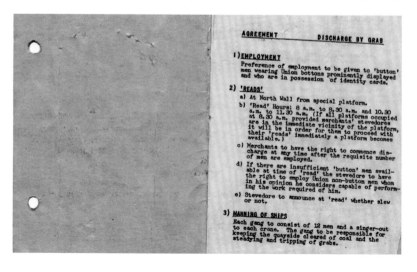

First page of agreement between MP&GWU, ITGWU and WUI, and The Society of Dublin Coal Importers, showing times of reads. (Donated by John Nolan to the Dublin Dock Workers Preservation Society)

now a major events centre, was the focal point of other read sites, adjacent to it or facing it on the quayside.

The dockers' names, or more usually their nicknames, were called. 'Seal', 'Oko', 'Salt Box', 'Big Bob', 'The Wire', 'Appler', and on, by name through to its completion, went many a read.[4] One stevedore of the 1940s and 1950s, who might be hiring 120 men at a read, is remembered for the ability to select virtually the first hundred by calling only nicknames[5]. At the other extreme were foremen who droned, 'You, you, you', while jabbing towards men with a rolled-up newspaper or a stabbing finger. As a variation on these forms of 'the you-you read', other foremen pointed a silent finger at their choices.

Number seven shovels and dockers. Left to right (seated): Barnie Moran, Owen Hoare, Big Paddy, Jonny Masterson and Miley Honer. (Donated by Peter Smith to the Dublin Dock Workers Preservation Society)

Because reads were held in a number of different locations, a daily choice was necessary for many men. The Custom House, Willies, Creighton Street, Spencer Dock, Cambridge Road: in which direction should one head? One prime consideration was to present yourself where you were already well known to the hiring company. If you were not chosen in one place, however, you might still race to another read. The docker needed good judgement – and some luck – in order to get to the most advantageous site on the day. More crucial than luck, however, was information. 'Dockers have enormous antennae,' said one supervisor. 'How they know is a mystery, but they always know when and why it's due and what cargo.'[6] Let us unravel some of that mystery.

Word regarding what ships were due by morning began to circulate in the dockland pubs each night. If this was not definitive information, come daylight knots of dockers would be found scanning the river mouth, from Butt Bridge or another vantage point, to see

Front row; Tommy Duffy, George Guiden, Andy Smullen. Middle row: Strannie Fitzsimons and Johnnie Barry. Back row; George Gray, c.1960. (Donated by Christy Fitzsimons to the Dublin Dock Workers Preservation Society)

which company had a ship docked. Or, one could call in to the 'seven o'clock shop', that is, recheck in the public houses that were open in the morning. An even better web of information is described by deep-sea docker Martin Mitten:

> Before the read, it would be around half seven, there would be one or two old dockers who would cycle around the port and they could tell you before the read at a quarter to eight or twenty minutes to eight that there was a ship up for Palgraves, there was one for Carricks, there was two up for George Bell, there was one up for Betson. And they could tell you where the ships were, and they could tell you what company they were for. They could also tell you how many ships were on the Crown Wall, how many were on the South Quay and who they were for … That gave the dockers the advantage of saying 'Well right, now there is only one ship for Palgrave Murphys; I wouldn't get a job in that from his three or four gangs. I wouldn't get a job there in Betson's. Paddy Nolan's, I might get a job there. George Bell: I'd fancy my chances there!'[7]

Once word got around, individuals headed for the platform or shipside where they felt they had the best chance. Reads for the day's ships were not entirely simultaneous. Availability of platforms, for example, meant the delay of some selections. Thus, those not picked at the first attempt could frequently make it to another site. Southside reads at Ringsend or the gasometer tended to be held before those on North Wall. Southside dockers often crossed northwards on the Liffey Ferry – or its predecessor, a privately operated rowboat – if not selected on their own side. Elbow-to-elbow with them on the crowded ferry might be northsiders who had already been ferried, without reward, once that day. Or dockers could race across Butt Bridge. Then, 'it would be a matter of jumping on a lorry going by, or jumping on a bike to get down as quick as you could in case that read wasn't over yet'[8]. As Martin Mitten said, 'The docker that had a bike was a millionaire: he was able to get up and down.'[9] Some of the 'millionaires' were even known to combine transport methods, putting the bike on the ferry. 'We were,' as deep-sea docker Willie Murphy put it, 'what you might call marathon runners. We could have qualified for marathons if we had went in for it.' Even so, often enough athletic prowess would still not get you to a second read before it had ended and your chances for the day were gone.

Beyond the base matter of merely getting work were other considerations. 'Peak jobs' of one sort were those which would lead to weekend overtime work. The 'half buzzer', half a day's work, finishing by midday, was the other extreme in terms of preference: the least desirable. One full day was a buzzer. Another preference involved the commodity to be worked. Among timber, fruit, coal, sand and the other commodities, individual deep-sea dockers had personal preferences. The contrasts and challenges involved in working the various commodities is the subject of Chapter 2.

A second, smaller, set of reads was often held at ten or half past ten. The routine was the same. The foremen 'would come along … and the men would congregate in front of them. They had a platform which would have been about four foot in height and they would mount that. And then they would be looking down on the men and they would read for whatever they required.'[10]

'Where they used to hang you'

The height of these platforms varied. Three to four feet high stood the lower sort. Just as often, however, the platform and its selector towered ten to twelve feet skyward, beneath which 'men would congregate like cattle in a paddock',[11] according to one deep-sea docker, 'looking up into the faces of the foremen, hoping to be selected for employment'.[12] The platform up at which you looked was 'very much like a hangman's', according to one of our interviewees: 'you remember – where they used to hang you'.[13]

Coal company agents and other selecting foremen might sometimes read from the shipside itself, looking down on the men amassed around the side of the ship on the quay wall. Such was particularly the mode in the centuries up until the early twentieth, when tides determined the time of the read. When ships could only enter the port at high tide,[14] men congregated at the ship where it tied up.

Dockers were hired in group units called gangs. Most ships required multiple gangs, as described in Chapter 2. The first group called at the read, the 'first gang', might have some choice of work on the ship or would be automatically designated to the most advantageous hatch. The first gang would often have a longer run of work time, for example, as work on a ship was finishing, only a smaller contingent of dockers was required to complete the work, so the first gang was always the gang that worked until completion, thus earning more money. The first gang was effectively equivalent to what was termed 'the best job', an expression officially appearing in formal docker labour/management relations documents.[15] Being picked early in the read was therefore

From the steps of the Custom House dockers could see what ships were docked. Loading dock crane can be seen in front of the sailing ship, c.1880-1900. Robert French photographer. (Image Courtesy of the National Library of Ireland, call no. L_CAB_00002)

everyone's hope. The first gang called was likely to be made up of men who daily appeared for the same employer. A single employing deputy might, however, be hiring for two or three ships, thus calling more than one first gang, second gang, etc. Deep-sea docker gangs will appear frequently in these pages, but for now we return to the read.

One docker always brought his dog to the read, in order to be that bit more conspicuous. The tactic possibly worked, but could hardly be adopted by all. For most dockers it was a case of 'putting up your head to try and catch the stevedore's attention'.[16]

There were very few ways that one might sneak into the work complement by cheating at the read. Joseph Quinn describes at least the following ploy:

> Now this lad, he would come in in the morning and he would always tell me to stand beside him because he was in the first gang. Then [the foreman] would call 'Quinn' and I would walk out with him, because I wasn't well known, you know.
>
> Now it used to happen to another fella, a fella called 'Mouse', and he had a brother and maybe a son. And there was three of them and the master stevedore would shout 'Mouse', and he would have the three of them walking out; and the stevedore would say: 'I said Mouse, not mice.'[17]

'Walking out' was, in general, the tactic of handing in your work papers, pretending you had been selected for a ship when you had not. This was a long shot indeed.

Uncertainty about daily work was a recurrent fact of docker life. In this respect, they differed from most workers. For most other workers, each day started pretty much like the last: half asleep or not, they would know where they were working and what they were going to do. In contrast, the docker's day started amid the jostle of a lot of people pushing for space, pushing for work. From a crowd of up to 500 men at a single read site on certain days, some would be chosen and some would not.

It was rather degrading to have to stand there and look up to a person and more or less beg for employment. And if you had done anything wrong on the previous day, low and behold, you didn't get picked. And you could stay there for long and many a day, and there was very, very little that you could do. There was nothing you could do, virtually.[18]

Some reads, in addition, were held in public places in view of passers-by. Jostling and shoving did sometimes occur.[19]

At a different kind of site for the read, according to docker Jem Kiernan, 'The men could be standing outside in the rain and [the foremen] would come out when it suited them to come out and pick the men for work.'[20] Despite the jostling at the reads and the large number of men on the quays, the mornings were not a raucous, clamorous time overall. Men joked in quiet tones. One participant's deepest memory of the day's beginning was of 'the inner silence of the damp mornings'.[21]

Even a read itself could be completely silent, as we have seen, with the foreman simply pointing. Still other foremen might add men to their work gang by growling to the individuals, 'Gimme your card.' Thus, at the read a man might feel that his worth is being decided upon. The boss would 'be up in the stand and he'd point "you, you, you, you" … He knew your name; [one foreman, for example] worked with me father, the whole lot. "You, you" – and you would be left out and you wouldn't get a job! It was very humiliating now.'[22]

It could get one down.

When you didn't get a job: the depression, that feeling. I don't know what it was … you couldn't believe that you were looking forward to getting a day's work and you don't get it.

You come up to a place and there is no work. You get two days one week, and the next week you mightn't get a day; you might be unlucky. The depression it put you in was terrible.[23]

Docker registration card, 1947. (Donated by Brendan Dempsey to the Dublin Dock Workers Preservation Society)

While success brought a nicely paid day's work, failure meant lengthy hanging about, from one read hour to the next, with nothing to show for the effort and time spent trying to get employment. One docker wrote this lilting rhyme:

> Down at the read by eight o'clock,
> And then again at ten,
> A visit to the bru,
> And back down again by two,
> The read it was a bad place,
> The system a disgrace.
> A good man could be left there,
> If they didn't like his face? [24]

Willie Murphy Junior's first job, in the early 1950s, was unloading a coal ship. He was 16 years old. He remembers going down to get his second day's work.

> Me mother bought me a pair of boots, out of that [first] job
> … And I never done another day's work! I wore the boots
> going up and down the docks looking for work, but I never
> got another day's work … They were big hobnailed boots
> for the next coal boat I was going to get. Jaysus … I got
> nothing again for that whole summer. There was over 1,000
> people down on the docks that time, so they had plenty to
> choose from … Every morning we went out a quarter to
> eight o'clock. Every day, we would go to the different yards
> and see if there was bit of work, see if the boats were up, but
> you were usually left standing there.

And this was the son of a popular deep-sea man.

When another docker first brought his son down to give him a taste of the scene, he took the lad to the read. The son's reaction was pointed. 'He said it was like slave labour. He wouldn't entertain it.' 'Cannon fodder',[25] 'degrading',[26] 'I hated being picked out like that',[27] 'humiliating':[28] expressions such as these were voiced on occasion by dockers, always about the read system. Such language might lead the listener to rather accept the analogy of the read to attendance at the scaffold 'where they used to hang you'.[29] Such a conclusion would be a mistake. Overall, dockers did not feel that they were in a degrading occupation, were not demoralised, and did not feel like slave labourers. They certainly did feel this way, it is clear, at low points in their working lives.

Wetness, as well as uncertainty, plagued the docker at the read, the Irish climate making outdoor waiting significantly uncomfortable. One might already have been soaked by rain on the trudge from home into the docklands, only to face more time in the open at the read. There were some, mainly abortive, attempts to draw the reads inside. For Dublin's Eucharistic Congress in 1932, a long shed was cleared of machinery and used to host Masses. This former storehouse then became a read room for a brief time. Its fate was similar to the purpose-built read room constructed at North Wall in 1959. The latter special building was used exactly once. The dockers thought the rooms too far from the main work zones, too small and too crowded; they feared they could not be visually picked out clearly enough by the foremen selectors (especially the man with the dog, presumably).

The port workers' paper kept at it, however, terming the 1959 read room experiment 'too niggardly in scale', and arguing that

> The dockers generally have shown monumental patience for a remarkably long period, and it is high time that their hardships were alleviated. Open air reads at the Wall End have long been a test of stamina; for the 'mainland' of North Wall Extension is exposed to all the winds that blow; and it is no joke on a bleak wintry morning to stand in driving sleet or rain to await employment.[30]

Another, later, shed-type read area and its tiny canteen was simply 'foul', according to one stevedore.[31] The rejected read rooms were each in their turn soon relegated to trade union or other organisational purposes.

There's Your Matches

A partial solution to the matter of obtaining work was to become part of an established group of men who essentially always worked together as a single unit. These ready-set and well-known gangs were often called whole, filling one full work crew for a ship. Though associated with a gang unit, at the read each man was still named individually. But the names coming up would be known to all once the foreman had started the read with a known unit leader.[32] Gangs regularly picked by a single employer were the 'house gangs' of that employer. As many as 30 per cent of deep-sea dockers worked in house gangs at any one time. Everyone selected had to be present at the read. If a gang member was late to the read, he usually could not be called. A gang member who was unavailable because he had already independently obtained work could jeopardise his place in the formation. Becoming a member of such a gang was, of course, far from a simple matter. Often such a grouping would consist solely of members of the same family. Marrying a sister might be your only recourse.

Blood membership of a 'known' docker clan was priceless. Some reads consisted of one sentence from the stevedore: 'Are there any Nevins there?' There were upwards of fourteen Nevins at their peak. The calling of the Nevins could polish off much of a single read. Clan connection was powerful, yet men without a prime docker family name also became members of top deep-sea gangs. Other individuals established reputations for skill, strength or simply as hard workers. Still others were 'known' mainly for reasons of personal popularity, or even simple longevity, either of which could help. To some of the less often successful men it seemed, rightly, that the same 'known' personages always got picked. 'Floaters' were those who always searched for the best option, free from group association. Floaters could be choosier about the kind of cargo they worked. Established gang members had to go where the gang leader led.

The read system encouraged self-interested behaviour, despite those loyalties to groupings and family. 'It was something shocking down there,' says a northside docker, 'baitin' one another to get into positions where you would be seen. That was every day.'[33] One of the Ringsend docker has this strong feeling about it: 'It's *me fein* at the reads … It is me, me, me and when I'm sorted out I'll see what's left for you.'[34]

Effectively avoiding the read moment, men were sometimes clandestinely engaged before the read through contacts with foremen earlier in the morning. This tended to be done in or around the dockland pubs. Known as dawn patrol, it was emphatically considered unethical by some dockers.

Far worse than the comparatively minor iniquities of *mé féin* or the dawn patrol was the corrupt system of kickbacks. More than one docker remembered days when men used to buy their work. This was usually done indirectly via a publican or a payout deputy, and was customarily called 'leaving down a drink' for the employing foreman.

When a ship had finished, men were paid off in pubs such as The Eight Bells and Butt Bar at Butt Bridge. The picturesque version of the method of pay out described here by docker Wilo Nelson also encompasses 'leaving the drink':

> When the ship was discharged, [the employer] gave the bulk of the money to one of his docker friends to pay off the rest of the men. He'd march into a pub and the rest of the dockers would go in after him. Now, the publican would always have plenty of change, and he give 'ten bob for you, ten bob for you', and so on. Then he'd go, 'five bob for you, five bob for you' … They couldn't make it up as fifteen shillings … And he'd say, 'there's two pence for you', until there was money left that could not be shared out. He'd put that into his own pocket. Seven pence or ten pence. Every man who got paid off left a drink for the stevedore. The publican would hold that money over … The stevedore would know that such a body didn't hand over a drink. Well, he got no job next time.[35]

Rarely, dockers resisted. Yarra Duffy had been moving cement all day.

> It was £2.10s for a day's pay and we were after shifting 260–270 tons of cement. You had to go up to the Butt Bar to get paid. Me and another fellow the name of Jack Curran went up there. This fellow Hayes was there with another man, a type we called 'the rabbit', you know, people who forked out for the work. This fellow comes up to me and says, 'there's your money: £2.7.6.' I said, 'I'm due £2.10s'. 'No', he says, 'Stephen [the publican] has to get a half a crown 'back.' I said, 'You give me £2.10s. If I want to give him half a crown that's my affair.' So then Hayes comes down to us and says, 'Are you not taking the money?' And I said

I wasn't. So he called the barman and got two half-crowns off him and rolled the coins in the notes and threw them on the ground in front of us. 'Don't come near me for work', he says.[36]

Another method of payment was via a drink for the 'rabbit', such as the paymaster called Billy. Each docker was expected to buy Billy a glass of whiskey. By the end of a payout, Billy had perhaps twenty undrunk whiskeys on his bar table. When the dockers were gone, the whiskey was poured back into the bottle and Billy was given cash by the publican.

Or, you paid in advance.

> The fella ... would put a drink down for him behind the bar, and say 'That's from so and so.' So the [foreman] would walk in and he'd say, 'So and so left that down for you.' And the foreman then, the next morning, he'd give that man a job because he was after leaving a drink for him, you know. Ah, that happened regular.[37]

These coins were traditionally left at the bar in a matchbox. You could also pay direct: There's your matches. I forgot to return them.

It was difficult enough to be popular as a working, onboard foreman if you were also selecting men at the read. 'He saw me,' a docker grumbles about a selector of a particular morning, 'but not with his mouth.'[38] Jem Kelly was promoted to ship foreman and abandoned the job, returning to the docker ranks almost immediately. He received this shock just after his promotion: 'I said good morning to a fella. And he said, "You didn't know me yesterday morning when you were picking out." So after that I gave it up.'

Stevedores were the ultimate employer of the docker. The stevedoring company was the docker's paymaster. The smaller stevedores traditionally carried out their own read, while the larger Dublin companies put the read in the hands of foremen. In dockland communities, the common term for the readmaster was 'the stevedore', although in fact he more usually was a deputising foreman. 'The boss' and 'the stevedore' were the everyday terms used by dockers. It was not that dockers did not know who was, and who was not, an actual stevedoring executive. Certainly, they did. Yet, many foremen jobbers got labelled 'the stevedore' in everyday parlance. Stevedoring executives did not engage in the matchbook practices just described. Dockers assured everyone, moreover, that some foremen and selectors were resolutely above demanding, or accepting, kickbacks. Well-established deep-sea dockers, especially those who were members of both regular gangs and known families, scarcely, if ever, encountered the need to kick in a fee for work. 'Backhanders' were nevertheless paid by dockers to obtain employment in some cases. Although the matchboxes and their shillings did pass extensively, it may have been mostly those who had no family connection who needed to buy their work. The full story of the stevedore is part of Chapter 3. For now, we turn to the buttonman.

Buttonmen

'Anybody who was a friend of the corpse' might get a job on the docks before 1946.[39] If you had met the foreman in the pub the night before you could be employed. Anybody, in fact, could just come down. Labourers, carpenters, teachers and lecturers, clerks and male shop assistants, everyone it seemed, picked up work on the docks. Naturally these interlopers were roundly resented by the career professional dockers. Still, the latter treated the transients with forbearance; the occasional workers were, after all, within the overall long tradition of casual dock labouring.

The ending of World War Two became a crisis in this regard. Commerce was minimal during the war. Few dockers had work. Many spent part of the war years in the war industries in Britain or in the British Army.[40] After the war, Irishmen returned in a flood. Many arrived on the docks looking for

Horse and carts waiting for bags to be unloaded. (Donated by John Nolan to the Dublin Dock Workers Preservation Society)

work. Some returnees had been long-time Dublin dockers before the war. Most had not. The 'traditional dockers', as they called themselves, the single-trade men, were now doubly vulnerable, to both returnee dockers and interlopers.

To provide some job protection for the traditional dockers, in 1946 and 1947 a trade union list of full-time dockers was drawn up by the unions. The employers agreed to give the men on this list full first preference at the reads. Those whose names reached the list became 'the buttonmen'. A button badge indicated their status. After the initial few

years of registration, during which seamen were also eligible to register as dockers, the list was closed to newcomers. Some 650 buttons were originally available. In fact, not all current full-time dockers seized the opportunity to gain a button.

Buttonmen now had to be selected before non-buttonmen at each read. No non-buttonman could be called until all buttonmen had been selected.[41]

The button itself, of which its holders soon became so proud, was originally the union badge. Union badges are associated with dockers in particular because they originated with the National Union of Dock Labourers (NUDL) during the 1890s. The (British) NUDL produced a quarterly metal badge, the 'docker's button', which was worn in Ireland, Scotland and England. Employers objected to the wearing of the button on the docks during the early decades of the badge's existence.[42] It became, therefore, a badge of courage for dockers. The Irish Transport and General Workers' Union (ITGWU), the successor in Ireland to the NUDL, soon followed suit with a button badge. In August 1913, during the historic Lockout, the ITGWU badge depicted the Red Hand of Ulster. For a time, the ITGWU ceased producing new badges quarterly, keeping the red hand emblem in honour of the men and women workers who shared the fate of the Lockout. Distinct dockers' badges, of every cut and colour, were issued by all of the trade unions having docker members throughout most of the twentieth century. DEEPSEA CARGO AND COAL DOCKER and DUBLIN DEEP SEA & COAL DOCKER are among the embossed variations emblazoned on the bright badges. The colour of badges changed frequently as a way of identifying who had paid their union dues. The Irish Seamen's and Port Workers' Union (ISPWU) had a number of different badges, one of which featured a dock work scene. Its successor, the Marine, Port and General Workers' Union (MP&GWU), favoured a single design. This showed the triple-knot of St Brendan the Navigator and a partial Starry Plough etched in silver against a deep blue background.

It was customary for dockers to stud their belt with their union buttons. Others wore them on their lapel. Strictly speaking, the docker's button was to be prominently displayed in some such form.[43] The belt was a good choice because, although a coat might be removed while working, a belt, for support of the small of the back for heavy lifting, was never removed.[44]

With the introduction of 'the button system', union badges alone no longer gave priority status to anyone who was not also on the official list of 'buttonmen'. Some dockers did not register for the new buttonmen list because they thought the plan would come to nothing. Or out of stubborn pride: I have to get a button for to get a job? No way! I'm down here all my life. This was a mistake the rejecters were to regret deeply. Now they were far less likely be picked. Old mates, now buttonmen, cast their eyes to these men with sympathy and pity. 'It was sad to see them standing there. They were so used to the old system.'[45] For non-buttonmen the read continued to be a demoralising experience You had to wait until all the buttonmen were employed. Whether or not he wanted to, the foreman had to employ a buttonman before a non-buttonman. Non-buttonmen working on a ship could sometimes even be supplanted by buttonmen, for example, if work recommenced on a ship after the gangs had been dismissed. Employers might wish to recommence with the same gangs, including any non-buttonmen who had already become familiar with the particular ship and cargo they had worked. This was not permissible, however, if there were buttonmen who wished to take the place of any of the non-buttonmen.[46] What's more: 'If non-Buttonmen and Buttonmen gangs are working the same hatch, then even if the Buttonmen are finished their portion of the cargo they have the right to claim the cargo of the non-Button gang in the same hatch.'[47]

The lament of the non-buttonman has been written by non-button docker Bill Preston. Preston titled this piece *The Docker's Song*:

As I was walking down the beach on a bright and sunny day
I saw a boat for Downey [48] it was floating in the bay,
But when I went to stand in the read, much to my surprise
There was a load of buttonmen, swarming round like flies.

...ick's house gang working the cement boat.
...k row from left: Michael McDermott, Danny Fox, Connolly, Willie Forbes, Stachier Carrick, Paddy 'Whacky'
...ick, Phil McDermott, Thomas Murphy, Eddie O Brien, 'Wootens' Mooney, 'The Little Flower' John McDermott,
...ie Carrick and 'Cocker' Montgomery.
...nt row from left: Willie 'Butch' McDermott, Joe Carrick, Michael Carrick, Phil Carrick, and two cranemen,
...y Cummins and unknown. (Donated by Lily McDermott to the Dublin Dock Workers Preservation Society)

There was Tom St. John and Oxo, Shoulders Bill, and Paul,

In fact there was enough relations there to lift it on the wall.

And this is what they said to me, 'are you a button man?'

I said, 'stick your job up your bum-de-bum', and turned around and ran.

I went to Paddy Nolan, a gentleman is he,

He'll even give your mate a hand when you are at your tea.

But when I asked him for a job this was all he had to say,

'I'll be reading here at ten o'clock, I've an ore boat on the way.'

At two o'clock that afternoon at Patsy Kelly's read,

He said to Kevin Kelly, 'There's a fellow that needs a feed.'

And Kevin said to Patsy, 'He needs one there's no doubt.

We'll have to give him a job today, so we'll put him singing out.'[49]

Now, I went aboard *The Hazel*, and my heart was filled with joy,

And the song I sang for the inside men was *The Wild Colonial Boy*.

Then I heard a voice behind me, it was a terrible roar,

'Get that coat and get off this boat, and don't come back no more'.

I wandered round for years and years, a victim of my fate,

Until I met St. Peter, he was standing at the gate.

He said, 'Come in, you're welcome', and he showed me where to go,

'You'll find the rest of the boys inside, but the buttonmen down below.'

I stayed in heaven a couple of year, and the truth to you I'll tell,

When I got my holidays, I said I would visit Hell.

Now the buttonmen that were down there they were nearly up the pole;

Tiger O'Brien was doing boss that day, and he had them shovelling coal.[50]

Blue buttons soon became the standard badge of the original list men. Red buttonmen then appeared in the late 1950s as a later secondary tier. They were the sons of dockers. Red buttonmen could only be called after the blue, but had to be called before the non-buttonmen. Soon too came the yellow card men, like the red buttonmen, secondary to the blue. It was blue, red, yellow and then the non-buttonmen, having no kind of colour status at all.[51]

The foreman could still make life uncomfortable for even the buttonman to whom he'd taken a dislike, however.

If he [the foreman] didn't like him, if he'd done something on him some days prior, he would still have to employ him. But that would be degrading because he would know this man's name, and he would leave him until he made the call 'any more buttonmen', and then the man would walk out and hand in his cards.[52]

The insult was clear to everyone present.

The button dealt a partial blow to the practice of buying work via a kickback to the selecting foreman. Because work was plentiful during the decade after the button system began, all buttonmen who appeared at the read were likely to have work. The motivation to 'leave a drink' for the foreman was, for a time then, largely restricted to non-buttonmen. More important in eliminating corruption, the foreman was no longer in the position to guarantee selection to non-buttonmen, because buttonmen might be present in sufficient numbers to fill his quota.

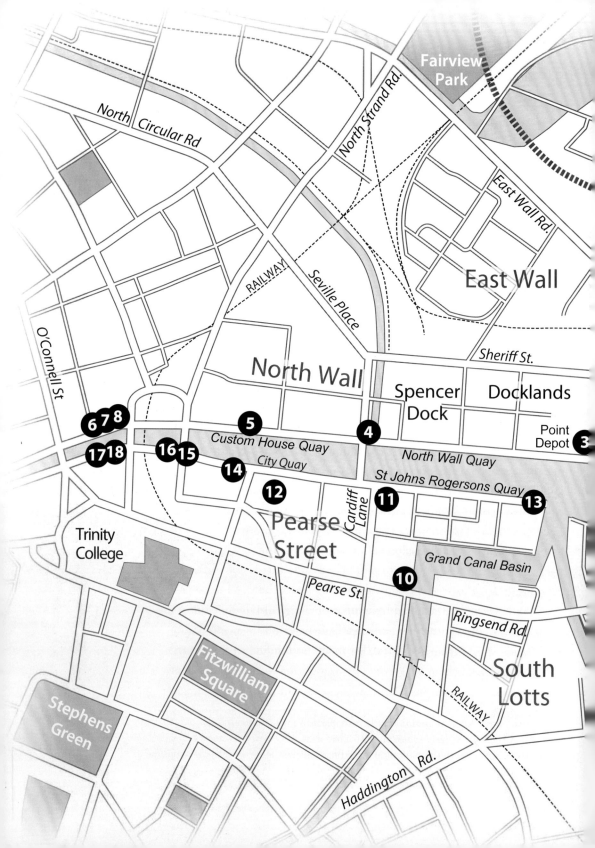

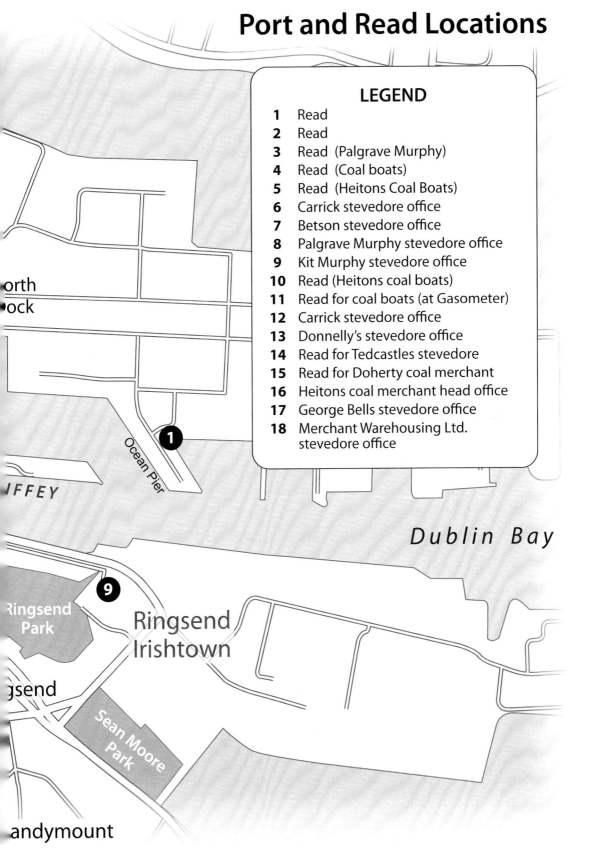

Port and Read Locations

LEGEND

1	Read
2	Read
3	Read (Palgrave Murphy)
4	Read (Coal boats)
5	Read (Heitons Coal Boats)
6	Carrick stevedore office
7	Betson stevedore office
8	Palgrave Murphy stevedore office
9	Kit Murphy stevedore office
10	Read (Heitons coal boats)
11	Read for coal boats (at Gasometer)
12	Carrick stevedore office
13	Donnelly's stevedore office
14	Read for Tedcastles stevedore
15	Read for Doherty coal merchant
16	Heitons coal merchant head office
17	George Bells stevedore office
18	Merchant Warehousing Ltd. stevedore office

North Dock

Ocean Pier

LIFFEY

Dublin Bay

Ringsend Park

Ringsend Irishtown

Ringsend

Sean Moore Park

Sandymount

Some space for foreman manipulation remained, though. Patsy Kelly, of *The Docker's Song* fame, was a foreman who had a son, a docker, who had no button. It is said that Patsy would sometimes call a certain docker to the first gang, knowing, according to participants, that the man had 'a terrible drink problem' and would probably not turn up for work the next day. The next morning on checking that all the members of the first gang were present, 'he'd more often than not discover that this docker was absent. So he'd bring in the son, who was then guaranteed a job until the ship was finished.'

This read system survived all technological and economic change up to 1971. Eventually the reads were centralised at Ocean Pier Gate and dockers were called alphabetically, regardless of whether they had a colourful button, who they had bought a pint for the night before or with what work gang they were affiliated.

When you had worked, your number was placed at the bottom of the controller's list for the next read. This was called the rotational system. Though the docker was still uncertain as to whether he would or would not get work, at least then non-employment carried no sense of individual failure. Feelings were mixed about this rotational system. Old gangs and friendships were split up. Suddenly gangs 'were all mixed up. You didn't know who you were working with' after the wrenching conversion to the rotational system. Or worse still, you would know your co-workers only too well: feuding men might be forced to work together and the quarrels carried onto the ship. What was most felt to be lost was the sense of individuality that resided in the choice of ship site. Yes, men were at the reads to get work: 'We were out every morning for to get work, and that was it!'[53] Yet, that was not all of it. Deep-sea dockers regularly chose their read site based on a preference to work a particular commodity, for a particular employer or with a particular group. That freedom of movement was valued.

The read system was challenging to say the least. That 'inner silence of the damp mornings' is remembered by some as a rough testing. There were many compensations, as we will see in later chapters. Even at the read, enormous fun was to be had meeting the lads every morning. While waiting, the jokes would be flying. It was the docker's lot that he could end up spending much of the morning with time on his hands when not employed at the first read. 'Most of the time you would go up to the Custom House. At the time the Custom House steps were all wide open … all the guys would just sit there and play cards, and chatting and reading the paper. The paper would be worn thin.'[54]

At next read time, it was across the quays to take your chances again. If still unlucky, it was back to the Custom House steps, the next read, the dole office (after 1933) or to the pub. It was a tough system. As deep-sea docker Martin Mitten sometimes experienced the personal singling out of the read: 'It was like picking cherries off a tree.'

For those who were selected, the quest ended as they 'handed in their cards', the employment book, to the stevedore and were told to go to *The Orestes, The Dunaff Head, The Durban Castle,* or *The Lanahrone.* With anticipation, the day's gangs made their way to the named ship.

TWO

BLUE BRIMSTONE, THE TWELVE-MAN REEL AND THE SINGER-OUT

You would not, as a matter of pride, leave that hook
hanging over your head.[1]

The number seven shovel has such a graceful, silver, pointed spade shape
that some dockers describe it as heart-shaped. It weighs twelve pounds
and lifts up to four stone of coal. You have to be strong to use it. You
have to work up to it, as few novice dockers could manage a number
seven in their first weeks. Blisters and cuts come with the initiation.
One of the tools of the docker's traditional craft, the number seven
was used inside ships in the work of discharging, as unloading a ship is
always termed. The vast interior of a ship is divided into separate holds.
Cargo is removed via hatches, openings at deck level. Other docker
tasks take place on the dockside or on the ship deck.

The 'bearer off' and the 'double topper' are two of the specialist
roles into which a work gang might subdivide itself – alongside the
trimmer, the busheler, the winchman, the 'singer-out' and many others.
Beginning with the coalies, this chapter follows the many-sided daily
work of the Dublin deep-sea docker.

rish sugar for USA: A consignment of 1,600 tons of Irish beet sugar is loaded onto SS *Irish ELM*
at Dublin Docks on Wednesday, 18 April 1962. The sugar is bound for New York and Baltimore,
Maryland, USA. (© Irish Photo Archive; http://www.irishphotoarchive.ie)

The Coalies

Coal has many uses. In the early part of the twentieth century, gas was used for cooking, heating and some of the lighting in the city of Dublin. But that gas was in turn made, until 1969, from coal. There were once over one hundred gas companies in Ireland, and numerous coal companies. Electricity, including that for powering the tramways, was primarily also generated by burning imported coal. Coal imports increased, particularly after World War Two. In 1938, the typical collier brought in 700 tons of coal from various ports. By 1947, however, the 'Liberty Ships' had appeared. These 10,000-ton ships, originating in the United States, have long remained a vivid part of the deep-sea docker memory. Six to eight of these then huge vessels might be discharging at one time at the coal berths in the port, with another three or more riding at anchor waiting for a berth. Most of the coal in the big colliers had to be shovelled out of the holds manually. This required a monumental amount of muscular labour.

The first task for most commodities, coal included, was 'sinking to berth'. The hold would have been filled to deck level. Sinking to berth meant creating a space from which to work at the very top of the cargo in the hatch.

Coal was shovelled into tubs, mainly using the number seven. The tubs were not vast in size: five feet across by three or four deep, holding from one ton to twenty-five hundredweight, was a typical size. The weighty coal could be heaved into a tub reasonably quickly by men working together. Four men worked each tub in a large collier, three in a smaller coal ship. Some blocks of 'Welsh steam' coal were, however, 'as big as a television set', [2] in the words of one Dubliner. Posing problems, some Welsh blocks were obviously not moved easily.

The tub sat in a frame that allowed it to be hoisted by a hook on the end of a rope or cable, running straight up out of the hatch to the pulley of a derrick[3] or crane. Many cargo ships carried their own derricks, giving them the bristly, unattractive appearance of an oilfield. Tubs could, via docker work that we will observe later, be cranked up onto the deck in the earlier days of merchant shipping and sometimes then swung directly onto dockside by the ship's derricks. Cranes lifting directly from the dock, rather than from the ship, made a steadier hoist. When available, the dockside crane usually took preference over the ship's derricks.

Down in the hold of the collier, coal dust thickened the deeper into the cargo the dockers dug. Larger colliers had four holds of 30–40-foot depths, whereas smaller colliers had holds of 12 feet. 'Coal dust, clouds of it';[4] the foreman couldn't see the men in the hatch. To thwart the dust getting a grip on their throat, many coalies sucked on a piece of coal to moisten their throats.[5] 'The sweat,' according to Willie Murphy, 'would be pouring off you.'[6] 'Sometimes you would get off ship: and the dirt and the black. You'd be like the fellas there on the telly: niggers! And your trousers would stand up straight on their own with the sweat and the dirt. And you hadn't great facilities for washing.'[7]

Coal dust, according to one of our informants, was ingrained into the coalies' skin. A pub as far away from the docks as the North Circular Road had a coalie as a regular. 'You could,' the publican claims, 'sweep the coal dust off the floor' where the coalie had been drinking. The same publican claims he once served the same docker when clean, rather than coal black, and could not, despite the docker being one of his favourite customers, recognise him as anyone he had ever seen.[8]

Bulky, steel-studded boots called 'Stingos' were the coalie footwear. Stingos are miners' boots, considered most appropriate for an occupation involving so much digging. Stingos could not be got in Dublin. Coalies would ask sailors to buy them in Liverpool. When the soles wore down, coalies might ask the bootmaker to add extra chunks of leather to one boot during resoling. The leather chunks helped in obtaining a foothold in the coal pile. One boot usually wore more rapidly than the other: the one on the leg you braced yourself with to lever up the full number seven. That boot got the leather chunks. A flat cap was also worn, although some found women's nylon stockings to be the best head protection.

Your cap, as well as protection, served to stake your claim to a work spot in the hold. Everybody shot in their caps; where it landed was where you worked. At other times, the number seven shovels were hurled in like javelins to spike a spot, to 'mark your berth'.[9] Many coalies had their names carved on the shovel handle; there was no confusing whose number seven was whose. With still other gangs, individuals just raced for a spot. Most aimed for the corners of the hold so they might avoid the danger of coal hitting them on the head, which would happen if you were on one of the inside tubs under the upward-rising loaded tubful. If the cargo had tilted during the ship's voyage one aimed for the lower end, where digging was easier.

Late night work was common, meaning that coal, black as it is, was dug after dark. Whatever light clusters the ship could provide enabled the coalies to see the shine of the lumps and blocks. At one, two or even three o'clock in the morning, coalies were sometimes still digging in the murky gloom. Old-time dockers spoke often of working all night in the 1950s and earlier. Late nights, in more recent times, occurred mainly on the final day of work when a ship was 'finishing'.[10] Earlier, however, the tide dictated much. Completion of a ship in time to float

Loading Sunbeam Jerseywear boxes into the hold of a ship at B&I, North Wall, Dublin, 1 August 1962. (© Irish Photo Archive; http://www.irishphotoarchive.ie)

out at high tide saved valuable time for ship owners and commodity shippers.[11] This could mean a very early morning start, or a late night, as the tide would have it. Often 7 a.m. reads, earlier than noted in Chapter 1, were a normal procedure when a ship was coming in on an early morning tide. Most men relished the long hours for the extra pay. 'One More Bucket' Ellis was especially keen to keep on working, as was the docker nicknamed 'Won't Go Home'.

To handle a number seven for the long hours which collier work meant, a coalie had to know how to grip it, with its cold metal handle-top. A subtly free and floating hold was needed. Too tight a grip brought blisters. The coalies were noted for their smooth and easy shovel-swing motion. They could appear relaxed while scooping and filling. Very long hours, however, and blisters rose anyway. The remedy for blisters recommended to beginners by old-time coalies was their urine.[12]

The back-and-forth beat of the crane and its descending hook lent both rhythm and necessity to the coalie's labour. 'It was constant work all day long to keep things going,' states one docker: 'a full tub up, and an empty tub down'. Each man could move 50 tons of slack in an eight-hour day, as 'the long-handled shovels', in James Plunkett's short story called 'The Plain People' about Dublin dockers, 'flashed busily in the dust-laden holds'.[13] One device used by experienced coalies to make the work easier was to trough down into the load such that the lowered tub would tip on its side when landing. You could then 'rawhead' the coal straight across into the tub without having to lift the bulk of it on the shovel. Thus, two coalies rawheaded, while the other two men on the tub delved – the tougher task – deeper into the bituminous depths. While digging a trough made filling the tubs much easier, it also created the danger of an avalanche of falling coal. When the floor of the hold had been reached, the square-head shovel, a little three-pounder, was used to scrape up what remained.

A mad, four-hour assault by the coalies was often required to discharge smaller colliers. Some ships which put in to Spencer Dock or opposite at the south quays, with the tide, would be promised by the agent to be completely discharged in time to sail on the next tide, creating an exactly defined work period. A very small collier from

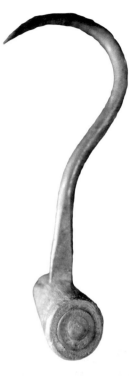

Dockers Hook. (Dublin Dock Workers Preservation Society collection, photograph by Aileen O'Carroll)

the pre-World War Two era, a ship under 200-ton capacity, could be finished in a 'half buzzer'. One completely discharged ship, a morning's work, then to the pub, and to the afternoon read.[14]

Coal is a combustible. Fire in the cargo hold wasn't unusual, and added to the challenge of being a coalie. 'When we would be digging out the coal there would be flames, leaping out at you sometimes.' On rare occasions, a hold full of coal had to be flooded to quell the blaze.

Yet, among dockers, coal was a popular commodity to work. Many long-time dockers worked only the colliers. Coal was a regular import and could therefore provide reliable income for those who became known as experienced coalies. The Liberty Ships, and subsequent even larger ships, multiplied the time necessary to discharge a collier, to a

Ship's plan of the Blue Funnel Line vessel M/V *Machaon*, showing where cargo is stowed. (Donated by Joe Potter to the Dublin Dock Workers Preservation Society)

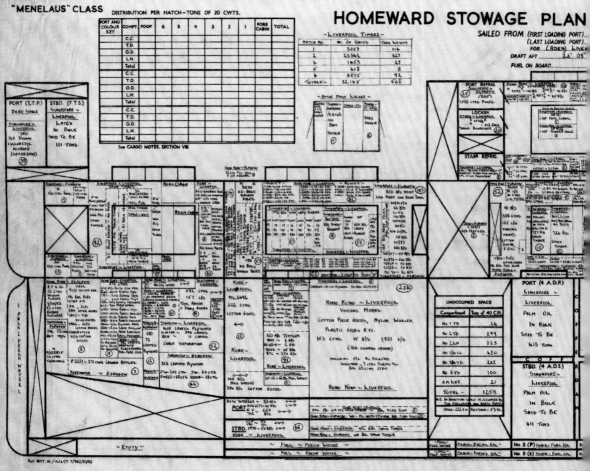

week or more. Being a coalie also carried a certain form of prestige over general cargo handling. At least two men, Collier Elliott and Collier Dennis, acquired their nickname out of this specialisation. Many regular coalies specialised even further, limiting themselves to the twelve-man-gang slack ships and English coal ships, such as the *Cabourne* or the *Kyle Queen*, in preference to the sixteen-man-gang Liberty Ships and Welsh steam vessels.

Ghosts, Green Tongues and the Mi-Mi

The belt of the Dublin docker carried two special accoutrements. One was the button of the buttonman. The other was his hook. Suspended

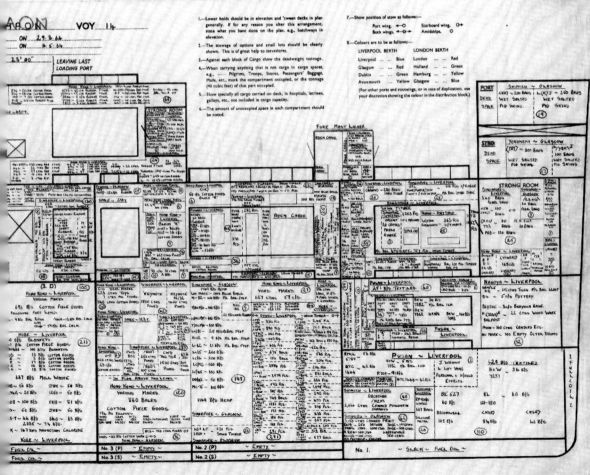

from the belt, the wooden-handled hook looked large and dramatic. It was another mark of the docker. According to one Dublin docker, their hook, their personal property, 'was their pride and joy'.[15] There were two varieties. The bag hook had a head studded with tack ends and was used to handle bales of cotton, bagged animal feed, potatoes or anything in sacks. Even occasional shipments of coal arrived bagged, as in April 1947 when dockers were unloading 5,000 sacks from New York, an American gift to the Irish people during post-war hardship times in Europe.

The J-shaped cargo hook was more conventionally hook-like in appearance.

The docker's hook appeared on the first button of the buttonmen – appropriately, alongside a shovel. Like the coalie's Stingos, the hooks were made in England, so the cargo man also needed a sailor friend to buy hooks for him. If, on turning up at the read, a docker found that he had forgotten his hook, he might be lucky and 'get a lend' from a friend, otherwise he wouldn't be employed. 'For heaven's sake don't lose that on me,' the friend would nervously plead, according to one docker.

Grain required considerable docker labour. Deep in the dim hold of a grain ship, 'bushelers' worked in pairs transferring the vast heap of grain which they stood into sacks. A bushel was a unit of measurement equal to 8 imperial gallons for dry goods. It was also the name of a pot or scoop that was used to fill sacks in the hold. One man held a sack while another filled it and attached it to the overhanging hook. 'Martin and I were mates. You had to change over. I'd fill ten bags; he'd hold ten bags. Then I'd hold ten bags and he'd fill ten bags. So the average 60 ton a day for two men they used to fill 60 ton of grain.'[16]

Often, bushelers were also required to stuff a stipulated weight into each sack.

Initially, hand winches, operated by four men manually turning a handle, hoisted the sacks out of the hatch. 'I often saw those men stripped to the waist,' one docker remembers, 'and their bodies glistening with sweat.'[17] Later, hand winches were replaced by steam winches driven by the ship's steam and, eventually, by electric dockside cranes. Winchmen were regarded as specialists. Stevedores insisted that not just any buttonman docker could be considered able to operate a manual winch.[18]

As the 'heave' or 'hoist' of sacks rose, a 'bearer-off' would ensure that they were kept clear of the sides and hatchway.[19] In some ships, there were two, or even three, hold levels below deck: a lower hold and a 'tween-deck', or two tween-decks. The bearer-off had, at times, his own platform high in the hold near the hatchway. Martin Mitten's father 'beared off', he told us, on a large, four-masted, sailing ship. Once the hoist was clear of the hold, dockers on deck, helped by the bearer-off, removed the sacks and placed them on a weighing scales, releasing the rope tackle. There a 'weighman' would check, for certain commodities, that each sack contained the correct amount of material, removing any surplus, or adding if necessary. 'Heaven help the busheler,' a docker asserts, 'if the weighman had too much scooping to do to bring the sacks back up to the required weight.'[20] Other dockers on the weigh platform then tied the sacks and 'kneed' them over to the ship's side,

Loading M.V. *Hardenberg* at North Wall, Dublin. Dockers loading a variety of export goods ranging from prune wine to coils of wire at the docks, 19 February 1961. (© Irish Photo Archive; http://www.irishphotoarchive.ie)

where they were collected by dockers or corn-porters and carried down the long planks to the waiting carts.[21] If quayside cranes were present to relieve the kneeing, the job of 'hooker on' became deck work. These dockers hooked on the hook of the dockside crane, detaching the ship's winch hook that had raised the hoist from the hold. Hooking-on, and detaching the winch hook, might be done immediately the hoist cleared the hatch – in mid-air – requiring dexterous, quick movements.

A docker summarised grain work in the early 1930s:

> You'd bushel the grain into sacks, 17 stone two was the weight: 4 bushels into a sack. It was brought up onto the deck of the ship to be weighed by a weighman

… The 'bearer off', he was known as the 'boy', he beared off the sack and put it into the scales. The Merchant Warehousing [Company's weighman] would put it into the scales, weigh the bag and get it to 17 stone two. Then there was a man carried it to the rail of the ship. Then there was another man carried it off the rail of the ship onto the wagon, or the horse and wagon, or onto the old steam wagon.[22]

The workday on grain ships ran, in the early years, from six in the morning to six at night, 6 a.m. being the recommencement time when discharge had already been under way on the previous day.

Left page
A tub of coal is tipped into a CIÉ rail wagon while inside the coal boatmen work with shovels. (Donated by Florrie Cunningham from Michael Donnelly's collection to the Dublin Dock Workers Preservation Society)

Right page
Working in the hold of a banana boat. Left to right: Paddy O'Toole, Mickser Tilley and Abber Byrne. (Donated by Ray Murphy to the Dublin Dock Workers Preservation Society)

Many grain ships carried lively, non-paying passengers. As the ships moved from port to port, rats would embark along the way. They would board the ship by running up along the tying ropes. Unlucky rodent raiders were halted by steel fenders encircling some of the long mooring ropes. Successful stowaways grew fat, feasting on the grain while the ship was at sea.

> Some of the ships used to be full of rats and all. They'd come down with the grain and the dockers would pick them up. This is a fact! This man used to pick them up and he'd pull out their teeth! This is true. He'd put them down his chest, you see. And you'd be standing down to fill the bushels, and he'd take the rat and put it on the back of your neck; and the dockers would be fainting. The men used to be terrified of the rats. They would run out of the hold: I seen them myself. Smaller rats ... they would run along the top of the grain and we'd be laughing. We didn't mind them.[23]

In 1914, an old-time solution was tried to solve the problem of rat infestation on the docks in some of the transit sheds. Ten cats were supplied by the Society for the Prevention of Cruelty to Animals for a period of two months. The terms of service were laid out as being 'one shilling per cat, plus a sum of fifteen shillings and sixpence per week for wages for a part-time attendant and milk and food for the cats'. 'It seems that the cats performed their tasks efficiently,' H.A. Gilligan wrote, wryly, 'since it was not found necessary to renew their contract.'[24] More likely it was decided that they were an unnecessary expense.

Raw sugar from Cuba also came bagged at the hefty weight of 24 stone each! Very hard work, but sugar, called 'demerara', was a popular cargo. It was one of the 'tonnage' commodities. On tonnage, dockers were paid by how much they moved. A lot of demerara could be moved in a relatively short space of time. A quota, 'the mi-mi', or minimum, pronounced 'mee-mee', had to be reached before the rate per ton kicked in on a tonnage commodity. The gang fought to quickly as possible pass the 96-ton mi-mi. A job where a lot of tonnage, and therefore a lot of money, could be made in a short time was called a 'snip'.

In contrast to tonnage commodities, timber and coal were examples of discharge commodities for which dockers were paid a flat rate for the cargo. Flat rate work was less profitable and was referred to derogatorily as the 'mini-mo', pronounced as 'meeny-mo'. With flat rate work, unlike tonnage or hourly work, it was to the docker's advantage to finish the job quickly, get paid, and try to move onto another ship. Tomatoes in their boxes, and other delicate commodities, were paid at a per-hour daily rate.

Giant bags of calcium, earmarked for paintbase, had to be lifted, down in the hold, to be slung on ropes for hoisting. Cement powder, twenty bags at a time, was also hauled out of the hold, swaying on the big hooks. The cement was carried, sometimes on the dockers' backs, from the ship's side, across the road into the stores, and perhaps further up a narrow plank, to be stacked twenty-four sacks high. Manhandling cement was reckoned by many to be the hardest work of all. It was the dead weight and the heat of the cement that made the going tough. The 16 stone of cement in jute bags would turn any man's back into a piece of raw meat in a very short time if he were not used to it.

Anything crated, bagged or packaged, cement included, were 'break bulk' goods, to differentiate it from the loose bulk commodities that had to be dug out of the ship, and which were the great labour-intensive deep-sea docker work for centuries.

Ore, like other bulk, was shovelled into tubs. The clattering of iron or copper ore against shovels and tub made a fierce racket. The number five shovel, smaller and rounder than the number seven but with an even sharper point, was used for ore. Copper ore could cause alarming side effects: 'If you put your tongue out and looked at it, it would be green. From working the copper ore, your whole palate, and your tongue would be green.'[25] It seemed nearly impossible to wash off the glow from copper ore. It became known as green ore. Iron ore and iron pyrites (the latter an ore for extracting sulphur compounds for the chemical industry) were known as blue brimstone. Copper ore was green, pyrites blue and bulk potash was pink.

Although some dockers rated ore to be as difficult to handle as cement, others felt it was not so bad once they had got the knack of it. On the ore ships, unlike the colliers, there were no set breaks. While the crane kept moving, the dockers took turns 'spelling off', catching a quick cup of tea or cycling to the pub, while others picked up the slack. The foreman looked the other way, happy enough as long as the crane's hook was being fed apace.

Digging, digging … so many commodities arrived in bulk in the holds. 'Treble X' was a fertiliser, a phosphate. Phosphates were dug out of the hold by sixteen men to each hatch, with four rotating tubs, four men to a tub, each tub bearing up to 2,500 hundredweight. With Treble X, breaking out 'the stow', the initial excavation into the cargo at the top of the hatch, was a challenge. It was often so hard in the hold that dockers had to wield picks at it before they could employ shovels. Sand, imported or trans-shipped from the Netherlands, could freeze in winter. Three to four feet of frozen sand required the dockers to drill into the ice to break it up before digging it out. Loose bulk cargoes of phosphates, potash and the like were termed 'fossil boats' by deep-sea dockers. Shovelling inside fossil boats accounted for a substantial amount of the labour hours of deep-sea dockers.

Nastiest to work with among the array of cargoes was guano, bird droppings used as fertiliser. 'It had an awful smell out of it. No one robbed it.' The stink of it wafted far from the shipside. As the dockers forked out the guano, it might begin to tower over them, cliffs of waste, more than man high. If it got too high, the mound could collapse, leaving the docker in danger of being overcome by the foul fumes.

> When you got a fall, a whole big heap would come down. Everybody had to get out of it, run up the ladder or they would be suffocated. There was ammonia mixed in it, like for to keep out the disease … to keep you from getting a disease. It was the ammonia; if you stood there you would just die.[26]

Unloading bricks in the traditional fashion required hand to eye coordination. From the hold, men threw up four bricks at a time to a colleague on the deck. This docker immediately pivoted at the waist to toss the four to another not far off, who in turn swung round to throw to another. This became a 'train' onto the quay and along onto a horse-drawn dray, or to be stacked. Such relay handling must be an ancient system. One Dubliner remembers working such a train out of a masted sailing schooner in 1952 at Butt Bridge.

Big slings were used to unload ready-turned poles from Scandinavia. Small ships might carry nothing but these long poles. With the long poles brimming all across the decks, as well as filling the holds, the pole boats were a picturesque sight. On a smaller ship, there could be as many poles on deck as below. Ten or so poles were positioned by dockers in a sling, to be raised by the hook. Wood pulp was handled in large three-by-four blocks.

Mahogany, other hardwoods, and timber were usually borne by large ships originating in Africa and elsewhere, part of it often also as deck cargo. The fleet, christened *Irish Larch*, *Irish Willow*, *Irish Poplar*, etc., also carried timber, appropriately. Wood stuffs have continued to constitute a staple commodity for the Dublin deep-sea docker into the third millennium. These days, timber is pre-bundled for the hoist, but traditionally slings had to be prepared, as with poles. Gigantic logs of mahogany were shipped in a raw state. To create a safe sling hoist for such rough monsters required considerable skill indeed. Sometimes timber had to be carried from ship-side, two or three planks at a time. Padding in the form of a sack around the shoulders protected the dockers' skin and bones. The best kind of sack for protection was a matter of much dispute. Some preferred soft sacking, others hard stuff. Wearing a full overcoat was unacceptable in the timber-work culture, however.

The fate of the *Anniston City* illustrates the laboriousness of timber.

The American steamer *Anniston City*, which arrived Saturday, had, for her, the unprecedented experience of remaining in the Alexandra Basin until the following Thursday. She is

3,450 tons register and comes from Vancouver via Glasgow and Belfast. In spite of the stevedores working overtime until eight o'clock every night, she is being robbed of the reputation for American hustling, owing to the difficulties experienced in discharging the huge baulks [*sic*] of timber, which comprise part of her cargo.

This was 1931, as reported in the 'Dublin Harbour Notes' of *The Irish Times*.[27] On a shipment of tons of loose timber, 'you'd be going', deep-sea docker Willie Murphy says, 'for a week to ten days. And that would be a hundred men of four gangs. That would be eighty-four men. Eighty-eight men, like, four winchmen, putting down four winchmen four singer-outs, and a twenty-man gang.'[28] A labour-intensive operation indeed.

If overcoats were scorned for timber work, they were worn by dockers at many times and in many places. A foreman informant speaks of his 'overriding memory of heavy black coats. They'd wear old suits, working men's boots, and the heavy black coats.'[29] Whatever the weather, the overcoat was discarded soon enough in hot heavy work.

Timber and poles were only one kind of commodity that were set into rope slings. Bags and sacks of varying contents often went into slings. Each such sling, for any kind of commodity, had to be firmly packed so that it rose and swung out across the ship to the dock without falling apart.

Cowhide for leather was exported as whole hides. Hides were initially carried aboard on the backs of individual dockers. Later this was replaced by a relay system, where the hides were passed from one man to another until they had reached the hold. Chilled or frozen half carcasses were covered with muslin before being handled.

Colts and geldings were exported, sometimes while yet unbroken. The big animals were loaded individually by dockers.

A prominent Irish racehorse fellow – he came down with twelve or thirteen geldings, young colts, young mares, not

Discharging timber poles, Paddy McAuley in foreground, 1947. (Donated by Jimmy Carthy to the Dublin Dock Workers Preservation Society)

yet broke. Terrible bloody job getting them on board and there was a fellow called Danny Gunne, who could do anything with animals. I was pretty good with them myself. A horse is nervous and if you're nervous you can do nothing with him. He goes mad if he senses that. If you're confident you can put confidence in him. You can walk with him you know. They'd be thousands of pounds. You'd have to coax them in, humour them in. It all depended on what he sensed, if they'd walk up a gangway.[30]

Cattle were the most numerous of livestock cargo. Drovers herded the animals into dockside pens. Dockers then fed and watered the livestock until it was time to shepherd them along the gangways. But cattle care had only just begun once the animals were on board. Dockers sailed to Antwerp, Hamburg, Rotterdam and other northern Continental ports, caring for the animals en route. This was good, easy work. The return voyage was a paid sea cruise with 'nothing to do except sit on deck chairs and cause trouble possibly'. Trouble there was, some of it resulting from the Dubliners' love of ports, especially Amsterdam's café life and alcoholic delights. Specialists in this work were called 'bullock men'. Many Dublin dockers did it, as did some seamen who were members, with the dockers, of the Irish Seamen and Portworkers' Union. A distinct button identified the specialists as the 'Livestock Section' of the union. Eventually, the cattleman function became an even cushier task. For reasons described in later chapters, the seagoing docker was phased out, but his 'ghost' continued to sail the waves. Cattle dockers were paid for tending cattle, but were dispensed with in fact. They were paid for staying away from the ship. Obviously, this was a plum job, and sometimes these assignments were shared in rotation by agreement.[31] Later, however, ghost docker pay went to the union rather than to individuals.

Hector Grey's boxed imports were among the more pleasant 'general cargo' work. Grey's low-priced 'toys and fancy goods' shops were a Dublin institution, making available, according to a 1960s advertisement, 'all your souvenirs, gifts and wedding presents'. As well as unloading the volume of cartons of fancy goods out of ships, some dockers also gained further work elsewhere from Grey. One deep-sea docker recalls how he often worked for Hector Grey:

> He had a shed out the back where he stored all these specials and he'd employ a couple of dockers, if he knew them, to go out there and sort it out because we knew how to – the lay of the cargo and its proper routes. We used to go out and straighten his shed for him periodically. He was quite a decent man to work for.[32]

Grey reckoned the dockers were more efficient, based no doubt on their familiarity with the commodities just quoted.

> He had a warehouse up there in Fitzgibbon Street. 'Go up there and check out the stuff.'

> … A day's pay … And said, 'wouldn't you get plenty of men around the town to do that for you?' 'You do it. They'd take days to do one day.' So, he had his head screwed on.[33]

Boxed general cargo such as toys could be piled in the hold onto trays for hoisting up and swinging off the ship.

Tea began to be shipped directly from the country of origin to Ireland in 1947, before which it was mainly trans-shipped from Britain. This Irish Government decision to terminate trans-shipping increased the size of the tea ships arriving in Irish ports, hence the bulk amount of tea chests to be discharged from a single ship. Up to 31,000 wooden chests could arrive at a time. Tea was only one of the commodities which shifted from trans-shipment in Britain to direct overseas import at this period. Deep-sea dockwork therefore increased in Dublin port.[34] This development coincided with a general increase in trade volumes after the end of World War Two. By 1964, a supplemental list of commodities with docker rates of pay provided by the large Irish shipping and ship broker agent Palgrave Murphy named sixty-nine commodities further to their already extensive primary list, including animals in crates, dinghies, pianos, and 'sanitary ware'.[35] Among the more voluminous cargoes from Canada and the United States, dockers handled wheat, timber, newsprint, steel, agricultural and other machinery and some fruits. From Brazil came coffee. Coal, somewhat paradoxically, was always entirely regarded as a deep-sea section commodity, even though some of it came from Great Britain.

Bananas landed on the South Wall from the Canary Islands on vessels which also served as cruise ships. Boxed and crated fruits, products of the Spanish and Cypriot sun, were arranged, six to twelve crates in a net bundle, to be swung skyward by the crane's arm. Despite being handily boxed, even fruit could sometimes be taxing, as when fruit boxes might fall into another cargo section, say granite or ore, break open and require picking out by hand.[36] With so many of the deep-sea cargoes, you could, when the hold was opened, smell that part of the world from which the ship had weighed anchor.

Handspikes, Bogies, Trimmers and Gins

Gangs were described as being 'long' or 'short'. Depending on the cargo and the dockside handling needs of the importer, either a long work gang of fifteen to twenty-two men or a short gang of twelve or eight was picked at the read for each hold of the ship. Gang size varied historically, becoming longest in the 1950s through to the 1970s. Traditionally, the 'twelve man read' was commonest, and indeed remained the formal norm into the 1970s. More men typically worked inside the ship in gangs of all sizes; what varied most was the number on the dockside. The very short gang with only two men landing on the quay wall was exceptional. This happened when the importing firm had a lorry waiting for direct loading by the two quay men. Bonuses were often paid to dockers on these very short gangs – so it was popular work.

A large ship had several hatches, all alive with dockers during discharging. An ore ship, for example, might have been worked on by four gangs, making forty-eight men. Three in each corner servicing three hooks in rotation was a typical 'inside' gang. More might have been inside, however, as some ships and some commodities required twenty inside men in a single hatch.

The division of men for work tasks into inside and dockside categories would have been decided at the read. This was done by the order men were called; the first named were the inside men, the latter the dockside group. Even the hold in which men were to work was assigned at the read: the first gang worked the deepest hatch. Within the gang, most individuals had their regular work mates, dependent of course on the uncertainties of the read.

In conjunction with shipowners, supervisory staff had influence over the dockers' methods of working. The senior foreman of a stevedoring company would have charge of several ships. Above him was a superintendent. The supervisors would advise the selected docker gangs in planning a ship strategy if the cargo was not one with which everyone was already familiar. For the most part, the gang had a free hand to decide on the specific work methods. Dockers were considered experts at their task. Each ship also had its own foreman, usually from the permanent staff of the employing company. The foreman was usually experienced, knowledgeable and able to take a leadership role on occasion, when appropriate. In no way did he tell the members of the gang what to do during their work. He assigned them inside or dockside and handed responsibility to them to get the job done. These assorted supervisors functioned also to exercise control – the foremen making rounds of inspection. This was not token surveillance: the foreman was a present force. 'You had to show that you were able to do it, because the boss would be looking at you. And if there was anything wrong you'd be looking in his face for the next few weeks [at the read] and you wouldn't be wanted.'[37]

'Ham foremen' were sometimes selected at the read from among the dockers. Ham foremen were 'casuals', chosen for the ship at the read. Ham foremen did no selecting. They were paid the rate of the men in the best-paid gang on their ship. If a ham was required he was normally the first docker picked for the ship at the read. A docker gaining a day's work as ham foreman was not marked off as outside the ranks of working dockers as were the permanent selecting foremen. A ham foreman could even be dismissed from the work complement before the ship finished, although this was unusual.

A large port did not maintain a dockside crane at every berth. When a dockside crane was available, work started as soon as the inside men had got into the hold and staked a place and a partner, while those outside waited for the first load to come ashore. In the absence of a quayside crane, the ships' cranes might be employed. Much preliminary work was necessary to activate the ship's crane system. Let us look at such a scene from the classic days when the dockers worked the many-masted cargo sailing ships.

The first work to be done was the setting up of various pulleys and hauling machines. The 'gin' was the pulley used for hoisting or hauling. Three or four gins would be arranged, fore and aft, utilising the ship's 'stays', the ropes supporting the sailing ship's masts. Connecting ropes led, through the gins, to hand-cranked winches set up to power the hoist of cargo up out of the hold. We have already noted the backbreaking labour in store for the winchmen, or wincemen, as it was sometimes pronounced, who would be winding the winch handles for the hoist. Following all this, two types of platforms were erected: one kind on deck to accommodate the weighmen, the other, partly across the hatches, was for the bearer-off.

While those on the ship were busy setting up cranes, ropes and pulleys, those outside had to bring the gangplanks over to the ship. The necessity for gangplanks demonstrates that cranes were often unavailable, and ships' derricks not suited to every commodity. A docker remembers dealing with placing those gangplanks: 'It was no easy job lifting those planks on a cold wet winter's morning, when they were either covered with snow or stuck to the ground with frost. If any man was seen wearing gloves, well he would never live it down!'[38]

On deck, dockers had much work in the early days moving cargo that had been winched to deck. They might have to haul it from the radius of one winch and derrick to the radius of another derrick or crane for the swing to dockside.

Wheeling cargo down the gangplanks was far from easy and though dockers learned shortcuts, these could make the operation a risky one.

> At high water coming down these planks with two boxes of Yankee bacon (about 15 cwts.) was a very tricky job, and the usual procedure was to slide down half way on the legs of the truck, then lift the shafts and let the momentum of the truck carry you right across the road. If you stumbled or slipped you had a good chance of ending up in hospital.[39]

Steamship winches could be driven by the ships' steam on steamships equipped with that facility. The distinctive rattle of the steam winch is memorable to those who have heard it. Still, the dockside reach of the early winches and cranes was short, requiring extra work on the wall. The 'guy hauler' was a specialised docker role, involving manipulation of the derricks. The derrick was pulled round by hand using a wire, the guy wire. This was necessary in order to position a derrick for maximum reach. When not thus employed, the guy-hauler moved sacks and other commodities on deck for the weighman; he became, that is, 'the boy', a bearer-off. Once cargo was landed, it had to be moved by dockers using rollers and handspikes. Handspikes were wooden bars used to lever or crow heavy items. The outdoor work continued in all weathers. Sacks draped across the shoulders were standard protection. The normal workday in the early days was from six in the morning to six in the evening, once work on the ships had commenced.[40]

Returning closer to the present, let us sort the dockside work of the more modern twenty-two-man gang. Eight men were inside on the gang we choose, thirteen were performing tasks dockside. Nine men were handling bogies. Bogies were low, flat carriers on small wheels, upon which the cargo was placed dockside. An expert craneman in a modern crane can land the hoist out of the hold neatly upon a waiting bogie (or wherever else on wall or dock is desired). The dockers could then immediately begin to manoeuvre the bogie in its next direction.

A poorly landed load, however, thrust the modern docker back to the earlier days of ships' winches: back to a lot of 'kneeing', shoving and handspiking. The biggest docker might pull a front loaded four-wheel bogie, while two others pushed from behind. A large-sized bale being moved on a hand truck required two men. Both the four-wheel bogie and the dockers' two-wheel hand truck (also called bogies) had steel wheels. To oil the wheels, the dockers scrounged grease and oil from the ships.

Four dockers in our twenty-two-man gang were 'tierers'. They stacked the commodity inside a warehouse or shed. Two men stacked at basic level, man high. They were tierers in the strict sense, while the other two were 'toppers', piling up the height of the stacks. The toppers stood on the stacks built by the tierers. A longer gang might have

Before forklift trucks. Anthony Montgomery and Larry 'Big Apple' Doyle. (Michael Donnelly collection donated by Florrie Cunningham to the Dublin Dock Workers Preservation Society)

one or two 'double toppers', tiering very high under the eaves of the warehouse. Specialist sorting, for example of types of timber, was often done by deep-sea dockers in the warehousing sheds or at dockside. It was because of such specialist sorting experience that dockers were in demand outside the port by, for example, Hector Grey. Other necessary sorting occurred when multiple importers received chunks of the same cargo.

A 'tipper', rather than tierers, toppers and sorters might be required by a different commodity. Tippers tipped loose bulk cargo into waiting lorries or carts, or into dockside receptacles. The tipper stood on the rim of a lorry, usually creating the emptying process by hand. This might, for example, involve releasing a hook on a hoist, the hook then being re-locked for the crane-arm's return swing. The tipper was the dockside counterpart of a hooker-on on deck.

Bulk cargo needing to be shovelled required a far higher ratio of men inside the holds. For coal there was a ratio of sixteen inside and four outside. This ratio could extend as radically as eighteen inside, plus only a single tipper and the singer-out whose job is described below. Although more men in many other typical gangs worked outside the hatches rather than in them – at the other extreme, that is, from the ratio just cited – the inside work was clearly considered by dockers as the classic, the 'real' Dublin deep-sea docker work. Inside work was harder than dockside work, especially in discharge. The inside men were those called first in the gang at the read. Those called next constituted an outside set to match the inside gang. Most dockers regarded being called first for inside work as an honour, and inside gangs competed for reputation just as full gangs did. A minority of Dublin deep-sea dockers, however, felt that some foremen called their favourites later in gang sequence in order to grant them the lighter dockside duties.

Once a gang was chosen, the likelihood was that it would continue unchanged until completion of the ship. If a man failed to show for any day's work on a gang, he lost his work for that ship, something too costly to the individual.[41]

A checker was always present to count everything but was not part of the docker gang, per se. Some checkers were former dockers, however.

The singer-out was the final gang member. The job was not physically demanding, and so it was typically done by someone less able for the power work. One part of singing-out was to signal when the load was ready to be hoisted. The task demanded needful attention and reliability for the craneman worked blind. His view of the load he manoeuvred was obscured by the edge of the hold. He had to know whether the heave he was raising was clearing the hatch sides cleanly. The singer-out shouted this important detail. The singer-out also checked the quality of the rising hoist. He might signal to the craneman to put it back if a bad sling appeared; then the inside gang would be directed to fix it. The inside men also warned of returning, dropping tubs and hooks, so the singer-out positioned himself on the seaward side of the ship, opposite the craneman's landside position. Thus, each of them could see one side of things. Piping and shouting directions for heaves out and empties back, the singer-out's job was a fulcrum part of the operation and was generally paid at the same rate as the rest of the gang. Although older dockers most often got the job, Martin Mitten began his deep-sea life, at age 18, as guy-hauler, singer-out and then hooker-on. Paddy Robinson, according to his own testimony, was a singer-out at age 12:

> to help me father rear the family ... He got me a job in Heiton's as a boy singing out. I shouldn't have been there. I was underage. I was in the job for five or six year: singing out, like telling the craneman what to do. As the labouring fellas used to say, 'the craneman's director'. A nice title for a fella![42]

Novices as singer-outs were rare, however. Usually, the singer-out was an older, experienced docker who could be most trusted to protect the gang. Indeed, some dockers regarded singing out as the most stressful of the variety of tasks, because of the strain of responsibility. A 'hatchway man', another of the gang, might also stand on the deck and with hand signals cautiously guide the swaying cargo towards the quayside.

In the early stage of his working life, a docker might be brought along progressively from one role to another, perhaps starting with some of the dockside tasks, moving on to become a guy-hauler (a 'boy') or a weighman before achieving power enough to fill the tubs in the hatch. One docker's first job was to stitch up torn flour bags, a job suited to those with young eyes but without strength enough yet for the heavy weights. Singing-out and hooking-on were, despite the two individual biographies just mentioned, far less often among tasks given to newer deep-sea dockers.[43] At the digging, one might have the chance to adjust to the lighter weights borne by the number four and five shovels before moving to the coalies' number seven. At the serious extreme, there was even a number nine!

Cranes and dockers loaded, of course, as well as discharging. Irish peat moss was exported to become the turf on North American racecourses. Nets full of jute bags of peat moss, or packages of Irish wool for export, were swung into the hold – to be stowed by the trimmers. Trimming was packing the load in a balanced way so that it did not shift at sea, using dunnage when necessary. Dunnage was wood or other light material used to further brace, protect and trim cargo to prevent damage. Spreading loose commodities such as grain into the wings of the hatch was a simpler trimmer's task. Trimming for seaworthiness was usually technically more skilled work than discharging tasks. A shifting cargo could sink a ship. Among London and Manchester dockers, loading carried more prestige than discharge.[44] Not so Dublin, where trimming carried far less renown in the deep-sea docker scale of distinction.

All dockers who 'followed' work with a regular stevedoring company became particularly skilled in handling the commodities specialised in by that operative. Some dockers took a zealot's interest in logistic problems. Given the complexity of the work, that is not surprising. One deep-sea docker was so keen a deviser of methods that he became nicknamed Nicky Knack. Nicky loved any logistical challenge, for example, how to get difficult cargo up out of the hatch, and was always working on some complex problem. 'Systemer' Farrell had essentially the same nickname. 'Up an Inch' is a pejorative moniker for someone who is over-exacting, while 'Burst the Deck' labels one who forces the pace of the gang inappropriately. Beat-the-Dark Geoghan and Heave-Ho Daly carried work-a-day nicknames, as did Turnaround Hawkins and Handspike McDonnell.[45]

When a ship was finished, the gang was 'sacked'. Such was the dockers' term, and the formal Dublin trade union term.[46] The employers also spoke informally of sacking when they dismissed a gang or part of it, although in written documents they 'return gang(s) to the Read'.[47] Gang size could be shortened or lengthened during work on a single ship to suit different phases of discharge. Thus, part of a gang might be returned to the read, or the stevedore might, conversely, himself repair to the read stand to select men to lengthen the gang.

Technological evolution altered dock work fundamentally. Under the pseudonym 'Old-Timer', one docker could weave the following lament as early as 1960:

> The young men of the present generation of dockers may think themselves very lucky that they are not expected to tackle the heavy labour that the dockers of fifty or sixty years ago had to undertake to eke out a very precarious livelihood. I wonder do our younger dockers today with all the modern appliances for handling cargo, such as mobile cranes and forklifters, four-wheeled trucks with rubber tyres, and silos, ever ask themselves how the work was done half a century ago, before any of those gadgets were thought of ? [48]

Yet despite the change mentioned by 'Old-Timer', 1960 was still clearly the great age of monumentally manpower-necessary Irish dock labour, when muscles did the power work, and when anyone not used to the effort could not lift his arms after a day of it.

When Something Goes Wrong, It's Serious

The dark, dusty and cargo-crammed hold was a workplace full of risks. 'The dangers in the hold of a ship are well known,' *Waterfront* explained. 'A falling bale or lashing wire can mutilate in seconds.' Accidents witnessed remain sharply etched in the memory of dockers. This one occurred when a lorry was backed up above deck level.

> The brakes slipped or something and the lorry came in on the ship. For quickness the lorry was on the edge of the

A hoist of timber poles. (Michael Donnelly collection donated by Florrie Cunningham to the Dublin Dock Workers Preservation Society) water, and it came right in on the deck and the whole thing bended. The chap that was at the back came down [with] the bags of cement … We dived down after him to try and get to him. He fell into the hold, into the ship where we were working … and about 4 or 5 ton of cement came down with him, burst all over the hatch. 'We were lucky, we were safe enough, but we couldn't see one another. We all tried to dive down, someone roared that there is man down with the cement, but he hadn't a chance. We got him up all right. I think he was alive going to the hospital.[49]

Another time it was under sugar bags that deep-sea docker John Hawkins and a workmate were buried. It proved difficult to get the two men out of the hatch. Hawkie was OK, but his mate never again returned to work.[50]

Another docker, covering up the hatches of a 'Yankee ship', had only battened down two of the necessary cover fastenings, 'instead of hooking on four. And he jumped on the thing and it bended and he went down 40 feet into the hold. Hit the beam of the twin decks going down. A young active docker he was. Jim Sweeney was his name.'[51]

In one case, a hoist broke loose and fell back into the hatch on the docker below. In another, the edge of a sharply-rising heave caught the docker and threw him against the wall. A 20-year-old docker called Wallace was killed when the grab swung into the hold and hit him, the craneman not knowing that anyone was down there. Much trust had to be placed in the hands of the singer-out and the hatchway man to ensure that hoists, hooks and grabs cleared the ship safely. Yet the singer-out could not save the life of the young docker who jumped into a bumper hatch of grain and was impaled through the neck by 'a lump of stick' stuck in the grain.

Footing, or materials to be handled, could be slippery from leaked fruit juices or other wet commodities. But it was the ordinary, rather than the extraordinary, circumstances which surrounded most accidents. Some situations depended solely on the individual's own care. A 'paper boat' discharging giant reels of paper could be especially dangerous

if the vessel didn't have stability arms. If you're lifting paper aboard with a ship's crane, you're lifting maybe 9 or 10 tons a tip. And you have the two cranes going out, two of them hitting the wall. As soon as the weight goes off, the ship rolls back the other way (so if you had stability arms that could help). But James was standing on a reel of paper and when the ship rolled back there were only three rolls of paper left in the hatch, nearly £3,000. He was still in the hatch, he was standing on one of them and when the ship rolled back he slipped off. The two rolls of paper came together. Dead immediately.[52]

'Every day someone would be injured,' says another docker, referring to the period of the 1920s and 1930s.[53] The risk continued. 'We've had quite a few deaths,' Michael Donnelly, docker trade unionist said in 1998, 'to my knowledge around twenty … When something goes wrong in our section, it's serious.'

Dockers took a pragmatic attitude to it all. They kept alert but didn't spend time worrying about the risks. 'You never looked at the danger: you'd have to be careful.'[54]

Breathing the dust in the holds was dangerous too. Digging phosphorous – including compounds and sulphur ammonia inside the hold – regularly caused men to bleed from the nose. Breathing flour dust could affect the chest. Most of the dust, from grains,

The 100 Tons Electric Crane at the North Wall Construction, 1926. The first electric crane in Ireland, it operated from 1905 to 1986, after which time it was demolished. (Dublin City Library & Archive)

coal, phosphorous, potash, was unavoidable. High winds could raise exceptional billows of dust. Ventilation fans were not usually provided on shipboard. And dockers were not so careful about that situation. They did not recognise it as much of a hazard, any more than did their employers. Dockers were paid bonus rates when dust was high, for example, when pink potash was 'white', the docker term for dusty. Imported asbestos, 'bagged blue asbestos', was fairly lethal stuff to suck into one's lungs when a bag split. Among dockers' normal tasks was sweeping up the dust and spillage remaining on the floor of the hold, including asbestos dust. Awareness of the dangers of asbestos came as late to the shipping industry as to everyone else. Considering it all, and looking back, one old-time docker declares: 'If I had known the dangers, I'd have preferred to go hungry.' Luckily, that docker, Mick Tierney, remained hearty and hale into his sixties or seventies.

Off the ship, on the dockside, lorries, railway cars and forklift trucks were constantly moving; men have been killed by train-cars and forklifts. Freight of all shapes regularly descended and rose in swaying arcs. The danger was clear. Often a docker steadied or guided the descending load onto the bogie or seawall. Jem Granger was dragging on a coal tub when another tub, hanging from a different crane, swung across, colliding with the first and crushing the docker between. His lungs were badly damaged. He survived only two years, unable to work, and barely able to breathe.

No Umbrellas

The sheer diversity of work kept the job interesting. The many commodities we have described dockers handling to this point by no means comprise the full variety of goods and cargoes which deep-sea dockers handled, the list of which could go on and on. Even the ships as workplaces changed. The change from sailing ships to propellor-driven steamships was far less significant than was the increasing size of ships. Hull sizes, and therefore hold and cargo space, increased gradually over the full millennium, and at an especially rapid rate after World War Two. With the variety and the changes, 'the time passed terrible quick.

It was never boring. You could go up seven days a week and get seven different jobs.'

Most of all it was arduous, tough, hard work. 'They raised their family out of industry' is the way one stevedore puts it.[55] Hours were long, as we have seen regarding both grain ships and night-time digging in the colliers. As late as 1968, an agreement between the Marine Port and General Workers' Union and the Master Stevedores' Association states: 'Normal hours of work shall be 8 a.m. to 9 p.m. (10 p.m. on the day the ship finishes).' Jokes to the contrary, deep-sea dockers worked hard, according to all observers. Tonnage pay was one incentive. There were individual exceptions. 'Some of them,' Willie Murphy acknowledges, 'used to come back early … to get ahead of themselves, to get the work done early', but Martin Mitten added 'unfortunately some of them used never come back, and some of them used to come back late'. These exceptions, annoying to many concerned, other dockers certainly included, added their own kind of colour to the scene. Tardy returnees and 'Irish rheumatism', the dockland term for laziness, had to be exceptions, for too much was at stake. Too much was at stake with the gang's work requirements. We have shown in this chapter how formidable the work enterprise was. Too much was at stake too with the individual's need to face the next day's read with a continued good work slate. Shippers praised the speeds of Dublin gangs: 'second to none', according to one shipping official.[56] Referring especially to unloading timber, deep-sea docker Brendan Dempsey asserts: 'We set records.'

The tasks themselves were carried out creatively, to save maximum exertion. Hooks were laid down so that bags could be dropped on them, rather than raising the sack to the hook. Tubs were tilted for rawheading. Shovels were handled with skill parallel to handling a camán. The work was done with careful intelligence such that physical effort was removed until absolutely necessary. The raw muscle of the docker, nevertheless, was essential to the Irish economy, and he applied that muscle with energy, power and pain.

An individual's personal valuation of the worth and importance of his work weighed considerably in terms of job satisfaction. Many dockers mention a sense of pride. Competition among gangs for the reputation as the best gang in the port is one aspect of pride. Self-esteem in the value of their work has been more than strong in the tradition of the Dublin docker. Despite both the read system and the gruelling nature of some of the tasks, job satisfaction is evident. Another aspect of pride is that there never was an 'umbrella' – a hovering, waiting unsupplied crane-hook hanging over the inside. Expressing part of docker self-esteem, in relation to that incessant, inevitable return of the hungry crane arm, one docker says, 'you would not, as a matter of pride, leave that hook hanging above your head'.[57]

THREE

THE PORT, HOBBLERS AND THE GULLS OF RINGSEND

I was so proud working with my father.[1]

Two unique features of the story of the Dublin docker are the prominence of hobbling in the development of dock work in Dublin, and the particular relationship between stevedoring and docker work. Hobbling connects centrally with the history of the port of Dublin, as well as with the unique development of stevedoring in Ireland. We look first at the up-and-down history of the bay and the port.

The Medieval Dublin Docks and the Evolution of the Port

Prior to the ninth century Dublin was little more than a small monastic settlement.[2] In 837, sixty-five Viking ships sailed in through Dublin Bay and up the River Liffey. With their arrival, Dublin became not only a thriving town with numerous churches, but a useful staging point for maritime trade, thanks to a handy pair of harbourings. Ships were unburdened, or loaded and trimmed, along the River Liffey for the long-distance sea trade as early as the late 700s. As the port developed over the next centuries, among the essentials for the increase

Spencer Dock Scherzer bridges built in 1912 to allow ships access to the Royal Canal and Spencer docks, north of the Liffey, c.1912–14. Robert French photographer. (Image Courtesy of the National Library of Ireland, call no. L_ROY_11592)

of commerce from the town's hinterland, markets and craft industries, were shore labourers to help handle chests, casks, bales and stuffs for the new merchant importers. The docker's work spans the history of Dublin. We trace now the story of the port as a rather changing and shifting worksite. We follow the hobblers and their connection to stevedoring. We see the emergence of dockers and the importance of family tradition in the docker heritage.

Winetavern Street marks the west end of Wood Quay below Christchurch, with Fishamble Street at its east end. This was the harbour's prime original berthing for deep-sea ships, its origins lost in time. Scandinavian occupiers solidified the embankment in stages over the early centuries. The other berth, as the settlement began to become a town, well before the end of the first millennium, was in An Dubh Linn, the Black Pool at the mouth of the River Poddle. Today this spot is marked by the gardens behind Dublin Castle. The harbour in the pool was along what was to become Parliament Street. This pool slip soon partially stagnated and Wood Quay then dominated as the discharge and loading wharf.

The Normans greatly expanded the docks after they occupied the city in 1170. Directly across on the north bank, the monks of St Mary's Abbey had a dock from which they traded with French ports such as Dieppe. Standfast Dick made the north bank dangerous for ships, however. The Dick was a reef of projecting rock not far from what is now Ha'Penny Bridge.[3]

In the medieval world, Dublin port was a leading emporium for North Atlantic commerce.[4] Wines, spices, iron and salt were the main imports ferried under sail through the bay and up the Liffey from the Continent and Britain. Rowed galleys and longships also navigated the river. Goat and cow hides for leather moved in the opposite direction, along with corn (as grain was traditionally known), livestock, bronze and silver work, hawks, and slaves and, in the earliest days of the Irish port settlement, wolfhounds and gold.

A large permanent wooden crane was in place by the fourteenth century for dockworkers to discharge ships.[5] The crane served the secondary purpose of weighing imports. This was an official function of the customs authorities and would have required a Dublin dockside workforce, as weighing-related tasks could not be delegated to the ship's sailors. The sale of goods then took place near the quayside. Merchants did not pre-order shipments as frequently as in much later centuries; thus the dockside workforce likely remained on standby to handle and move for the buyer, as well as for the shipper.

The crane stood at the west end of Wood Quay, at the bottom of Winetavern Street for many centuries, often reconstructed and improved. Although some stone was used for these improvements earlier, it was not until the early seventeenth century that the first fully stone quays were built in Dublin.

During the late Middle Ages and Reformation period, Dublin dock workers, or ships' sailors, loaded and trimmed sawn planks of Irish wood for the overseas markets. With considerably more difficulty, they also struggled with massive unhewn oaks that were being cleared from the island for export. The pews in Rouen Cathedral were made from Irish oak. Salted salmon, whiting, pollock, cod, herring, hake and smoked sardines were also loaded at the crane, along with woollen cloth, linens, ready-made cloaks, yarn, tallow, candles, butter, salt beef in hogshead and the earlier staples, skins and grain. Honey was added to the imports, and Dublin, like the rest of the world, continued to take as much Bordeaux wine as it could get.[6] Rolling big round wooden hogsheads constituted much of the discharge labour in the earlier centuries; so many commodities being shipped in barrels. Some of the discharge and loading work was done, during the 1500s and 1600s, in the small inlet slips that indented the Liffey riversides during those centuries.

A burst of quay construction in the late seventeenth century finally gave those unloading ships a broader, stronger, lengthier worksite. By the year 1700, stone quays had been erected on the north side of the river from Arran Quay to Bachelor's Quay and on the south side from Usher's Island all the way to George's Quay at Moss Street. New cranes, two or three of them, were situated for docker work at Old Custom House Quay, near the modern Clarence Hotel. Considerably further out towards the mouth of the river, in 1713, Sir John Rogerson organised the infill of land and construction of a quay on the south side of the river stretching towards Ringsend. Rogerson had been a Dublin City Councillor who was granted ownership of this wasteland marsh zone. In return, he privately paid for construction of this significant section of the Dublin quay system.

The gap which had been created between Rogerson's monumental extension wall and George's Quay was filled in by the corporation in 1715. This became known as City Quay, as did the residential area that sprung up behind it. Generations of dockers and their families would come to live in City Quay. Meanwhile, north and south of the Liffey channel, fronting the bay, wharfs were also being built. Bayside Strand North originally lay along the line of the present Custom House, the waterfront beginning its widening diagonally into the bay near what is now the Abbey Theatre. Liberty Hall stands in what was a dock indenting the north quays in the eighteenth century. This was Mourney's (or Marney's) Dock, which had in its turn replaced earlier Iron Quay. The north wall of the Liffey channel extended itself faster than did the construction of any bay-facing eastern wall. The Liffey quays therefore continued to be the chief work site of the Dublin docker.

A uniquely Irish form of construction was employed to create sections of the embankments forming the quay walls. Kishes are turf baskets, particular to the Irish boglands. Kishes were filled with small stones and sand to be sunk inside heavy rock outer quay walls. There were 1,000 kishes from Monasterevin recorded as providing for these works in 1715.[7] So common was this form of embankment construction, that, in Dublin, the building of new quays could be officially spoken of as 'continuing the bank of kishes'.[8]

The Custom House of the present site was built between 1781 and 1791, despite the opposition of some of the gentry living in the nearby Georgian houses, and three separate docks were built around it. Shortly thereafter, across the river, Grand Canal Docks, between Ringsend and Sir John Rogerson's Quay was opened with much celebration. Twelve cranes were to grace these southside deep water facilities, which were entered at the mouth of the River Dodder. The shipping trade failed,

however, to make use of these fine resources. Examination of the Ordnance Survey map of 1837–8 makes plausible that it was simpler to sail straight past Ringsend and to berth and unload at the North Wall a little further up the Liffey channel, rather than to negotiate entry into Grand Canal Docks. Thus, the fine Grand Canal Docks never became a hub of docker activity.

Sailing ships of the early eighteenth century might have carried malt for the brewing trade, or bricks for the growing building industry in Dublin. Grain had now become an import commodity, and a

Large tanks on the lorry contrast with the old-style barrels on the quayside, showing the move from manual labour to mechanical. (Fexro's collection, Dublin Dock Workers Preservation Society)

significant one. Spread-sail, four-masted corn ships carried grain from Australia to these islands. Here is a detailed account of the cargoes dockers stowed and trimmed in 1830.

> For the year ending 5 January, 1831, there were exported from Dublin 7,461 bales of bacon, 41,105 firkins of butter, 40,00 barrels of wheat, 20,744 barrels of barley and bere, 153,191 barrels of oats, 16,482 loads of oatmeal, 10,356 sacks of flour, 103 barrels of malt, 88 hogsheads and 259 casks of hams, 3,300 crates of eggs, 10,084 tierces of beef and pork, 1,701 boxes of candles, 1,750 packs of feathers, 6,781 bundles of hides, 365 casks of lard, 693 bales of leather, 800 puncheons of whisky, 29,800 hogsheads of porter, 3,648 boxes of linen cloth, 2,100 bills of printed cottons, 3,500 packs of wool, 69,500 oxen, 58,000 pigs and 80,000 sheep.[9]

The imports for discharge for the same year are equally colourful: '340,000 tons of coal, 3,350,000 pounds of coffee, 52,000 chests of tea, 2,000 bags of pepper, 15,000 hogsheads and 2,200 bags of sugar, 1,150 hogsheads of tobacco, 7,100 pipes and hogsheads and 1,500 cases of wine, 11,600 logs of timber, 2,000 great hundreds of deals and 3,500 great hundreds of staves.'[10] Deforestation already complete, Ireland was by then importing timber.

Despite expansion, all was far from well for either the port or the dockworkers over these many centuries. A terror for men near the docks was the press gang. The British Crown had an absolute imperial right to shanghai men for service in the Royal Navy. Dockworkers, however, as well as mariners, were in danger of impressment not merely because they were able-bodied and in the vicinity of the port but because 'landsmen' were also directly, and by that designation, sought for 'recruitment'. 'Recruitment' was blatant impressment when volunteers did not meet the quota. The 'call' for landsmen wanted could even exceed that of seamen levied.[11] The sudden savage rush of the press gang was a fear for a century-and-a-half. But a several-centuries longer peril was the bar.

A Bar in the Mouth

Dublin bay proved to be troublesome water as an entryway for a busy port. Six miles long and five and a half miles wide, this is how Marmion described its loveliness in 1850.

> This bay, which has been represented to have a strong likeness to that of Naples, has no resemblance to it whatever; but it is not therefore the less beautiful. Entering it from the sea about sun-rise, it presents, probably, one of the finest prospects in nature. The land on both sides forms two peninsulas: on the south is the fine range of Wicklow mountains, faintly blue, towering in the distance; nearer, and along shore, the harbour and town of Kingstown, Killiney Hill, and Dalkey village and island present themselves to view; on the north, the hill and harbour of Howth; Lambay and Ireland's Eye form the boundary: while in the deep centre, the metropolis is faintly seen, with its attractive Light-house, robed in white, standing like a watchful sentinel to mark the entrance to the harbour.

Lambay and Ireland's Eye are islands.

This peaceful physical beauty described here masks a turbulent navigational history. Silt brought down by both the Dodder and Liffey rivers added itself to sands from the sea to form natural shallows in the bay. Ships also dumped unwanted ballast in the bay. The result was the growth of two huge sand humps called the South Bull and the North Bull, obstacles that were to cause considerable obstruction to navigation. Between the Bulls, the combined power of the two rivers etched a fragile channel. As we have seen up to the early fourteenth century medieval ships sailed the channel, with the tide, all the way to Wood Quay.[12] As centuries elapsed, this passage was to become more difficult.

The list of hazards was long. The channel itself routinely moved around in the bay as currents and winds shifted sands and silt. Finding the channel could be a challenge in the open expanse of bay before the modern breakwaters were built. Anchorage was a second problem.

Ships needed deep water in which to ride at anchor while awaiting the tidally permitted hours for approach to the port. Such deep water was unavailable in Dublin Bay. Large vessels were forced to wait instead in the bottomless roadsteads in the Irish Sea east of Dun Laoghaire or at Dalkey.[13] Delay at anchor was, however, more than a matter of waiting for tides.

Dublin port history includes centuries during which the amount of moorage space was inadequate. Until 1791, the Custom House was located in the heart of Dublin city, far up the River Liffey. The first Custom House, constructed in 1620, was at the end of Crane Lane in today's Temple Bar (on what was known as Old Custom House Quay). In 1707, a new building was erected a short distance away on what is now known as Wellington Quay. Merchant ships were legally bound to proceed to this point. At any one time, up to seventy ships could be moored and stacked eight deep against the quayside. Such congestion kept vessels which might be waiting at sea longer at anchor in the outer roadsteads than would otherwise be necessary. Gales, ever a threat at sea, became an enhanced problem because of the lack of port anchorage. The anchorages outside the bay off Dún Laoghaire were open to the tempest: it was hazardous floating, delayed in the Irish Sea in a gale, especially for sailing ships. But even the bay itself was not much better. 'The bay of Dublin,' the city assembly complained in 1808, 'is an open bay and a most dangerous roadstead for vessels during the continuance of strong north-easterly or south-easterly winds from which points violent storms frequently proceed during the most dangerous seasons of the year.'[14] All of this was compounded by the bar.

The bar was an underwater reef running through the middle of Dublin Bay. At low tide it offered, in its natural form, just under six feet, 1.8 metres, of water, in the channel, making it necessary for most ships to run it at high tide. The trough of a deep wave could dip to three feet of water at the bar.

'Dublin haven hath a bar in the mouth,' wrote a seventeenth-century commentator, 'with an ordinary tide you cannot go the key of Dublin with a ship that draws five feet of water.'[15] At ordinary high tide, that was, of course. Thus, even at fullest flood many ships were in peril crossing the bar. The bar was marked with a 'beoie or perche' in 1582, but buoys were not a solution.[16] Many ships were wrecked on the bar, with considerable loss of life.

The bitter cry of the merchants of Dublin about the treachery of the bay, especially the bar, is a 500-year chronicle of appeals to the Crown, and other damning documents. The problem of the bar was finally solved by the 1840s through decades of scouring by a clever currents-channelling construct called the Bull Wall. This was built on the recommendation of Captain William Blyth in a report published eleven years after the *Bounty* mutiny. This wall, against the North Bull, funnels the force of the ebb tide hard out against the bar, just where the bar crosses the shipping channel. A couple of decades of this daily punishment, and the bar was permanently grooved. The port could now blossom, and did in the late nineteenth century, especially, as we shall see, with the construction of Alexandra Basin in 1885. But the centuries of problems had created a Dublin docker tradition which has connections down to the present: the hobbler.

The Hobblers

'The badness of the harbour,' lamented a commentator in 1674, 'did occasion the decay of trade.'[17] Decay because ships were avoiding the

Left: River Liffey, Eden Quay and the Custom House. Engraving/print showing sailing ships far up the Liffey (Dublin City Library & Archive) Right: *SS Munster* docked at North Wall, Dublin, also showing factories and warehouses that surrounded the quays, 15 July 1959. (Image Courtesy of the National Library of Ireland, call no. INDR2149)

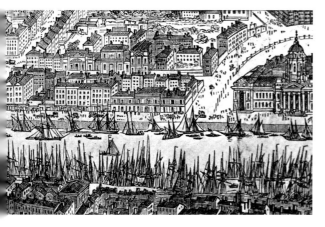

quays of Dublin; discharging elsewhere. Dalkey was by far the main beneficiary port. Coliemore Harbour in Dalkey became, especially between the fourteenth and sixteenth centuries, a primary port of call for the province of Leinster. Salt, iron and wine were among the commodities being discharged at Coliemore, which was fully a rival to Dublin City as a port.[18]

Coliemore Harbour as a port of discharge was a rather imperfect solution. Both commercially and legally, most cargo was either destined for Dublin city, or destined to pass through her. Dalkey was a difficult, slow land journey away from Dublin. A second alternative, however, existed. A Dubliners' petition to the Crown as early as 1358 hints at this alternative, one which is of special interest to the history of the Dublin docker. The petition bemoans 'that owing to the dangers of the harbour of the city of Dublin, no large ships laden with cargo will venture thither and that consequently merchants have usually sold their goods on shipboard within a distance of six leagues from the city'.[19]

Sale was taking place well outside of Dublin port. More important is a singular aspect of the history of the Dublin docker and Dublin stevedore. Whether goods were already consigned to an importer or were for sale: discharge itself was being performed at sea!

At sea discharge is transfer of cargo from ocean-going vessels into 'lighters'. Lighters are smaller craft of shallow draft, able to negotiate inferior depths. Discharge in the Irish Sea came to be taken charge of by a coterie of self-organised entrepreneurs known as 'hobblers'. Originally men from Ringsend, particularly, offered these services. A hobbling boat carried four or five men, usually four oarsmen and a steersman, and a lug sail. Rowing hard over against the cargo ship, they swung hooks onto her deck to secure the vessels together, and, after negotiations, began the transfer.

Discharge at sea was hazardous. Often cold and wet from sea spray, the hobblers hauled the sacks, boxes, or planks up from the ship's hold. The ship's winch, if the ship carried derricks, could be used during sea transfers, everything done balancing carefully on vessels tilting in the swell. Men had to be careful not to get their numbed hands caught as the smaller boat bounced unevenly versus the rise and fall of the larger vessel.

The hobblers did not know what cargo they would be handling until arrival at shipside. They simply raced to the ship to offer their service once the vessel had appeared on the horizon. It took several trips to complete such a discharge, ferrying the goods to Coliemore, Dublin, or Ringsend.

Once the channel of the Liffey had deepened, the hobblers as they had for centuries, sailed out to perform one or both of two tasks. The first was to act as pilot and tug, guiding the ship into port and mooring her at the quay wall at Dublin Port, now no longer called Ringsend. The archaic version of the term hobbler, in England, is hoveller, possibly deriving from the verb to hovel, or bring into shelter. The charge was two pounds for piloting and mooring, with another two to follow for piloting the ship back out to sea on the tide of her return voyage. This made sixteen shillings total a man for each of the five-man crew.

Contracting for the full discharge of the cargo in port was a second plum, which once more fell to the hobblers, with the same negotiation taking place as on deck for the at-sea discharge into lighters. The hobbler quoted a price for discharge of the cargo in port. Although the amount was ultimately paid to the dockers by the shipper, ship owner, or importer, the negotiation for docker labour costs took place at sea between the master of the hobbling boat and the ship captain. Although the charge for unloading was negotiable, the cargo ship could negotiate with one, and only one, Dublin agent: he who had locked onto the cargo vessel first.

Hobbling became fiercely competitive. When cargo ships appeared on the horizon, a race among the hobbling craft ensued, for the first of them to grapple the incoming ship gained, by mutual agreement, the right to service her. 'Up with the hook, grip the rail, and then fall in behind her.'[20] The first one to get her hook into her had her. Lyrics Murphy's father and grandfather were pilots and hobblers.

> They carried what they called a hook, a wooden pole with an
> iron hook at the top of it, with a rope spliced on to the iron

Discharging hogsheads of tobacco from Norfolk Virginia at the Point, 1931. (Donated by Michael Donnelly to the Dublin Dock Workers Preservation Society)

hook. You also had from ten to fourteen fathom of grass rope. The idea of the rope was that it gave a bit of a stretch, like elastic. When you'd hook a steamer it might be doing ten knots.[21]

Ringsend men may have entered hobbling earliest because Ringsend had begun to supplant Dalkey as the alternative to running the full perils of the ascent to Custom House Quay, Old or New. It was towards Ringsend that the Liffey-reluctant vessels had begun to drift. The earliest discharges at sea were brought in and discharged at Ringsend Dock.[22]

Competition was not merely among the 'Gulls of Ringsend', as the Ringsend hobblers were known.[23]7 Dún Laoghaire, however, pursued the enterprise with notable success too, as did townies from

Butt Bridge and East Wall. Dún Laoghaire boatsmen sailed a two-ended skiff, faster under sail, against the square stern Ringsend yawl, which was sturdier in heavy seas. There were some thirty competing hobblers in the 1930s. *The Irish Girl* and *The Irishman* were two of the especially fine hobbling boats. Most boats were family owned and crewed; the Kinch family made their living on the two boats just named. Smith, Lawless, Gough and Pullen were further Ringsend hobbler surnames.

'Highwater' Flanagan was a hobbler of such legendary scruffiness that he was mistaken for a pirate by some ship captains.[24] Bulletproof Power, Wee Chucks Byrne, Kick-the-Stones Fullam and Bluenose Murphy are among other hobbler nicknames. The hobblers were often fishermen in their other walk of life, who added hobbling to their interests. Strong, hard rowing, however, not fishing skills, was vital to competitive success.

The hobblers might spend days at sea in order to lay first eyes on a ship breaking the horizon. 'You'd go out and watch for them day and night.'[25] 'They'd go as far as the Rock-a-Bill, or Wicklow Head, or the Kish Lighthouse, because there was an awful lot of opposition [*sic*] in those days.'[26] The South Stack lighthouse, off the Welsh coast was often in view.[27] It was not possible to carry hot drinks, but they asked lighthouse keepers and passing ships for tea.[28] Bullock Harbour near Dalkey, was the overnight haven if storms interrupted the vigil.

Hobbling was formally prohibited by the Ports and Docks Board in 1936. The *Jealous of Me*, a Dún Laoghaire skiff, had foundered in the bay in December 1934, drowning three young hobblers, Richard and Henry Shortall and John Hughes. This tragedy is cited by dockers as the cause of the supplanting of the hobblers. Their functions were, as we shall see, being superseded. Hobblers were an extra-legal and unsystematic element in a port striving to modernise. The clampdown would have come on another pretext, or in a different form, had the *Jealous of Me* not been lost.

A few dockers continued, in the hobblers' tradition, to work multiple trades. 'Boatmen' were those who tied up the ships with huge ropes to the moorings. Some dockers doubled as boatmen.

there was a whole inter-relationship between the fisherman, and the dockworkers, and the seamen, and the people who tied up the boats … If they weren't tying up boats, they were doing a bit of dock work, or doing a bit of fishing, or whatever was available on the day: whatever was happening on the river. Well, then [combining all these] you got your living out of it.[29]

Although we have explained docker skill as specialised expertise, many of the men who did cargo handling for most of the millennium before the early nineteenth century followed multiple occupations, or, as commonly, were general dock labourers. In the Irish censuses of 1901 and 1911, only relatively few individuals named their occupation as docker. This despite the fact that the term was in common use at the time.[30] Among those with multiple occupations, one docker was apparently also an undertaker. Dubliners, naturally, could not miss such a nickname windfall. On the quays, he carried the nickname Chase the Corpse.

Seafaring remained an option in the career of a significant number of dockers. For the latter,

'it was traditional. If the work was good on the docks they stayed. If the work slacked on the docks, which periodically you got very bad times you know, they'd [be] joining the first ship that would take them. And off they'd go to sea.'[31]

The crew signing-on process in Dublin often remarkably duplicated the docker's read.[32] 'Wilo' Nelson, a well-known Dublin docker and foreman, was the son of a Scots sailor. Wilo too was briefly a seaman at the beginning of his career. Another docker had eight sons, all of whom became dockers, but seven of whom had some experience at sea. 'Sailor' Kiernan, Sailor Sims and Burnt Sailor Murphy are among dockers bearing seafaring nicknames.

Willie Murphy Junior went down to work at 16-and-a-half. After initial success at the read, the work dried up. One day, walking down the quay he heard that a ship carrying machinery was looking for crew. Presenting himself to the captain, he said

'I hear you are looking for crew?'

'I'm looking for a fireman,' he said. 'How old are you?'

I said, I was 22, in my gruff voice, like. I was 16-and-a-half.

And he says 'Do you know anything about fire?'

And I said: 'I have done a bit here and there, like, you know'.

So he says, 'Well, go home and ask your mother if it is all right', so of course, he knew I wasn't 22.

So I went home … and I told her I was going on as a galley boy … working as a junior. If she had known I was going as a fireman, she would have killed me.

That was my first trip to sea … And the chief engineer, he didn't want me down there. He had a look and he says 'Not another one!'… [There was] this big chute that you bang, and down comes the coal and you shovel it in. So the first shovel of coal I got, the boat gave a little roll and I rolled over to the chief engineer, so that by the end of my trip, he sent me up to the Captain. The Captain says don't worry about it, so he gave me the fare home … So that was the end of that. That was my first experience.

After that, he stuck to docking. Those who tried the sea didn't always come back, however. The brother of one docker jumped ship in California in 1919 and wasn't seen again until 1963. Having met a Dutch woman, he settled down outside Chicago. Returning after over forty years, he found his family living in the same flat in Moss Street in City Quay in which they all had lived in 1919.

A further link between seamen and dockers was via the trade unions. Seamen's unions rather dominated, or incorporated Dublin docker unionism for periods. We pick up the story of docker trade unionism further in Chapter 4.

Seamen also became dockers. As the button system was being formalised, seamen could opt in. Being members of an allied occupation, especially from the trade union point of view, seamen could register for a button and switch to being dockers. Familiarity with ship's winches led many of those who then left the sea towards the winchman specialisation.

The Stevedore on Top and He Looking Down[33]

Hobbling and stevedoring were intimately connected. A stevedore is, in the original linguistic sense, a docker who loads vessels – literally, a packer of cargo. The term originated in Spain, as *estibador*, where it is still the Spanish word for docker.[34]'Stevedore' still carries this original meaning locally in some British ports. There, stevedore and docker are titles for two different types of cargo handlers. Stevedores are considered, in those ports, the more specialised, and the more skilled.[35] In Dublin, however, the stevedore has long been the agent who supplies dock labour to shippers. The stevedore is the docker's employer. The alteration of the meaning of 'stevedore', from docker to employer, occurred simply. Hobblers were at the centre of this transmutation of language.

The hobblers often contracted, off the coast at sea, for discharge of incoming ships. This contract was entered into by the master of the hobbling boat. The hobbling master was thus in charge of supplying dockers. Because 'stevedore' had the more prestigious ring to foreigners, the master contracted to supply 'stevedores'. The master of the hobbling boat became the master stevedore, or head of the docker gangs. But, as he was also contractually the supplier of labour, he was seen by those he contracted with as the master-in-charge-of-supplying dockers/ 'stevedores'. In this sense, the master stevedore was the employer.

No one in Dublin, however, ever called a docker a stevedore. The designation thus fell first to the hobbling boat master alone. Then some port-based entrepreneurs began also to supply docker gangs for ships, and adopted also the term master stevedore, or simply stevedore. It was, in Dublin, a term of clear and distinct meaning.

'Stevedores' in the very broadest sense of the word came in two colours. In Dublin Port, there were the 'paid bosses' and the stevedores proper. 'Paid bosses' were used by the coal companies. Receiving a regular weekly wage, the 'paid bosses' job was to recruit 'coalies', dockers expert at coal handling. These were foreman employees rather than stevedores proper, as Willie Murphy explained; 'The stevedore were a different race of people to the bosses, you see a boss got a basic weeks wage, he was guaranteed x number of pounds a week.'

In contrast, as Willie Murphy outlined here, the stevedore didn't receive a fixed wage.

> The stevedore he worked on a tonnage basis with his agent
> … He would make a deal with the agent and he would say

Grand Canal Docks and Sir John Rogerson's Quay on the south of the river Liffey, 1926. (Dublin City Library & Archive)

'OK, so much a ton?' and if it was on a daily basis he would put so much on each person that he'd employ, and he'd be paid accordingly … he would get a cut for himself and done very well.

'Stevedore' could be a nasty enough epithet rolling off the tongue of Dublin dockers on some occasions. 'Not a kind word to say about them'[36] is one Dublin stevedore's experience of the docker's attitude to stevedores. 'Always suspicious,'[37] he adds. An early basis of docker resentment against stevedores stems from what dockers regarded as usurpation of a position in the port which they considered their own; a usurpation that worked severely to the disadvantage of dockers.

Alexandra Basin, on the north side of the river Liffey, 1926. (Dublin City Library & Archive)

Hobblers were little more than members of a team, doubling as boat crew and docker gang. The contracting master stevedore of the hobbling days was effectively the docker himself, at least as dockers remember it. The independent 'master stevedore' hobbler was at most a gang leader; certainly he was not a non-working middleman. Then, somehow, white-collared businessmen arrived as stevedoring companies, 'The stevedores today,' one stevedore explained 'probably had no skills at all about handling ships, they have to handle computers and balance sheets, they are businessmen.'[38]

Historical reality is more complex. Yes, the docker-as-his-own-agent existed.

The smallest stevedoring outfits were difficult to distinguish from work gangs ready to go. And there were the hobblers, the small timers. On the other hand, a tradition of entrepreneurial employers also runs from well before the beginning of the twentieth century. James Connolly was, in 1900, denouncing the Dublin stevedores, so named, as 'tyrannical bosses over the men'.[39] What was most tyrannical in Connolly's eyes was the dirt-low compensation that could be paid these dispensable, casual labourers. The evil arose from competition among the stevedores to secure the contracts for discharge or loading vessels. They competed via undercutting one another on their tonnage or whole cargo quotations. The loser was the docker, who could only be paid what the stevedore had quoted, less the stevedore's own profit. Connolly saw the docks as the most complete form of the exploitation of labour in Ireland.[40]

The direst aspect of this merciless situation was solved in 1912, at least for a period of years, apparently through the persuasive finesse of James Larkin. Larkin, against the odds one might think, succeeded in gaining the ear of the stevedores, then convincing them to stop competing for contracts by way of using their latitude with regard to pay rates and manning levels. He persuaded them, rather, to set a standard rate of pay for the port and to establish adequate manning levels generally.[41]

Stevedore's were very small businessmen. The staff of the traditional stevedore, if we exclude ships' foremen, consisted at the most of a paymaster who only worked at payout, and the publican in whose premises payout occurred.

Although some stevedores could be harsh or exploitative, and although the extraction of a kickback to publican, paymaster, foreman, or stevedore has a long enough history, nevertheless, docker cultural memory is correct in identifying the early stevedores as most often working-class men, and in some cases, working men. Men moved, moreover, in and out of stevedoring, further making the initial line between working docker and employing stevedore a porous and rather open one.

Billy Carrick was a nineteenth-century docker and hobbler; Monk Donoghue was a contemporary port worker. Together they formed a stevedoring company. Archie Murphy was a hobbler who formed another. Both of these firms were still operating in 1971, when the classic period of docker work covered by this study was altered. 'The Carrick' was the title often bestowed by dockers on the successive heads of the Carrick family. The Carricks lived in Creighton Street off the south wall of the Liffey. One stevedore remembered:

> [The stevedore] used to get out of bed, wash and shave and walk up to the corner of Creighton Street, which is on City Quay, and the men who were following ...would congregate there. No stand, just on the path. Pick out the number of gangs, say eight men plus a singer out. 'You go to such and such a ship'. And that's the way. And down on Ringsend you'd have a similar operation.[42]

Another stevedore read the selection from outside his cottage door. And yet another from his bedroom window! The Carrick firm hired plenty of Carricks, and the Murphy firm many Murphys – all of them kin. The Carrick stored shovels for the dockers, also right there on Creighton Street.'[43]

Cowld Shoulders Darcy, Georgie Gough and Patrick Downey were further nineteenth-century stevedores whose family members, like the Murphys and Carricks, remained dockers and port workers through the twentieth century. Georgie Gough, of Irishtown Road, was popularly known as the mayor of Ringsend. He had no children, but his brother was a hobbler who later became a docker, a busheller. Patrick Downey, although entered as illiterate in the census of 1901, was a successful stevedore, whose twentieth-century descendants continued stevedoring, and were also general labourers.[44] The Newmans of William Newman and Sons stevedoring company, by contrast, also owned a motor company on Kildare Street, and 'always dressed like rich gentlemen'.[45] Descendants of Cowld Shoulders, a northside, Sheriff Street family, carried the nickname 'Cowlers' in the mid and late twentieth century.[46]

A different kind of professional businessman joined the pursuit of stevedoring, alongside the local labour suppliers, as commerce became more involved. Larger and more complex ships required more in-port services. The stevedore became a general agent caring for most of the needs of shippers and ships. Spare parts from the ship's chandler for repairs were purchased by the stevedore. Port charges, according to the tonnage of the vessel, were paid to the port authority on behalf of the shipper by the stevedore. Warehousing for goods which were not directly removed from the quays was arranged. The stevedore advised the shipper and is his agent. Even more crucial than increasing complexity, in the change of things from hobbler to formal organisation, was the possibility to communicate more easily in advance of arrival. Stevedoring firms with permanent offices, secretarial staff, filing systems, and legal acumen began to draw the stevedoring business. It was not merely the sinking of the *Jealous of Me* that caused the demise of hobbling. The larger, more formally organised companies arrived shortly after 1934 for two reasons. Firstly because of the increasingly sophisticated in-port requirements and secondly because the hobblers as competitors had been eliminated.

Some stevedores specialised, as Carricks did in cement. J.D. Twohig, headquartered on Burgh Quay, specialised in tea ships, and might be employing only every couple of months. Eventually, Palgrave Murphy emerged as the largest. Palgrave's, referred to as 'The Company' by dockers,[47] were agents for several shipping companies, and often had a ship daily. The stevedore firms contributed a subscription to the Dublin Master Stevedores' Association according to their size. For the year 1949–50, the Ringsend Murphy company, now headed by Kit Murphy, following Archie Murphy, paid in £5.10s, the smallest subscription, while Palgrave Murphy contributed £57.7.3,

Like the dockers, the stevedores focused on the arriving ship. The contract may have been negotiated in advance, but the moment of truth was when the 'boatmen' tied the vessel to the moorings. A fast discharge is good service provided by the stevedore to his clients. This meant, to the stevedore, a good docker gang ready to go. The stevedores felt that they knew the dockers, and especially that they knew what combinations of men worked together efficiently in gangs. 'We have a good gang,' the stevedore might sigh with relief, knowing the work would go expeditiously.

Some of the skill in working together displayed by Dublin dockers derived from the long tradition of fathers bringing their sons into the occupation.

He'd Put a Son in His Place

Dublin dockers were proud of the occupation, as we saw in Chapter 2. Their families shared that pride; it made part of the family name. Sons often followed their fathers into docking. Neighbourhood prestige was only part of the reason for this continuity. Good jobs were never plentiful in Dublin; the chance for a good trade on the doorstep was therefore another motive for occupational succession. The docker had a dual legacy to pass on: status and money. Not a lot of money, perhaps, as we discuss further in Chapter 5, yet an income of true significance in working-class Dublin. When dockers spoke of family heritage, all of these factors were included. Mentioning first his father, one docker explained: 'when he died and I took his place … I was the only boy … Well, I was privileged, like, to start at 14 years.'[48]

It was usually not difficult for the father to find a way in for his sons. A new face at the read could be quickly matched with an old name. Here are simple further strategies.

I have no doubt that my father spoke to the stevedores whom he knew and said 'that's a son of mine over there; if there is any work give him a job by all means' …

What used to happen in latter years was … fathers … were seen in the read standing behind their son and pointing to him; and the stevedore would say, right that must be Willie Murphy's son. [He'd call] 'Willie Murphy', and when he would call Willie Murphy, the younger Willie Murphy would walk out and get employed. But Willie Murphy [Senior] had already been employed [elsewhere earlier] and gone off about his business.

So that is how they would get to know them.[49]

Considerably more enterprising than standing behind your son pointing is this:

My father was a top docker … he'd often go out in the morning and he'd get a job here and he'd put a son in his place … and he'd get a job somewhere else and he'd put a son in his place. And he'd have all the sons working and maybe then he'd go down to the pub.[50]

This wouldn't always work, to say the least. The foreman might be both wise to what was going on and unsympathetic with the practice. Putting a son in your place this way required some collusion. The son inheriting his father's name or nickname didn't often win his father's fortune at the read quite this easily.

Some boys kneaded their way in gradually. I mainly made my progress filling tubs for my brothers; maybe fill his tubs at dinner hour and that. When he'd be up at his dinner, I'd go down and fill up the tub … [You progressed] gradually until you thought you were fit enough to get into a coal boat … You use your own head, it was up to yourself to learn.[51]

Stepping in this way to give members of a work gang a break was not unusual. Those who stepped in were called 'spellers'.

Other sons drifted in more experientially. One docker's son had left school at 12 and a half to work as a butcher's messenger boy. One day, his delivery round took him down to the quays.

> I was coming away one morning and I saw the guys discharging a brick boat at the Butt Bridge into Heiton-MacFerrin's yard. I'm watching these guys discharge by hand. It was an old schooner, an old sailing boat and she was just there at Butt Bridge. So I spent the morning working with them. They were working onto a horse and cart. They were just throwing, hand to hand, two bricks, four bricks at a time. So I got in the train and started doing it, and each time that I stepped in for someone, he stepped over to the pub … I was relieving all the guys on the wall and each one would go over for a pint and come back. So they gave me five shillings.

> Well I was sacked when I went back: from the butcher's job. I was three hours relieving, I was enjoying myself that much I never went back to work until later on that afternoon, so they sacked me. That was my first taste of dock work.[52]

Not his last: he became a docker. Jem Kiernan had a sudden initiation.

> I was on my summer holidays from school. That was in 1935.

> I remember my mother sent me down to the dock with some tea and sandwiches for my father who was working discharging a coal boat in Spencer Dock on the Sutton's bank. I was 14 years old at the time. My father came over to me and said 'son go home and take them short trousers

off and put a long pair on you.' So I looked at him and he said 'Go on, I'm after getting you a job working with me.' So I rushed home and changed my trousers and went back down to him. I remember getting down into the hatch of the coal boat.

I was looking at the dockers digging the coal out of the boat and loading it into the big tubs and the crane in on to the bank owned by Suttons. I was so proud working with my father. James Nutsy O'Toole and Tommy Basset were working on the boat. I knew from that day on I was going to be a docker.[53]

As a measure of the importance attributed to family, *Waterfront* included a regular feature entitled 'Famous Families of the Port'. Here the Shaws are dated from the nineteenth century.

Those were the days when the brothers Fred and Richard Shaw were in the front rank of deep-sea workers. The Shaw brothers were known and respected throughout the 'Point', as North Wall Extension has been known from time immemorial, and they left a name for honesty and probity which has endured to the present day.

Fred, when he died, left only one son, named Fred also. Fred Shaw followed in his father's footsteps: working for many years as a deep-sea docker. Fred was a pillar of trade unionism, in times when unions were still looked at askance. A son of Fred's is today prominent at the Point, and is carrying on the tradition of his great forebears. So the famous name is perpetuated.[54]

The Forbes and Behans were families who supplied the larger part of a 'house gang' as were the McDermotts, Nevins, Doyles and Carricks.

A register of 348 deep-sea dockers compiled around the time of the development of the button system reveals seven each Carricks, Fullams and Lawless. Among the most numerous surnames, eight Downeys, ten Nolans, fourteen Byrnes, and, heading the list, sixteen Murphys.

Dockers' daughters married dockers' sons, according to our informants, and so the family trees became entwined.

> It is amazing, how closely knit the whole thing is. And people don't realise it, that there is so much inter-marriage all around the place … You know there would be six people at the read, six different men with different names, whether they'd be second or third cousins, twice removed or whatever, but they would be related somewhere along the line.[55]

Given the significance of all of the forms of inter-connection mentioned here and in Chapter 1, it is not surprising that some dockers reckon that one must be a known figure in the port in order to be called at the read at all. If not, 'It was not worth his while going down there, you know, because they wouldn't know his name, although they could possibly point to him out at the read and employ him. But that would be as a last resort.'[56]

The button system recognised and institutionalised the importance of family connection. When a man retired through ill health or old age, he could pass the button on to his son, brother or uncle. This kept docking a family profession. [If] there was a son who was living at home, he would be looked on as the provider of the family. He would get the button, rather than an elder brother who might be married. It was given to keep the family together … to help the family out more than anything else.[57]

In some cases, the transfer wasn't automatic. Some families, we are told, had to 'stand up' and make an issue of it in order to get the button passed on.

If a father was sick, he could also transfer the button to his son, but this had to be for a minimum of six months. Once recovered and able to work, and six months having elapsed, the button returned to the father, the son having to relinquish it.

The shipsides were nothing new to the sons of dockers, as we have seen, and will see further in Chapter 5. Yet the day came when, after years of listening to docking stories, of overhearing jokes between father, brothers and uncles, of spelling occasionally, now it was your turn to join the man's work world. Even for those with a family connection, the first weeks on the docks were far from problem-free.

While it was up to each docker to learn for himself, within the gang, work was usually divided up in a way that accommodated the new docker. Additionally, it was known for novices to rush lunch to spend the spare time practising alone on the empty ship so they could appear more skilled more quickly.

Not practising, but in the pub, on one of his earliest ever lunch breaks, Martin Mitten gained advice from an old-timer.

> This old docker, Lord rest him, Martin Hogg, he was …
> And he said to me … he knew my father and his brothers
> and that and he said, 'Martin' he said, 'are you going back
> to work?'

> Says he, 'have you a sandwich in your pocket?' 'Make sure'
> says he 'that you have a sandwich in your pocket.' Says he
> 'when you are at the tub and feel weak and you have no
> sandwich in your pocket you will get weaker, if it is there, you
> will be all right, it will help to strengthen you at the time'.

He took the old man's advice and so earned the nickname 'Bunter', because, like the overweight comic-book character Billy Bunter, he always had a 'chuck' sandwich in this pocket.

Some of the advice was more personal. A father sending off his son: 'Our hands were raw, there were blisters everywhere. So my Da sent me down to the toilet to urinate in me hands and leave them … It hardened them. It would help kill the pain. It would take the tenderness out of it.'[58]

The advice to urinate on your hands was part of the trade wisdom passed on to some.

In return for their help, and in recognition of the years they had put in, old dockers were respected. And space was made for them in the work gangs – with the cooperation of foremen and stevedores. Part of this respect resulted simply from the kind of men they were considered to be. Martin Mitten was 78 when we interviewed him, but he remembered the generation before him, 'they were great men, marvellous'. Trust in the older men continued too: they were often put singing-out.

Some felt that the long memory of dockers led to intransigence. Not merely loyalties, but methods and technologies of the past often kept their grip on individuals. One deep-sea docker who was also a trade union official asserts:

> We had an awful lot of people, and they were like ostriches: they would bury their heads in the sand, and they couldn't see progress. Sometimes we would look too far ahead for them to catch up you know. They would say our grandfathers and our great-grandfathers done this, and you couldn't get them to move.[59]

This man's point was immediately proven at our interview when he was interrupted by a colleague. 'No,' retorted the second docker, 'it was heritage! More or less like principle!'[60]

Today there is little opportunity for sons to follow their fathers down to the deep-sea docks because the size of the workforce has so far shrunken. Some of the great family docker names are no longer called in the early morning. Many dockers would still like it if their sons could continue in their footsteps. One says, wistfully, 'every docker used to have sons to carry on the tradition'.[61] 'Oh I would have liked it,' admits another, 'if one of them had gone there, at least one. The name is gone now; there is no one there now.'[62]

If You've Ever Seen Liquorice Allsorts

Alexandra Basin was called 'The Pond' by dockers. The basin is the deep-water centrepiece of the lengthy extensions constructed eastward into Dublin Bay on the north side of the Liffey. Lying behind the North Wall Extension, the Alexandra pier complex was opened in its original sections in 1885. Twenty years later one of the port monuments, the 100 ton crane, was erected. The 100 ton, now dismantled, stood on the North Wall Extension. It rose 150 feet above the dock, and had a clear lift of 75 feet above water level. Although also used for general purposes, it was the lift for heavy machinery such as generators. It was a majestic sight seeing the big crane hoisting a 100-ton locomotive straight out of a ship.

The North Wall Extension itself took from 1871 to 1937 to create. The year of completion saw the beginning of the gradual move of deep-sea functions of the port over from the south river.

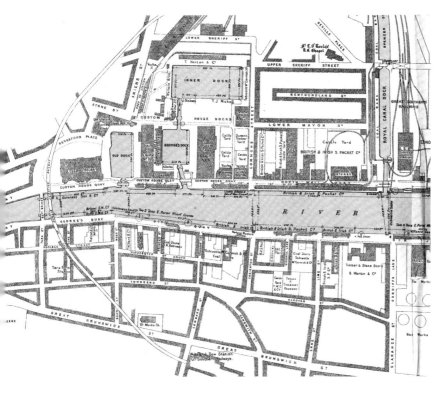

Detail from map showing Custom House Quay, North Wall Quay and the Grand Canal Dock, 1926. (Dublin City Library & Archive)

The Dublin Bay-facing East Wall had become a completed quay in the mid-eighteenth century. It was restructured in its present form about 1950, and named Ocean Pier.

The Pond and the river-facing wharves now became the deep-sea section of the port more purely, cross-channel docking concentrating around east at Ocean Pier. By 1971 there were more than sixty cranes in the port. The inlet docks near the Customs House – George's Dock, the Inner Dock and Spencer's Dock would decline in use because the ships became too big to enter through the entry-channels and locks.

The first result of the decline of the inlet docks was to increase docker work out on the river quays. Even though The Pond was absorbing much deep-sea dockwork, the Liffey channel up to Butt Bridge was fully deep water and its quays and cranes could continue to handle the large ships which could no longer enter Spencer's or the other narrow docks. Thus Dublin's commercial centre, at some of the busy major bridges, remained the worksite of many dockers, while others toiled further out of sight in the extensions around The Pond. Only through the later 1960s and 1970s were the quay sites gradually abandoned and virtually all docker work moved into the basins.

In whichever location, the docks were a riot of activity. There were all sorts of work to be done on the docks and all sorts of people to do it. The port had regular workers: warehousemen, railwaymen, customs officers, crane-men, importers' personnel, timberyard-men, stevedores. Importers and buyers at some periods of history bargained on the docks. Many of the port's people worked closely with the dockers, while others were occupied very differently. And there were irregulars around the quays, from occasional yardworkers and spellers to 'hoggers', 'boilers' and 'woodeners', men who were on the docks literally to suck slop alcohol. Hoggers poured slop Guinness, and anything else remotely alcoholic, into barrel lids and openly swilled the day away, chalking their faces in the process with red and blue barrel markings.[63] Woodeners, or boilers, worked especially on whisky barrels, into which they poured scalding water. They then rolled the barrel around, allowing the heat to draw alcohol from the wood.[64]

This was the docks: bikes stacked against the walls waiting for their owners; horse-drawn wagons, steam wagons and lorries, replacing each other in their time; gas company narrow gauge railway cars resting on sidings running close along the docks, surrounded by a motley assortment of waiting Dublin carters; female street traders from the Thomas Street or Parnell Street stall markets, who had learnt that bananas have arrived. Coal hawkers, using their own horse-drawn wagons, could cart away, jangling bridle and creaking car-bed, from a ton to a ton and a half. It was pandemonium of din and continual movement as, behind all this, ships clanked against the quayside. 'Any Monday morning' exalted *Waterfront* in 1960:

> here is the Dutch boat pulling in with tomatoes and general cargo. Hear the seagulls calling as they circle round her, as if to bid her welcome. Watch this one as, from the clear sky, he dives in effortless flight to light atop her mast. Now she's berthed and the work begins.

> Hear the clatter as the hatch covers are mechanically folded up, just like a concertina. Watch the crane as she lowers the hook to the hold, and dips her jib as if in salute. Listen to the creak and groan of the winch as she takes the strain. See the full 'bogies', half a gross or more of 12-pound trays pulled by the brawny one, and shoved by his mates into the shed by the ship. Watch them being sorted and stacked in their separate marks, in various coloured wrappings, blue and white, red and gold, green and orange, giving a gay and festive air to the toil and clamour of discharging. What a bustle! What confusion! Now the lorries queued outside the gates (some since last Friday) are in to load. Bustle and confusion did I say? To an onlooker it seems a nightmare, with lorries pulling in, vans backing out, 'breasters' running hither and thither with trays. What bedlam! What an uproar!

More: the smells of all of the commodities dockers were discharging. And, there were the seamen from everywhere, adding the accents of Dutch, German, Hindi and other languages to the Dublin city accent and the medley of other calls and sounds. Ships berthed, in one newspaper list of 1946, from 'Finland, Holland, Sweden, Norway, Denmark, USA, Mexico, Canada, Belgium, Persia, Newfoundland, France, Portugal, and Spain'.[65] And all the while, the empty tubs are being attached to the hook and hauled back to the boat, to be returned, filled by the inside gang as the dockers worked apace.

'All Sorts', the popular sweets, are a seemingly endless patchwork melange of pieces, colours, zig-zags, shapes and sizes leading a Dublin docker to make the analogy: 'if you've ever seen Liquorice All Sorts, you've seen the docks'.[66]

FOUR

GOD DIDN'T MAKE HALF-DAYS

You needed a union to protect you and fight for you.[1]

The economic life of Dublin city passed through the docker's hands. Those hands were highly skilled to the task of handling vital commodities at the funnel of the economic supply system. A strike by dock workers closed the port, idling other port workers, and bringing commerce to a standstill. In an island nation, the ports were vital. Import stoppages have publicly noticeable effect. A port strike affects the shelves at the local shop and supermarket. Thus, it was perhaps among the most publicly impressing of industrial actions. Some of the dock strikes have been of enough duration to affect the economy generally. Other Dublin workers, as a knock on, experienced lay-offs as their firms had to cease operations because of a lack of imported materials or parts.

Dockers strategically managed their economic niche, with all its disadvantages, to maximise their leverage and their gains. Uncertain of employment, Dublin casual port workers were considered 'ruthless in seeking payment to compensate for this uncertainty and provide for the days of idleness or absenteeism'.[2] We have discussed the importance of the trade union badge in docker history in Chapter 1, and the relationship of seamen's unions to Dublin dockers in Chapter 3. Although this book is a working-class history, it is not a trade union

Cattle on the way to the port passing St Laurence O'Toole's church, North Wall. (Donated by Joe Mooney to the Dublin Dock Workers Preservation Society)

history. We will not extend to a complete history of Dublin docker trade unionism and general industrial action. It is important, nevertheless, to show how the weapon of strike was used by dockers, both in the work culture, and in the management of their economic niche.

Dublin dockers were at their most prominent point in Irish trade union history in the first two decades of the twentieth century. The National Union of Quay Labourers organised Dublin dockers in the early 1870s.[3] In 1875, the Dublin Quay Labour's Union had 1,500 members. The cyclical peaks and slumps of an industry influenced the capacity to organise. Union membership seems to have collapsed during the depression of 1879. The next organisation to take hold was the National Union of Dock Labourers (NUDL). Cork man Michael McKeown was appointed Irish organiser, and after a Belfast Strike in 1890, the organisation spread to Dublin. Again, however, membership declined. Willie Murphy Junior, a deep-sea docker like his father, suggested that in the early days in many ways dockers were very much a non-union workforce. One reason for this was the link between family connections and employment opportunities.

> You see there was an awful lot of families, and they would see themselves as self-employed through the family, the family traditions ... they wouldn't identify with trade unions because they were working for the family, you had the Carricks, the Nolans, the Betsons and they worked as families.[4]

The decline of the NUDL was to last less than fifteen years. Four months after arriving in Belfast in 1907, the Irish Trade Union organiser and ex-docker Jim Larkin could claim 4,000 members for the NUDL. Belfast dockers were among Larkin's most enthusiastic adherents up to that point. Dock labour in Dublin was different from what Larkin had left behind in Belfast and in England. In both Britain and Belfast, 'constant men', permanently employed, were significantly among the docker work complement. In the struggle to improve conditions for port workers in Belfast and the British ports, alliances between casuals and constant men were a valuable tactic for labour organisers. Constant men were rarer among Dublin dockers in 1907, presenting Larkin with an even greater challenge. Yet by July 1908 he had established 2,700 members in Dublin.[5]

Most followed Larkin, when in January 1909, he set up the Irish Transport and General Workers Union (ITGWU). It is not recorded whether, in 1909, the founders of the ITGWU had dockers in particular in mind in deciding to organise general workers, thus casting their net to include casual workers in the new union. In the event, dockers were, tellingly, the first members of the ITGWU. They were indeed the young union's very 'backbone' in its early years, according to C. Desmond Greaves.[6] In 1915, the thirty-three representatives for the main, number one branch included four coal boat men, two grain bushellers and two general labourers[7]. In 1920 dockers were the fourth largest occupational element of the union nationwide.[8] The role of dockers at the forefront of the Lockout of 1913 has been widely documented.

Other unions representing dockers during these early years included the short-lived Irish Dockers and Workers Union, established in 1914, but dissolved by 1917[9] and the Amalgamated Transport and General Workers Union (ATGWU) established in Ireland in 1922, though headquartered in England.[10]

In 1924, the dockers, once again, followed Larkin to a new union when two thirds of the Dublin base of the ITGWU, split and joined the Workers Union of Ireland (WUI) which was founded by Larkin's brother, Peter.[11] One docker referred with pride to his father's connection with Larkin.

> One of the great men that we must all pay tribute to was Jim Larkin. He started to really bring the dockers up off their knees. You know my father was a founder member of his union, he was a founder member of the Workers Union in Marlborough Street, he kept with him. He thought he [Larkin] was a saint. He was compared to a lot of people. He never drank.[12]

Incentive Rates Schedule

(Tier II applies when the earnings achieved under Tier I reach £2.00)

CARGO CODE	CARGO	TIER 1	TIER 2
101	Bags – Unslung (4½p applies after 250 tons)	2p,	3½p, 4½p per ton
102	Bags – Preslung	2p,	3p per ton
103	Bags – Palletised	2p,	3p per ton
104	Bags – Palletising in Shed	4p	per ton
111	Black Wire	1½p	2p per ton
121	C.K.D.	4p,	5p per ton
131	Containers up to 20'		7p per unit
132	Containers 20' +		9p per unit
141	Fishplates & Chairs	4p	per ton
151	Fruit – Cartons	3p,	4p per ton
152	Fruit – Dried	3p,	4p per ton
153	Fruit – Fresh	3p,	4p per ton
154	Fruit – Trays	3½p	5p per ton
155	Fruit – Bananas	3½p,	5p per ton
156	Granite	3p,	4p per ton
157	Asbestos Products, all types (Export)	3p,	4p per ton
161	14 man gang – General Cargo	2p,	3p per ton
162	16 man gang – General Cargo	4p,	6p per ton
171	Hardwood – Bundled and Loose	2½p,	4p per ton
172	Plywood Veneer Loose packages	3p,	4p per ton
173	Plywood Veneer Bundles of Packages	2p,	3p per ton
181	Liner Board	1½p,	2p per ton
191	Match Logs	No rate fixed	
201	Meat – Boxed (Manning & Rate to be discussed see Par. 6)		
202	Meat – Carcase	6p,	8p per ton
211	Pallets, full or part ship all commodities	2p,	3p per ton
221	Paper – Loose	2p,	3½p per ton
222	Paper – Preslung	1½p,	2p per ton
223	Crepe & Tissue, Unslung	3p,	4p per ton
224	Crepe & Tissue, Preslung or part	2p,	3p per ton
225	"Nornews" and similar	1p,	2p per ton
231	Pigiron	No rate fixed	
241	Poles, Preslung	2p,	3p per ton
242	Poles, Unslung	3p,	4p per ton
243	Poles, Preslung, Loose outside the radius	2p,	3½p per ton
251	Pulp, Loose	4p,	6p per ton
252	Pulp, Preslung	1½p,	2p per ton
253	Pulp, Units (Banded Bales 6 or 8, not preslung)	1½p,	2½p per ton

10   11

Agreement between The Association of Dublin Stevedores Limited and the MP&GWU and the ITGWU, showing 1978 rates for unloading cargo. (Donated by John Nolan to the Dublin Dock Workers Preservation Society)

The same docker fondly remembered how as a young boy he used often to see Larkin in the Savoy picture house. Imagine the wonder a child must have felt seeing an imposing and famous figure, in such unexpected surroundings: the dark of the cinema, at the afternoon showing. 'It was a shilling and he would be in there in the afternoon, and he'd have a pipe, and he'd be looking at the films. He never drank, he only smoked the pipe. He was six foot one. He was huge.'[13]

Tom Byrne, docker and seaman, came from a union family. His father would join in garden parties organised by Larkin. Long trestle tables were set up by women, tea was served and political speeches made. As a teenager, Tom joined the Workers Union of Ireland boxing club and remembers the Céilí dancing classes held in the union hall.

The union band, known as The Suffering Ducks, decked out in a fine uniform, accompanied Larkin as he went on his organising tours.[14]

Rivalry between the WUI and the ITGWU existed to such an extent that during the 1925 coal strike Workers Union of Ireland men pelted ITGWU dockers at the Alexandra Basin with lumps of coal and stones.'[15] Here is how *Waterfront* reported on the animosity.

> In the twenties, as more mature men will remember ruefully, the Port was split from end to end, and worker fought against worker. Incalculable harm was wrought, and the long upward struggle was not only halted, but heavily retarded. Not until the thirties were the threads picked up again, and the great forward march resumed.[16]

In 1933, yet another union emerged in Dublin Port, the Irish Seamen and Port Workers Union. In July, Irish and Scottish sailors went on strike, unhappy with a new agreement between their union, the National Union of Sailors (headquartered in England), and the shipowners. Ultimately the two groups of sailors left their parent organisation. The Irish founded the Irish Seamen's Union based in Ireland and established the Coastwise and General Workers Union catering for Scottish seamen. At a July meeting in the Mansion House in Dublin, sailors, firemen and dockers declared their support for the striking seamen: 'we endorse the action of the firemen and seamen in repudiating the tyrannical agreement forced on us by officials of the National Union of Seamen, the tools of the Shipping Federation.'[17] Within weeks the Dublin sailors were joined by 600 dockers, who had left the ITGWU, and from then on the new union was known as the Irish Seamen and Port Workers Union.[18] Historian Francis Devine contends that the dockers were motivated to join the new union by their weariness at the continuous intra-union quarrels between the ITGWU and the Workers Union of Ireland.[19]

The *Irish Times* report of the first AGM of the Irish Seamen and Port Workers Union noted that 'according to its founders it will be both anti-communist and anti-capitalist'.[20] The need to make an anti-communist statement may have been provoked by the launch of the Communist Party of Ireland, which held its founding meeting earlier in the summer. Fear of outside agitators was in the air. English MP William Davis warned of 'paid agitators' who were 'helping to create industrial struggle' some of whom 'were not citizens of the Free State'.[21] There is no evidence that this claim amounted to any more than hot air. Joe Ellis, the General Organiser of the union, further stated that they would endeavour to give the rank and file real control of the union, doing away with the rule of officials. *The Irish Times* report continues, 'It was their opinion that if a section of men had a grievance that section was the body to deal with it and to decide what steps should be taken to remedy it. No official should be able to dictate to the members in any way'.[22] This position not only reflected what was common practice among dockers, as we will see below, but also can be taken as an attempt to further distinguish the new union from the National Union of Sailors which was accused of imposing decisions on their members. By the mid-1950s the Irish Seamen and Port Workers Union began to recruit workers from dockland factories, and was renamed the Marine Port and General Workers Union to reflect its expanded changing membership base.[23]

A government report in 1945 characterised seamen and dockers as 'highly organised, but [with] much interunion rivalry'.[24] Intra-union conflict was to emerge once more in the late 1950s. The setting up of the Irish Seaman's Union in November 1957 was the trigger to strike action by the MP&GWU. The Irish Shipping Owners

Heitons coal trucks on a quay. (Donated by Peter Smith to the Dublin Dock Workers Preservation Society)

Association said they would henceforth only recruit seamen from the Irish Seamen's Union. In response docker members of the MP&GWU refused to unload vessels belonging to members of the Irish Shipping Owners Association. The association argued that their refusal to hire members of the MP&GWU was because there had been incidents of unruly behaviour by seamen aboard ships and the MP&GWU was not willing to take measures to prevent re-occurrence.[25] However, the obvious implication was that the Irish Seamen's Union was set up by the employers to break employees away from their union, and it was criticised for being a company union. *The Irish Times* described the shipowners as not being 'wholly above suspicion'. It set out – using the weapon ready to hand in the form of Irish Shipping Ltd. – to break the union.[26] About 1,000 deep-sea dockers were affected by the dispute that lasted over three months.[27]

The resolution that occurred on 24 February 1958 was curious. The number one branch of the MP&GWU, which represented seamen, split to form a new seamen's union, leaving both the MP&GWU and the Irish Seamen's Union without any seamen members. Thus the Irish Seamen's Union dissolved on 30 September 1959 and the newer Seamen's Union of Ireland became the primary union representing seamen. Newspaper reports at the time hint that some sections of the MP&GWU had decided during 1957 that it was time for the seamen to form their own union.[28] Frances Devine suggests that this desire resulted from a conflict between Des Brannigan, the Communist General Secretary of the MP&GWU and senior Catholic figures.[29] Des Brannigan stated that members of the MP&GWU executive were strongly influenced by John Charles McQuaid, the Catholic Archbishop of Dublin and that there were 'always attempts to undermine me as General Secretary'.[30]

The historical link between dockers and seamen was broken, though the docker interviewees insisted that the number one branch though now empty, remained in existence in the hope that the seamen would one day rejoin them.[31] The MP&GWU was to become the largest union for deep-sea dockers and the ITGWU for cross-channel dockers. By the late 1950s, 95 per cent of deep-sea dockers were in the MP&GWU; in the cross-channel section 75 per cent of dockers were in the ITGWU, 10 per cent in the WUI and 15 per cent in the MP&GWU.[32]

Among the official strikes and other industrial actions of historical note were the great Dublin Lockout of 1913, oft commemorated in docker trade union events, the general strikes of 1919 and 1920, the national dockers strike of 1923 in resistance to wage cuts, the calamitous port disruptions of the 1920s, pitting worker against worker, which involved the split of the WUI from the ITGWU.[33] In 1966 they struck for the introduction of a forty-hour week (without loss of pay).

This was part of a co-ordinated drive by Irish Trade Unions for a forty-hour, five-day week without loss of pay.[34] The *Irish Independent* at the time worried about the effect this later dispute would have:

> Most reasonable people would agree that in the present circumstances there was no great urgency about pressing claims for shorter working hours or other marginal conditions by strikes that would cause serious loss of wages not only to them but to other workers, as well as loss in production. A reduction in the working week from forty-two-and-a-half to forty hours without loss of earnings would be equivalent to a 6 per cent increase in wage rates, leaving aside altogether any reduction in output.
>
> This country could not carry this year a general 6 per cent increase without facing a further considerable rise in prices and almost incalculable consequences to its export trades.[35]

Undeterred, the dockers ploughed on. On occasion, they took to parading up O'Connell Street. Here is how the event was described in *The Irish Times*.

> A few elderly men sitting on the steps of the Customs House lifted their eyes from Sunday newspapers as six bands

and contingents from different unions smartly moved into position.

The colourfully attired bands drew more attention from the dense crowds that lined Eden quay and O'Connell Street than the placards and banners. Everyone seemed to appreciate the sunshine – an unexpected, late summer favour.

The O'Connell Fife and Drum Band led the parade and was followed by the colour party bearing the national flag flanked by The Plough and The Stars.

The ITGWU Band had a prominent place, leading a big contingent from this union which has many members in the port and port area. One big banner read '1913–1963 Dublin Dockers Locked-Out.' Close to the Howth Pipe Band was a large white banner which read 'An injury to one is the concern of all.'[36]

The five-week strike ended with the introduction of a five-day, forty-hour working week, with no loss of pay, with overtime rates applying at the weekends.[37] Pensions, medical benefits and sick pay were also felt to be necessary, though in the 1960s the dockers themselves set up a mutual aid fund, aimed at filling the gap left by government and employer. Strike threats in the early 1960s brought the read in from the elements as a transit shed was finally provided to protect from the rain during the early morning selection.[38] Both dock worker and stevedore joined in calls for the provision of basic facilities such as toilets, read rooms and a restaurant. One superintendent bluntly related his problem to *The Irish Times*: 'If I'm down on the south quays on business and I want to relieve myself, I have to jump into my car and drive all the way back to my office on the other side of the river. That's disgraceful.'[39] Following years of agitation by a voluntary committee a canteen was opened at Alexandra Road in 1966.[40]

When it came to getting agreement on fundamental changes, movement could be slow. In his investigation into conditions in

English ports, Lord Devlin remarked that 'Dockers, it has often been said, dislike change, even for the better.'[41] Union officials and stevedores said the same in Dublin. In 1961, weekly pay by cheque was introduced. The process of introduction was long and fraught. The proposal was accepted at one point, only to be rejected at another. Ultimately it took up to six meetings to get full agreement.[42] One union official interviewed described how frustrated some members of the Association of Dublin Stevedores (ADS) would get at the dockers union representatives. One day they would argue from a particular viewpoint and agreement would be reached, and the next day they would come in and argue the exact opposite. When one member of the ADS asked what caused them to change their argument, he got the reply 'it was a different day' and that was the end of it. The ground was always shifting.'[43]

The changes that were to affect dock workers the most were the introduction of buttons in the mid-forties and de-casualisation. In 1961, this was introduced for men in the Channel sector, then in 1971 it was extended to those working in the deep-sea docks.[44]

The road to these changes started on 28 June 1946 when 500 cross-channel dockers went on strike for a fortnight annual holiday with pay.[45] Some 500 checkers, storemen, carters and other port workers refused to pass their pickets.[46] As casual workers, dockers were not covered by the Holidays (Employees) Act, 1939. This issue had been raised over the years, including on a number of occasions in the Dáil.[47] Big Jim Larkin's son, a Labour Party politician, exclaimed in the Dáil in 1944:

There is no one in the Government or in the judiciary who can find a remedy, who can create the position whereby a casual docker will get what he is entitled to, a week's holiday. The dockers work long hours, sometimes they work continuously for thirty hours, but they get no holidays. I should like to draw attention to a case that was brought up in the courts. The Government brought the case to test whether a docker was entitled to a week's holiday. It was

Seamus Redmond, general secretary, MP&GWU. (Donated by Brian Murphy to the Dublin Dock Workers Preservation Society)

a most extraordinary action. The man who was brought up had worked one-and-a-half years in the one year—he had worked more than 500 hours overtime. These men are remarkable in many ways. They work almost to the point of destruction of their physical powers; as long as there is work there they will do it. The man who was brought up on the test case had worked 584 hours overtime.[48]

With the exception of urgent medical supplies, the unloading of goods into Dublin was halted. The export of cattle ceased. As the summer unfolded with no end to the strike in sight, dockers' unions offered to allow the release of 377 crates of eggs, provided they were given to charitable institutions.[49] The Irish Trade Union Congress, meeting in Dublin reported on the strike that 'the dockers are on strike for that [which] most other workers have already secured' and heard representations calling for de-casualisation.[50] Dockers in Belfast and Derry refused to handle consignments of eggs that normally would be shipped through Dublin.[51]

The strike ended on 3 August. The settlement stopped short of the demanded fortnight holiday. Those who worked the longest hours obtained nine days' leave – nine days for now. On foot of the settlement, Sean Lemass, the Minister for Industry and Commerce, promised to introduce a scheme to abolish casual work the following year.[52] Once dockers were employed on a permanent basis, they would be eligible for twelve days leave.[53] The Harbour Act of 1946 established a harbour authority and Section 62 provided for the possibility of setting up a dockers register.[54] Buttons were issued the following year – this being an improvement, for the lucky few.[55] 'The button meant you had to get a job before an outsider. At that time a stevedore could come along and pick anyone for the job, so long as they were button men … it was the poorest form of security, if it was security.'[56]

Tensions developed between button and non-button men:

It was very near coming to dangerous trouble … the non-button men and the button men nearly come to blows … [the non-button men] were all different, some of them from dockers families, but most of them were fellas just after coming down and drifting into the quays, and they were resenting the fact which is natural that we had the pick of the work, but we had all the service in the years there, they'd have to be employed after us …

… we'd get picked out and they'd have to stand in and get what jobs was remaining.[57]

The reality was, that the non-button men continued to face the worse effects of the read system. William Murphy felt that the button system was the worst move for the union because it introduced divisions among dock labour. 'Let every man take his chances,' he argued, as they had done in his father's day, 'let it be an open read and there'll be no enemies.'[58]

The button system ended with decasualisation, which introduced fallback money, a payment given when no work was available. Now dockers had a guaranteed income. The humiliation of the read was replaced by a rota system in which men were called alphabetically, everyone getting a turn.

After the 1946 strike the Minister of Labour asked the Labour Court to carry out an investigation on casualisation on the docks.[59] In 1951 this report was circulated to government departments for consideration. Yet it was a decade before decasualisation was introduced for cross-channel dockers. In return for the additional job security, cross-channel dockers agreed to lift a five-and-a-half year ban on container traffic. Deep-sea dockers had to wait an additional ten years before they too were guaranteed regular income. Sadly, for all the importance of the dockers to Irish Labour History, very little has been documented of their union struggles post-1913, with little analysis of the negotiations around these dramatic changes to dock work.

With just cause, given that improved working conditions derived from union organisation, pride in their trade union heritage was strong. Dockers, *Waterfront* proclaimed are:

> the esprit de corps of militant trade unionism. They blazed the trail in the early days, and have been in the vanguard ever since. If the dockers break, the Port is broken. And they must never break, because too much depends on their solidarity and spirit, not only in the Port but throughout the city and country.[60]

However, to the rest of the world docklands were hotbeds of industrial unrest.[61] In Ireland threatened strikes and pessimism and problems over strike resolution received notice in the national newspapers. Clashing with feelings of pride, there was also often a sense of being maligned and misunderstood. Here an exasperated *Waterfront* rails against the press:

The Docker and The Press
Keeping Truth Out of
the News!

'Truth in the News', says the slogan of the National ? Press [*sic*]. As far as dock-workers are concerned, the term is mere mockery, for down the years the workers of Dockland have been the victims of misrepresentation of every conceivable type in our Irish dailies, who in many respects, out Vogue 'Vogue'.

… The outpourings of every hole-in-the-corner committee or self appointed clique on this question is given the full glare of publicity, but the views of dock workers are carefully suppressed. Dockworkers indeed, are seldom mentioned except, possibly, when some court case is being reported in which the accused claims to be a docker. In this event the report is given front page treatment, to show people at large what a tribe of morons exist, in that discreditable place, Dockland.[62]

Did dockers deserve their militant reputation? There are a number of ways to approach this question: were they quicker to strike? Was violence more often a feature of docker strikes? Were they more likely to engage in unofficial strikes?

Certainly internationally, dockers were seen as more likely to strike than those in other workplaces. Those reporting on industrial relations in English ports after World War Two laid the blame for the industrial unrest squarely on the exploitative nature of docking work. In the UK, dockers were held to be more casual than building workers, and dockers' wages were subject to greater variability. Casual employment and wage fluctuation caused uncertainty, bred resentments and led to antagonism between worker and employer. This viewpoint was also reflected by those writing on situations in Ireland. Here Des Geraghty reports in *The Irish Times* in 1976:

> The need for labour varied. This created the basis for the casual port worker – the tough unskilled manual worker of the popular imagination. Insecure in employment yet he was considered ruthless in seeking payment to compensate for this uncertainty and provide for the days of idleness or absenteeism. Yet – this casual employment system was created by the stevedores, the port employers, to avoid responsibility for what the men call the 'down days' and still have sufficient works to cope with sudden expansion in trade.[63]

James Dunne, head of the Marine Port and General Workers Union also placed emphasis on the uncertain organisation of work.

> A docker is militant because of the traditional nature of his work. He is a product of a system whereby port employers down the years have used or abused his services, depending upon their requirements. Eventually there evolved a feeling – and I think this applies to dockers more than other workers – that they had to fight for everything that they thought was in their own best interests.[64]

In the UK, an increase in industrial action in the period following the Second World War led to the commissioning of a number of reports to investigate the problem. The Devlin Report placed dockers as fourth in the British Strike League, 1930–8.[65] Devlin proposed decasualisation as a solution in 1947, as it was the casual nature of the work that was held to be responsible for industrial unrest.

Dock work was certainly unpredictable. However, it is difficult to ascertain whether dockers were more likely to strike than more regularly employed workers. Maritime researcher Jesmar Hamark argues that there is very little concrete international evidence in support of these claims.[66] The absence of hard statistics is in part because it is difficult to obtain reliable information on strikes. Strike frequency refers to the number of stoppages per employee. It is a useful way of estimating how strike prone an industry is. In Ireland, there are a number of problems with the strike frequency data collected from 1960 to 1980. To be included in the statistics, a strike must have lasted at least one day and involved, in total, ten or more workdays – which rules out very short stoppages.[67] Additionally there was some non-reporting of stoppages which though small in size or brief in duration should have been included in the statistics.[68]

Another difficulty with the figures is that they don't give information just on dockers. Instead they gather together different occupations into

Marine Port and General Workers Union Conference, Salthill. (Donated by Michael Donnelly to the Dublin Dock Workers Preservation Society)

larger industrial groups. If we look at strike frequency by sector we can see that the most strike prone sectors from 1922 to 1981 were mining and turf production.[69] Dock workers can be found in the Transport and Communications group, along with train and bus drivers. Out of the six industrial categories, Transport and Communications are towards the bottom of the strike frequency league table; from 1922–1941 they are in the fourth position, from 1942–1961 they are in fifth position and from 1962–1981 they are back in fourth.[70] Michael Donnelly, Marine Port & General Workers Union felt that it was a misconception that dock workers were more strike prone than others. Overall, these broad figures would tend to suggest that he was correct in his assessment.

However, it is undoubtedly true that dock strikes are among that small class of strikes that receive greater attention than those in other areas. This is chiefly because of the impact they have on other industries and on the economic life of the country. For example, a strike in 1966 not only affected those who worked on the docks. The 600 men who were laid off during the strike as importation of necessary car parts ceased, also felt this wider effect.[71] Dock strikes are powerful, and it is this that gives rise to the impression that dockers are particularly strike prone.

All Out

Dockers were known also for their sense of solidarity. 'They were always very loyal to one another,' Michael Donnelly remembered, 'they would call one another all the names under the sun but they wouldn't let anyone else do it. Nobody else could do it.' Des Brannigan, once leader of the Marine Port and General Workers Union, remembered returning to work on the docks in the deep-sea end. Stevedores, perhaps remembering the irritation he had caused when a union official, refused to call his name at the read, leaving him standing. The situation looked to continue until a number of dockers took action to support him, 'They put it very bluntly,' he remembered, 'if he doesn't f***ing work, nobody else is going to work.' As simple as that. No subtlety about it whatsoever. And that prevailed.[72]

Small-scale loyalty could be magnified to the port as a whole. The call of 'one out, all out' had real meaning. This sentiment is common among dockers throughout the world. An inquiry into unrest on London Ports in 1951 noted 'the strong tradition of solidarity'.[73] This solidarity extended to dockers in other ports, and indeed in other workplaces. During a dispute in 1973 dockers in Cork, Waterford, Belfast, Drogheda and Limerick refused to handle goods diverted from Dublin.[74] Dockers described how in 1966, Cork dockers gave them support. 'Cork fraternity came up and marched through Dublin.'[75] Solidarity between unions was also seen in 1966 when the Workers Union of Ireland loaned £5,000 to the MP&GWU who were in the midst of a protracted strike, while in 1957 when the seamen were on strike the dockers gave them three shillings a day out of their wages. Co-operation extended to ports overseas. 'We had connections,' Willie Murphy declared 'the dockers had an allegiance … with the Manchester dockers, the Liverpool dockers … If we had a boat that we blackened, and it went to Liverpool or Manchester, they wouldn't work.'[76] A keystone of the docker's strength was trade union solidarity.

A Scab is a Scab

Another charge laid on the door of dockers is that their industrial disputes can be particularly contentious and prone to violence. As a dock strike could have immediate and costly effect, employers and government had particular motivation to end them as quickly as possible. Jesper Hamark argues that for these reasons, to an unusual extent, the hiring of strike breakers was used as a tactic to break dock strikes. Indeed, this was the tactic employed in 1913 when William Martin Murphy of Dublin United Tramway Company and two Irish newspapers locked out employees who were members of the new union ITGWU, and used strike breakers to keep the trams running. 'Scab' was a particular damning insult within dockland communities.

Nellie Cassidy's father spent three months in jail for hitting his next-door neighbour with his number seven shovel. Wives shunned

John Brown and Patrick Costello address a meeting of dockers regarding the breakaway of seamen from the MP&GWU in a shipping dispute, 1957–8. This meeting took place near the Point, just inside the gates at the North Wall. (Donated by Michael Donnelly to the Dublin Dock Workers Preservation Society)

wives 'and the women, once you took any husband's job they wouldn't look at you. No, because they were taking the food off your table.'[77] Martin Mitten watched his mother and other women throw scalding water from the top of their tenement houses during the 1925 strike which pitted members of the ITGWU against the Workers of Union of Ireland, both sides accusing each other of providing scab labour.[78] The Dublin Coal Merchants Association locked out members of the ITGWU and the Workers Union of Ireland, as members of the two unions refused to work together. Members of the ITGWU returned to work, leaving the Workers Union of Ireland members locked out.[79] The hostility between union members that ensued was to be long remembered. Children fought and shouted at each other 'my father never scabbed it like yours'.[80] A local lane became known as scab alley as that was where ITGWU workers were housed.[81] The Workers Union of Ireland accused the ITGWU of bringing in strike breakers outside the city and giving the union cards so they could work in the coal yards. During this strike, a bomb was thrown into the Custom House where they were sleeping.[82] A police escort was needed for the short walk from the Custom House where they slept along the quays to the dockside. As attempts were made to move coal in horse-driven carts, locked-out dockers ran along side with whips aimed at the horses to make them jump and topple the cargo.[83] Armed policemen were deployed to protect the drivers, two with each cart. Willie Murphy, who was 12 at the time, recalls 'there was a number of them injured and thrown in the river'.[84]

The accusation of scab was not forgotten. Tommy Bassett was a teenager in 1925. He grew up surrounded by docker families and started work on the docks himself at age 19:

> They never forgave a scab … didn't forget him or forgive him. And that was generations passed down to sons. It never left. Even if you met him in the street you wouldn't recognise him or give him the time a day. Oh, once a scab, always a scab.[85]

Nellie Mc Cann who was 15 at the time of the 1925 strike, remembers how one man from the southside 'went by the name of scab all his life and nobody'd talk to him nor work with him'.[86] After the strike was over, a docker accused of strike breaking would be isolated, he wouldn't find people on the docks who were willing to share a pint, he could only drink with a fellow outcast, forced to travel far from the docks, 'had to go somewhere foreign to drink'.[87]

Willie Murphy's father who was on strike at the time would say to his son 'I'll never work with scabs. I never scabbed.' Willie Murphy remembers finishing a boat and retiring to a pub on Spencer Dock for payment to be shared out among the gang. The money for the

Membership card for the Irish Seamen's and Port Workers' Union, 1944. (Donated by Brendan Dempsey to the Dublin Dock Workers Preservation Society)

job had been given to one of the dockers to distribute to the others. One of the twelve was known as a scab. Each man was given his due until it came to the scab, who asked 'where is my money?'. The story continues, 'He says "there it is" and he hit him a box. Ah he put the scab flying and you'd want to see that scab fellow running.'[88] When Michael Foran began working in the coalyards in the early 1960s, one of the companies he worked for was Heitons, an employer involved in the coal strikes of the early twentieth century. Though those strikes occurred years before he was born, there was still a stigma attached to working for them. Older coal men would at times refuse to talk to him, 'there was still bad blood among coal men over scab labour and Heitons had a bad name … for breaking the strike. There was still that lingering in the early 1960s, along the quays, along the coal yards.'[89]

Wildcat Strikes and Telephone Figures

Dockers are also considered to be more likely to take part in unofficial industrial actions such as wildcat strikes, go-slows and other forms of direct action. In the nineteenth century, Glasgow dockers used a go-slow strategy known locally as ca'canny.[90] It is hard to quantify whether wildcat strikes, often small, and of short duration and so absent from official statistics, were more prevalent on Dublin docks than other Irish workplaces. On a number of occasions the stevedore organisations complained that the union had lost control on the docks. Some, however, linked the prevalence of unofficial action to the particularly open relationship between stevedore and docker that existed, where grievances were dealt with directly rather than referred to personnel departments or union representatives.

> Even the warehouses and storage depots operated the casual system, keeping the regular workforce at a minimum level and expanding the workforce with daily casuals as required. Consequently industrial relations developed in a very immediate and straightforward manner. Casual workers rarely had the opportunity to give notice or engage in protracted negotiations. Improvements in wages and working conditions demanded immediate attention.[91]

From the dockers' perspective, if problems weren't dealt with immediately, the ship would have literally sailed and with it the ability to negotiate.[92] From the ship owners' perspective, a ship kept in port by stoppages could incur considerable extra expenses. As tides were missed, extra port charges had to be paid. Often it was more expedient for the stevedore to acquiesce quickly, and pass on the charge to the shipping company, than to wait and argue for a better outcome.

Differences tended to be settled noisily on the quayside with onlookers from the ship and quays. Members of the Port Committee, elected by the dockers, would be called down to the shipside to help settle the problem, calling for a show of hands when a proposal was reached.

Willie Murphy was on the first port committee in 1936. He had a particular argument with a stevedore, who – as to be expected – was also a relation. 'I used to be at loggerheads with him, you know, always at loggerheads ... I used to make claims ... and he used to hate me for it.' He describes one such confrontation. On occasion a boat filled with sand arrived from Holland. The top layer of sand, three or four feet deep, was frozen solid. As the dockers were forced to use drills to unload the boat, they looked for an extra payment known as 'hardship money', to cover the additional work they were required to do. The stevedore said to Willie when he asked for more pay, 'I never heard of this. I'll lose the job over you.'

> You know he was always threatening ... Well it might be half true. We accepted it with a grain of salt.
>
> He used to say 'Who is going to represent the men?'
>
> 'I am going to', I said.
>
> 'Are you prepared to go down and see Mr this, that and the other?'
>
> I said 'And you'll come with me too,? You'll have to be there?'
>
> 'Oh I'm not coming', he said.
>
> 'You better', I said 'I'll bring some of the boys with me but ... you'll have to
>
> organise a meeting with them [the shipowners] you know'.
>
> And eventually he said 'right'.[93]

At this time, the dockers would normally get 30 shillings for unloading sand, that is £1.10 shillings.[94] On top of that they hoped to get an extra

Jimmy Dunne and Frank Ellis, presidents of the Marine Port and General Workers Union. (Donated by Michael Donnelly to the Dublin Dock Workers Preservation Society)

£5. So the gang asked the shop steward to negotiate with the stevedore for that amount. The union representative continued: 'They were looking for a fiver, telephone figures as usual.' The stevedore threatened that 'he'd lose the job so we'd lose the job'. Willie admitted that the numbers asked were unlikely to be granted. 'I realised that what they were looking for was ridiculous, but in any case it paid off in the long run.' In the final agreement, they were paid the normal thirty bob a day, but also an additional three-and-a-half to four quid for unloading 400 tons of sand.

One stevedore, perhaps frustrated by delays, felt that these shipside disputes allowed the strongest man, the loudest man, the tough guy to influence the vote, others following for 'fear of his size or being slagged'.[95] A union official, perhaps frustrated by impossible negotiations, similarly commented 'It all depends on who the guy was. If the guy was a big tough guy, the little fellow would be afeard not to back him up.'[96]

The grievances could be real but in the opinion of a trade union official 'a lot of them were imaginary grievances … you would get an

individual that would get his pride hurt'. Hot heads, sharp words, on the spur of the moment tools would down and work stop. Arthur Kelly, docker, tells the story of a stevedore who found himself in trouble on first arriving in Dublin. He was involved in an altercation with dockers over who would unload the furniture for his new house. On losing the job, the dockers responded by putting a ban on the unloading of his furniture from the ship. 'They could put a ban on anything. His house was left bare and he never forgave the dockers but a ban was a ban as far as the dockers were concerned.'[97] In the short story the *Plain People*, the union official expresses in equal measure his difficulties and admiration for the workers he represents.

> There was no such things as Labour Courts and Conciliation Boards twenty years ago. And then, the crowd I deal with are different … they use the old methods. They don't understand agreements. There were very few agreements in the old days. They live in an old world, I suppose. I guarantee you won't change them any more than I can. But even though they're out to lynch me at the moment, I'll say they are a good bunch. You won't find better. They stick to their idea of fair and square.[98]

The feelings expressed in this fictional account were mirrored in the accounts of union representatives. Arthur Kelly remembered times he and his fellow representatives were warned off. Angry dockers would threaten that the Liffey was close at hand. These words spoken in the heat of the moment were not something he worried about, it was just part of the day-to-day and the threats were never made good. Still, he remembers an instance in the 1950s when a union representative ended up on the wrong side of a fist when he tried to tell a hostile crowd something they disagreed with.[99]

A degree of privacy was introduced to negotiations when, from 1963, claims were decided on at the weekly meeting of the Claims Committee, comprising three permanent representatives from both unions and the Dublin Master Stevedores Association. A majority was needed to carry a decision. The rule and regulations under which dockers worked developed, like common law, out of countless disputes and negotiations. In the Deep Sea section, by the 1960s these were documented in a ledger known as the Agreement and Rules Register, carefully indexed to cover situations from definitions of the best job to agreements on Sunday working, with amendments added and dated as they emerged. It was a complicated and detailed document that outlined various manning levels and rates of pay across a variety of commodities. Michael Donnelly explained that the difficulty with his job was that 'to protect the innocent you've got to defend the guilty'. That was even if when he suspected a claim was spurious or unreasonable, he couldn't risk not pursuing it all the way, as precedent set in one instance could have unfortunate applications in another.

Yet ultimately it was a process with which all parties were comfortable. In the late 1960s a Labour PartyTD[100] praised the committee for maintaining industrial peace in the port, describing it as 'an effective committee … which can resolve at local level, at the place of employment, within hours, with independent chairmanship, the issues that arise'.[101] The Labour Court, established in 1946, was additionally used to resolve larger industrial conflicts. Liam McGinn, Secretary of The Dublin Master Stevedores' Association, in a letter to the *Irish Press* commended union and stevedores for ensuring industrial peace on the docks through the use of the Claims Committee and constant open dialogue between all parties, concluding 'between us we have produced a solution to unofficial strikes which it might be well for other industries to consider'.[102]

More Money than a Bank Manager

As might be expected, most negotiations were concerned with rates of pay. How much did dockers earn? It is a difficult question to answer. Dockers differed fundamentally from many other casual workers. When work was good he was a big earner. 'I made more money than a bank manager,' Jem Granger often mused to his daughter and others. Granger's career as a coalie spanned the period up to 1963 when he was felled in an accident. Many dockers brought home very good money some considerable proportion of the time. The swagger of pride is unconcealed in docker tales of big earnings, 'the sugar boats was a goldmine'.[103] Politicians, such as Charles Haughey and the 'top brass' of the stevedoring companies were invited to the annual dinner dance in the 1960s. They came, Martin Mitten boasted because 'we had more money than they had'. The Department of Finance noted in the 1950s that 'while dockers' work is of a casual nature their earnings are on the whole high', adding that if unemployment benefit is taken into account they did better than other casual workers such as turf or agricultural workers.[104]

Tommy Bassett passed two foremen one day in the 1960s, just as they left the pay office. They were paid a regular wage with no overtime. One said to him, 'show me your week's wages'. He had £33, while they only had £25.[105] The date of this conversation isn't given but it can be assumed that it is in the mid-1960s as we know that is when foremen were paid £25 a week.[106] At that time, the average worker in manufacturing would expect to bring home just over £14.16 shillings a week. The basic pay for a deep-sea docker (that is working Monday to Friday without overtime) was just under £16 a week.[107] Perhaps the passage of time coloured Tommy Bassett's memories of how much he earned on that lucky week, but even allowing for exaggeration, with

Tom Boland lifts a number seven shovel. (Donated by Ray Murphy to the Dublin Dock Workers Preservation Society)

Deep-sea coal docker button. (Dublin Dock Workers Preservation Society collection, photograph by Aileen O'Carroll)

Red deep-sea and coal docker button. (Dublin Dock Workers Preservation Society collection, photograph by Aileen O'Carroll)

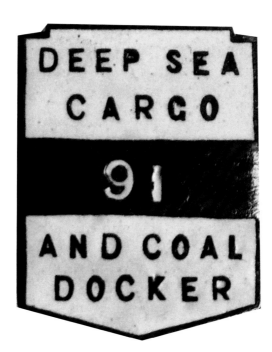

Yellow deep-sea cargo and coal docker buttons. (Dublin Dock Workers Preservation Society collection, photograph by Aileen O'Carroll)

Crates of plywood for Kantor being hooked on to the crane using the steel chains and hooks in the hold of a ship, *c.* later 1980s. (Donated by Alan Martin to the Dublin Dock Workers Preservation Society)

Union badge of the Marine Port & General Workers Union, designed by
Des Brannigan, former MP&GWU president. (Francis Devine's collection)

Dockers sitting on a bundle of timber while waiting for more bundles to arrive from the ship, *c.* mid-1970s. Left to right: Mick Kilroy, Jenna King and Paddy Kelly. (Donated by Alan Martin, photographer, to the Dublin Dock Workers Preservation Society)

Dockers standing between No. 9 and No. 10 sheds, 1960s. Left to right: Gabriel Downey, William 'Lonnie' Donovan, Thomas 'Tucker' Murphy, Gilmoro Redmond and Paddy Downey. (Donated by Brian Murphy to the Dublin Dock Workers Preservation Society)

Loading a Heitons coal truck at the Point, 1963. (Michael Donnelly collection, donated by Florrie Cunningham to the Dublin Dock Workers Preservation Society)

OUR LADY'S MEMORIAL

DUBLIN PORT

Subscribers Certificate

This is to Certify that ......THOMAS McAULEY,......

.....................DUBLIN PORT & DOCKS RIVER PLANT.....................

subscribed towards the cost of erecting the Memorial to Our Blessed Lady
at the Port of Dublin.

(Rev.) Edward J Rhatigan .... Chairman

.... Hon. Treasurer

.... Hon. Secretary

ISSUED TO SUBSCRIBERS OF ONE GUINEA

Subscribers' certificate for Our Lady's Memorial, Dublin Port. (Donated by Jimmy Carthy to the Dublin Dock Workers Preservation Society)

Irish Seamen and Port Workers Union march. (Donated by Michael Donnelly to the Dublin Dock Workers Preservation Society)

overtime and bonuses, it was possible to substantially add to one's weekly income. Yet each week was different, as he explained to the foremen, 'Don't mind him, sez I, you'll have the £25 next week. I mightn't get 35 shillings.' A report on docker earnings confirms how much earnings varied.[108] In the first week of September 1948, two dockers earned over £11, while twenty-six earned less than £3.

Builders would often come down to the docks for a fortnight in August. If the work was good they found they could get more than on the building sites, and having tasted the extra money, the temptation was to stay. Accounts of near poverty in the interviews are counterpoised by the big money stories in the biographies told by dockers and their wives.

As this is a substantive ethnographic study and not a statistical one, we cannot state exactly what dockers' annual incomes have been.

Information on pay rates is of limited use, limited because income differed from one individual to another. Jem Granger was a popular man. He was also a notably effective worker, enjoying a reputation accordingly. He always had work. Others did not have it so often. The non-buttonman in Chapter 1 lamented his workless wanderings. Granger was not fully representative of the dockside. Men like Jem were an elite of the Dublin working class, a big earner because of his power to extract additional payments in a wide variety of ways, and it is to these we now turn.

Dirty Money, Hot Money and Donnage Hours

In the cross-channel sector the cargos were more predictable, the ships more regular and so numbers of gangs required and most rates for unloading could be decided in advance and documented in a green book for all to consult.[109] In the deep-sea sector there was more variability and thus more opportunity to increase one's wage. Particularly lucrative were the Marshall Plan years, 1947 to 1957, when 10,000-ton coal boats needed to be unloaded. A docker could finish one ship and start immediately on another. Big money could be made if you were being paid a flat rate per ship, were a fast worker, and were able to work seven days a week, getting time and a half on Saturday and double on Sunday.

Unusual cargo, it could be argued, required special skills or came with additional hazard that required compensation. Most stoppages were linked to claims for what was known as 'dirty money' – extra pay for handling the most miry and nastiest commodities. The Claims Book of the Dublin Master Stevedores notes that on 19 February 1969, a dockers' gang went up out of the hatch, on strike in demand of extra pay for unloading sulphate aluminium. Consider Egyptian figpaste 'about 10 tons [of] which had spread through layers of cases and floor of [the] hold through compression and heat' on one occasion: dirt

The docker's newspaper *Waterfront* was produced from 1961 to 1972. (Dublin Dock Workers Preservation Society)

WATERFRONT

VOL. 2 No. 4   *THE PAPER FOR THE PORT*   APRIL, 1962

Produced by the Workers for the Workers.

A Monthly Magazine for all sections and all grades in the Port of Dublin.   **PRICE 3d.**

DANGER ON THE DOCKS !

STRIKE IN CROSS-CHANNEL SECTION?

THERE is serious danger that industrial action may have to be taken by the Unions as a result of the failure to reach agreement on the dockers' pay increase. The latest offer was turned down, as is generally known, and now anything may happen.

Gleams of sanity were beginning to manifest themselves in shipping circles in the last year or so. Great difficulties have been overcome ; and even the apparently insoluble container problem was taken in hand by a determined and united effort.

The net (and happy) result was that we have seen hardly a day's stoppage on the docks. Elsewhere throughout the country industry has been paralysed by strike after strike. But in the Port of Dublin, despite the bad name some Press writers like to give us, peace pevailed and the wheels were kept moving. Crises were not wanting. A hundred times they threatened, and a hundred times were averted. Both sides kept talking, and talking saved the day.

The conference table was the answer . For, while the delegates argued with the employers, and adjourned to meet and argue again and yet again, the work went forward. The ships sailed and trucks rolled ; cargo-handling records were broken and the prosperity of the Port increased. Often people grew sick and weary of the interminable conferences on this question or that, but there can be no denying that progress was made, some measure of agreement and better understanding reached.

And, all-important to the Port and its citizens, while the conference room was in occupation the work went on, and no one was the sufferer.

This in our opinion is sanity. The conference room is the place to resolve disputes and not the strike arena, with its concomitant of suffering and hardship. It is better to talk than to fight ; better a cold war than a hot one ; better to argue even when agreement seems hopeless than to explode and break up into conflict.

It would be too bad if now, after so much has been achieved and so long a peace maintained, a major strike were to be allowed to break out. The employers must know that the offer is inadequate and should be raised. They must know that the dockers have shown exemplary patience, in view of the fact that they are one of the few sections which have not yet benefited in the eighth round. And they must know that a strike at this juncture, with the container issue still not completely cleared up, would be disastrous in the extreme to the Port and to all concerned.

We have never believed in strikes. They are too costly to the men and to everyone taking part. But we believe there is one really imminent this time and there is only one way to avert it.

Keep talking !

That way dividends won't suffer.

And neither will women and children.

" Look at C.I.E., comrades ; look at Aer Lingus ; look at the E.S.B. I tell you, the only way to make sure crime DOES NOT PAY is to let the State take it over to run ! "

in the extreme![110] Dirty money claims provided, however, a circus of gambits by the dockers to argue that a cargo was impossibly sticky, foul, polluted, dusty, filthy or mucky. Soggy cargo was objectionable too, such as wet reels of newsprint, or the wet bales on the *City of London* in January 1963. Spillage alone could lead to such claims; and, who knows how spillage occurs? The contest would, at any rate, be joined between dockers and stevedores as to whether dirty money should or should not be paid in a disputed case. The chance for dirty bids became popular during the 1960s. Before then, dirty work was simply the dockers' work.

Various ruses could be used to bump a pay packet. Donnage was the term used to describe the materials used for packing, stowing and securing fragile groups in the hold of a ship. Donnaging work was paid separately from other cargo work. Donnage hours themselves, were rounded up to the full hour for every fifteen minutes' work. If a docker worked more than fifteen minutes handling the packing, he was paid a fixed rate, which was known as a 'donnage hour'.[111] The docker was meant to work for the full hour for this fixed amount. In reality, he would often work fifteen minutes and then go back to handling cargo. On going back to the donnage, he would be paid for a new 'donnage hour'. One superintendent explains how it was done:

> In theory you were supposed to get an hour's work out of them. If they were an hour's on it, that was all they got. Generally what they did [was] they would do a bit of it [donnage] and they would work at the cargo. Then they would come across more [donnage] – or even the first donnage they may have handled might then have mounted up in their way and they would have to move it again because there was nowhere else to put it, so that they would maybe have to get paid twice for the same donnage, and of course the employers didn't like it at all.[112]

In Chapter 2 we saw that for some commodities dockers were paid for how much they managed to move – tonnage rates. Scammers could work fifteen donnage minutes, turn to tonnage, then later work another quarter-hour donnage. When maximally successful, this could produce four hours pay for one-hour donnaging, while interfering little with one's day's accumulation of tonnage totals.

'Hot money' was an older custom. Extra money was payable when the temperature in the hold pushed too high. Internal combustion in the cargo would be the natural cause. When the temperature rose in this way, the superintendent sent for 'the doctor': a chemist with a special thermometer, who wore a white coat for the inspection. If, when the doctor took his reading, the temperature was at a certain degree, extra pay, hot money, was payable.

Fires also occurred, from unnatural, as well as natural causes. Dockers had their own thermometer. As coalies struck nearer the floor of a coal ship, the end of the job, and of the pay for that job, was looming. Fire in the hold, and its extra pay, seemed a boon. If a small fire existed, but was not creating enough heat, sticks and paper might be pushed in to encourage the blaze. In the absence of an existing fire, big oil rags, used to wipe men's hands when greasy with oil, could be soaked in oil, planted, and set on fire. At ten o'clock one morning in Alexandra Basin, such a fire brought the call for the doctor. Down into the hold went the man in white. Suddenly a big cheer went all over the docks. 'They got it! They got it! They all got it! Everyone was cheering. Everyone knew what was after happening. Sixteen quid they got.'[113]

Fires in the holds were not a major danger. Casualties did not result. Slippery and dusty conditions, the dirty cargoes, could, and did, on the other hand, cause injury. Such conditions were among the factors which, as we saw in detail in Chapter 2, made the occupation of deep-sea docker a relatively dangerous one.

Ghost Workers and Other Absent Dockers

If dockers were chiefly concerned with increasing their rates of pay, the stevedores were unhappy about manning levels and restrictive practices that had grown up over the years. Once assigned to a vessel, dockers could not be transferred to another during the course of the day, even once the work was finished on the vessel they had been assigned to. The result of this practice was that on the occasion when the docker was let go early, he received payment for a full day's work. Stevedore and employers tried to get the work finished by the 12 o'clock Angelus bell: 'They would cut you to the bone for the half-day,' remembered Martin Mitten. To him the pealing of the bells brought with it additional income, income obtained as a result of successful strike action. He recalled that the argument put forward to the stevedores to establish the claim was 'God didn't make half days, he made whole days.'

In the early twentieth century Dublin Port was the last stop for cattle raised in the west of the country, fattened in the midlands, transported to Dublin and then driven, often on foot, through the city for live export on waiting boats to the Continent.[114] In the 1940s and the 1950s the cattle ships were a particular source of conflict. The following official Dutch complaint of extortion in 1953–54 targets the ghost cattle dockers, mentioned in Chapter 2. Paying its respects to the Department of External Affairs, the Royal Netherlands Legation reminds that:

> as pointed out by the Legation at several previous occasions, the Irish Seamen's and Portworker's Union has been regularly demanding payments for cattle attendants whenever a ship carries cattle to the Netherlands, although the shipowners have had to dispense with these men's services as they were a continuous source of disruption and petty offences.

> The Netherland Government has noted with respect that this situation, where by fulfilment of their demands was obtained by the threat of strikes, not only continues but has even been aggravated by a new instance of extortion. Whereon M.V. *Trito* was delayed in the Port of Dublin by bad weather recently, the union, on the 15th January 1954 put forward an additional claim of £10 and twelve shillings for four men who were not actually employed during the delay to relieve the cattlemen who are regularly paid although not employed either.[115]

Each shipment of thirty cattle was supervised by one ghost. A ghost foreman was paid an additional £2. Ghost workers may have been both without form and function, but had to have paid relief! That was until 1966 when, at that point, the ghosts were made redundant.[116]

Absenteeism in a more conventional sense was, however, another matter. Long-term absenteeism, for six months or more, could result in the loss of a button (unless the docker was suffering from ill health).[117] Despite the unquestionable hard work generally put in by dockers, short-term absences appeared to be a regular problem on the Pond. It was a particular problem in the late 1960s when work was plentiful.[118] Three kinds of reasons explain these absences. Three, that is, after elimination

Dockers and seamen on protest march against lockout. Led by John 'Slim' Brown and MP&GWU president Jimmy Dunne on Guild Street. (Donated by Michael Donnelly to the Dublin Dock Workers Preservation Society)

of severe illness or injury; we have seen that, if a docker desired to attend at the read or the ship, he did so, ill, injured or not, if at all possible. Cargo selection was a major factor for dockers. The roughest commodities had to be handled nonetheless; and everybody handled them plenty. Still, sometimes individuals avoided the reads for potashes, green ore, blue brimstone or timber. Older or weaker buttonmen would for good reason hold off for an easier ship. Those men gravitated, on such occasions, towards the reads for ships carrying the more easily handled commodities. Sometimes, even no work at all seemed preferable. 'When there was a fosset boat in,' Martin Mitten, a deep-sea docker confesses, 'we would make sure we were idle.' An exaggeration this, clearly, as this man in fact worked many fosset ships, and remembered how he would bleed from the nose after unloading the sulphur ammonia.

Other dockers, secondly, regarded themselves as specialists in certain cargo, and tried to restrict or channel themselves accordingly.[119] Flat rate jobs were also often avoided for their lower pay rate than hourly work. Weekend work paid better than during the days. It was the buttonmen, especially, who could exercise these choices, once the button system was in place.[120] As they were now certain to be called first, they could reasonably expect to gain more attractive work than that on the ships laden with the toughest commodities. Some would present for the better paid weekend work, leaving the week to others. Non-buttonmen were always likely to be waiting at the read for any opportunity. During the heyday of the buttonmen, the hardest labour was often borne by the non-button dockers.

Absences by regular dockers were, secondly and differently, also high at the Christmas and New Year holiday period. Winter found a few more of the regulars to be unavailable daily than the warmer peak preference months of May and June. Except for the first three weeks of December, when the onrush of Christmas gift-giving brought all hands to the read. When work was plentiful, and therefore dockers were working every day, men sometimes did not present at the read simply to have a day off.

All of this rather flies in the face of claims presented earlier that dockers were out every day for work. At certain chosen times, they were not. But, is any of what has just been mentioned absenteeism? From the employing stevedore's viewpoint, it is. The dockers were not, however, permanent employees. May one accurately speak of absenteeism when the whole scheme of things is that workers are only wanted when the ship is docked and the cargo ready to be moved? Absenteeism is a concept meant for regularly paid employees. Casual dockers were perhaps somewhat entitled to their own agenda, all things considered. Not appearing at certain reads on certain days was part of their overall manipulation of the economic niche.

Over the years, particularly as new technologies were developed for use on the docks, manning levels became a point of contention. Forklift drivers employed by shipping companies could do the work of six men but the stevedore was still required, by union agreement, to hire the same number of gangs in addition to the forklift men. Ultimately the introduction of containers was to fundamentally change, and to some, destroy the occupation entirely. When a mobile crane was introduced which would effectively cut down on manpower, Arthur Kelly recalls how as the crane trolleyed along the quay, a half-dozen dockers solemnly paced alongside, each with a hand on the crane. 'There's the funeral procession,' one stevedore observed to another: 'the mourners are moving up the quay'.[121] Perhaps they had an idea of what the future had in store?

FIVE

THE HOME FRONT

We married jewels … they accepted our way of life.[1]

In the dark of the morning, the city sleeps. A docker leaves the warmth of his bed, up early to unload a banana boat that must ship out on the next tide. It could be ten at night, when he finishes unloading and heads for the warmth of a nearby pub. For one docker the Saturday tradition was to stop in after the bar to pick up a treat for his wife. Who were the women who waited for pigs' feet and onions, wrapped in paper, who depended on money left on the mantelpiece? What was it like to grow up in a docker's family? Away from the quays, the ships, the pitch and toss schools, the bars and the craic, what was life like for those at home, for those whose fathers, husbands and brothers, were dockers?

At the turn of the twentieth century, many dockers' families made homes in rooms in tenement houses.[2] A third of the Dublin population lived in these crumbling buildings and many persisted until the 1960s. For 21,747 families in 1911, home consisted of no more than a single room. In some areas, up to 100 people were crammed into each decaying Georgian house. Dockers remembered a childhood in the 1930s or 1940s spent with eight or nine family members in one room. Conditions were deplorable. These buildings rarely had indoor plumbing. The entire house had to share one toilet, known as a 'pipe', which was outside in the back yard.

The Dempsey family outside their family home, Cardiff Lane. Front: Paddy Dempsey Jnr and George Dempsey. Back: Frank Dempsey, Unknown Woods, Theresa Dempsey, Brendan Dempsey and Fran Dempsey, c.1948. (Donated by Brendan Dempsey to the Dublin Dock Workers Preservation Society)

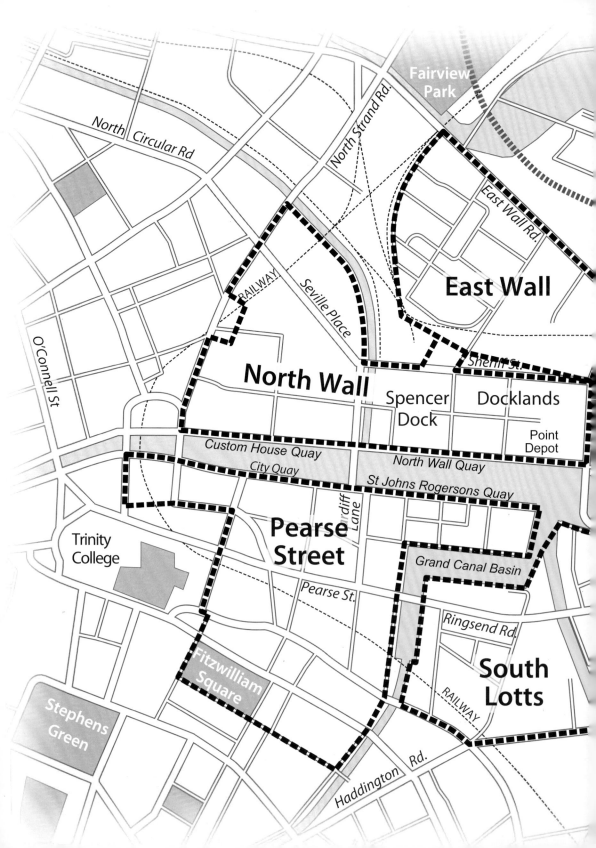

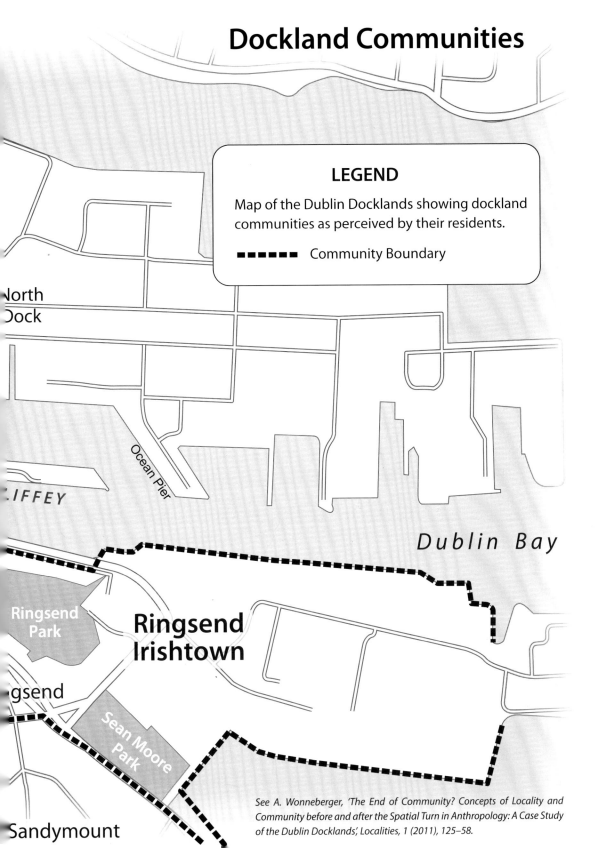

Dockland Communities

LEGEND

Map of the Dublin Docklands showing dockland communities as perceived by their residents.

▬▬▬▬▬▬ Community Boundary

North
Dock

Ocean Pier

LIFFEY

Dublin Bay

Ringsend
Park

Ringsend
Irishtown

gsend

Sean Moore
Park

Sandymount

*See A. Wonneberger, 'The End of Community? Concepts of Locality and
Community before and after the Spatial Turn in Anthropology: A Case Study
of the Dublin Docklands', Localities, 1 (2011), 125–58.*

Conditions were cramped – an extra room, an indoor toilet, meant a lot. Martin Mitten, remembering his childhood in the 1920s, said, 'We were king because we had our own toilet and wash and throw.' He lived in a flat on the top floor. Finding a bright side to the situation, he commented that 'when you were praying, you knew you were nearer to heaven then if you were on the bottom'. He remembers clearly how crowded it was.

> When I lived in Moss Street we had two rooms, a front room and a bedroom. My father and mother slept in the front room [which was] the feeding room all thrown in together. At that time there was John, Terry, me and then there was Nan … that was the sister. Nan would be sleeping somewhere near the door, and we'd be in two beds. One brother set the bed on fire twice, smoking.

Fire was an ever-present threat. For many an open fire was depended on for heating and cooking. When times were good, coal was used. During World War Two, and times of greater poverty, turf was relied on instead. Often there was no electricity. Dockers remembered using oil lamps. With a 'boup' the oil would run out and the *Our Boys* magazine would have to be put aside for the next day.

We Thought We Were Moving Into a Palace

In many great port cities, dockers and their families live close to the city quays. In Dublin, the dockland community was split in four. South of the River Liffey, dockers lived either around City Quay/Westland Row or Ringsend/Irishtown. On the northside, one community was based around the North Wall, while the other clustered around the East Wall and North Strand. Each parish identified itself as separate from its neighbour, though in truth they shared much in common, not just in terms of the importance of the docks as a source of employment but also in the way families lived.[3] A partial list of registered deep-sea dockers from 1957 shows that just under 60 per cent of registered

First dockers' dinner dance c.1960. From left to right: Doreen Doran, Ned Smith, Berna Corrigan, Jem Kiernan [Gabby Hayes], Mae Smith, Marie Mitten and Tommy 'Yorkie' Corrigan. (Donated by Berna Byrne Corrigan to the Dublin Dock Workers Preservation Society)

deep-sea dockers resided in one of the four dockland communities; the majority had their homes either in City Quay or Ringsend. Yet by 1957 just over 40 per cent lived elsewhere in the city.[4] As tenements were cleared, registered dockers spread from the dockside to the new suburbs and made their homes in almost all parts of the city. Dublin was a dockers' town.

In the thirty years before the Second World War public housing projects were built in the north docks area and around Ringsend. Tenements were cleared and new flats were built on the old sites. As a child, docker's daughter Phyllis Nolan moved from a small cottage to Markievicz House, a large flat complex with 171 apartments.[5] From an open fire for cooking to electricity, 'we thought we were in heaven … just to put on the light … baths even'. Others moved west into the city, remaining close to the river, north and south but away from the port. New suburbs were built in Beaumont, nine kilometres north of the port and Crumlin ten kilometres south of the port.

In the decade leading up to the outbreak of war in Europe, new public housing was built in the Liberties, a couple of kilometres from the port but also much further inland; Inchicore and Kilmainham were close to the south Liffey banks, with Stoneybatter and Finglas to the north side. After the war projects were developed aimed at increasing the quality of housing available in the south docks and Ringsend. The city also continued to spread to the new northern suburb of Coolock.[6]

Yet for many inner-city Dubliners, tenement housing – unsanitary, overcrowded and crumbling – persisted as a serious problem well into the twentieth century. The collapse of two tenement buildings in 1963 brought to public attention the worsening conditions of the aging buildings. On 2 June, on the southside of the city, two elderly people were killed when a four-story house collapsed on Bolton Street. Only ten days later, in the heart of the southside dockland community, a house fell in Fenian Street, killing two young girls, Marie Vardy (aged 9) and Linda Byrne (aged 8).[7] In response to growing unrest about the housing crisis, the government introduced a new programme of building. In the city centre blocks of four and five-storey flats were erected and the highrise apartments of Ballymun were built.

However, as far as the older dockers were concerned, anyone from about 'four mile outside' was a 'culchie'. Martin Mitten told of meeting a long-lost relation who had left Dublin 'when there was all tenements, rat infested and everything'. On returning he was astonished at the increase in prosperity among the people he had grown up with. Used to the long distances of the United States he was also amazed that Crumlin was considered to be far from Dublin. His docker brother remembers him saying 'I thought you said [he] lives in the country? He's only a stone's throw out of the city – it's about four or five mile.'

To the dockers, those four or five miles made all the difference. The dust and dirt of the docks was far behind. 'There was nothing there but fields,' Willie Murphy remembered, 'it was a wilderness when I moved out there in 1939. We were the last house … There was a space left for shops.' Gardens were also provided, much to the dockers' delight. 'The back garden I had,' he exclaimed, 'now, if I was a farmer I could have earned my living there growing vegetables and living on that is as true as God.'

Some were unhappy with their new homes. Although there were buses that could get you to the quay for the eight o'clock read, it meant leaving the house before seven, rather than walking a couple of minutes down the road. One who described himself as 'born and reared in City Quay parish' wrote to the dockers' newspaper *Waterfront* to complain:

> I am out here in Ballyfermot and have to pay 1/6 a day to get into my work on the docks and home again. I would rather have two rooms back in the old district than a mansion out here … I don't understand why more flats were not built on the river. Some people say it is not healthy. But there is more sickness out here than I ever saw in City Quay … I worked in London for a few years, and even rich gents and ladies there fight to rent stables in the city and near the embankment which they turn into living accommodation, which they call mews flats … if it is OK for rich folk in London, and not unhealthy, why shouldn't it be OK in Dublin?[8]

Willie Murphy did not settle in the suburbs. He explained that his journey by bike into the docks would require him to cross a canal. With his bike on his shoulder, holding the lock gate with his other hand, he would carefully cross over a narrow canal bridge. Once he wasn't careful enough:

> I lost me grip. I had a few beers on me … and I went in and I had to swim with the bike on my shoulder … 'Well' she said 'that's the end of it, I'm not having this'. So the next

Lever Brothers, Castleforbes Works, 1935. Back (left to right): unknown, Annie Maher, unknown, Kitty O'Shea. Middle Row, left to right: Christina Mylod (*née* Stacey). Front (left to right): May Donohoe, unknown, unknown, Sarah Clarke, Unknown, Lena Daly (*née* O'Beirne). (Donated by Brendan Dempsey to the Dublin Dock Workers Preservation Society)

night when I come home, there was a letter on the knocker, 'Gone to Townsend Street'. Everything was cleared in a day and that's what was left for me … I had to ride back in from a house into a room.[9]

As his son explained 'he was stopping too many times for a few jars on the way home. His tumble in the water was the last straw, she wasn't having that. No, she stopped it'.[10]

In Dublin, as in many other working-class urban communities, children lived on the street. This description of London working-class children shares much in common with children in Dublin. 'Whoever was at hand – passing by, looking out the window, talking at the door, sitting out with their knitting or preparing vegetables on the doorstep or pavement chair – would administer comfort or scolding or threats as required, no matter whose the children.'[11]

Watching out for children was a community affair. A good child was rewarded with food, 'if you were lucky you got a cut of bread and butter and jam'.[12] If a child was bad, word would get back to his mother.

> Most of [the women] all stayed at home. There were tenements beside us in Moss Street … a woman would send you for a message and you would get a cut of bread, but if you were impudent or the other woman complained to your mother she'd maybe give you a lick and another lick if there were any more complaints. They wouldn't take guff or anything.[13]

While the children ran around below, the women would chat and keep an eye out for trouble. There was very little traffic on the road, so the streets were their parks. The first game would be skipping rope. Girls swung far and wide from a rope tied to a lamppost. Phyllis Nolan remembered her sister, small and light flying high, only to lose her grip and hit the ground hard. Knocked unconscious she was rushed to hospital. Then there was 'pickey beds' a game similar to hopscotch.[14] On the ground, 'beds' were marked off and numbered. A small round ball known as a picky was filled with mud and thrown on a bed. One, two, three, four, the goal was to hop into each bed, avoiding the line and rescue the pickey. Handball is a traditional Irish sport, and a nearby wall made a good handball court. Football was and is a favourite. 'We played pitch and toss up to the wall at Haydens,' explained Willie Murphy Junior, 'we played rounders. We did a bit of boxing. There was the … clubs that were around at the time and the Comhairle Le Leas Óige. Most of us joined them when we were kids, from about 8 up to 12 or 13.'[15]

Established in 1943 by the Minister of Education Comhairle Le Leas Óige (Council for the Welfare of Youth) was established under the chairmanship of Fr Dennis Vaughan, an appointee of the notorious Catholic Archbishop of Dublin, Dr McQuaid. Fr Vaughan hoped that this and other youth clubs would assist boys in their intellectual and moral development and move them 'from the street corner and toss school into the better atmosphere of educational centres and the more natural influences of the home'.[16]

Though they were often warned to keep away, the docklands themselves were an exciting albeit dangerous playground. Children climbed the timber stacked three stories high in the timber yards, running the length and breadth.[17] They would watch the cattle being driven through the city and play with them as they were held in pens waiting to be shipped. Jack O'Reilly remembers the animal yards as a favourite hiding place when he was 'mitching' from school, 'sometimes we would sit on the back of the sheep and pretend we were sitting on the backs of horses'.[18]

Passenger ships, gleaming in the darkness like a grand hotel would berth on the quay close to Phyllis Nolan's home. Her father would warn her away from the shipside for fear of the sailors. With her mother, she'd sneak up to see the passengers dismount, sometimes carrying their winnings from a show on board – a teddy bear, a doll or a sugar stick.

Children were also expected to work. They contributed to the household from an early age. The younger ones helped out with fetching and carrying water, looking after the other children, buying the daily bread and often bringing down lunch to their fathers working on the docks.

Bringing dinner down was for many boys an introduction to dock work – the first step to joining their fathers as dockers. Stew would be put in a bowl and wrapped in a red handkerchief to keep the heat in. Willie Murphy remembered how he would also bring a billy-can of boiling water to make tea. Unfortunately, the water often got cold in transit, so the young boy would slip into the galley of a ship and heat it up. Most importantly, he brought a bottle of stout with him, which he got from the local pub. If his mother didn't have 'the price of it', he'd get it on credit. When he arrived down on the docks with the dinner his father would sometimes share a little of it with him. His father would pour some of the tea into the lid of the billy-can for him to drink.

'My father used to work night and day,' Phyllis Nolan remembered, 'he'd have to finish a boat to let it go with the tide. Ah he was always working, he knew his grandchildren better than us.' At the age of 11, she would get the ferry to Alexander Basin, a big can covered by a lid in her hands, in her pocket a note for her teacher excusing her lateness. On a windy day the ferry could be rough and frightening. She would sit with her father and share in the meal, sausages, rashers and fried bread piled on top of each other, sprinkled with a bit of salt. Her father would give half away, anyone who was missing their lunch was offered some of his. Rose Ann Doyle also remembers:

> My mother used to send me down to the docks to my father to bring him down a billy-can full of tea. He would be digging the coal out of the big coal boats and he would see me walking down towards him. He would come up from the cargo hatch and come over to me. I would sit on the boat and have some tea with him before bringing the billy-can back home.[19]

Sometimes when the dockers went for their morning break to the pub, they'd pay the children to continue the work. One docker remembers how his father would tell him and his four friends to 'come on down'. While the adults went off to quell the thirst, the children took their place in the hold. Climbing into the dark and dusty hatch of a coal boat, the friends would find four empty tubs. 'We'd fill the four tubs, the four of us and he'd give us three pence for the four tubs when they'd get back. We went up to a shop in Moss Street …There were fizzy drinks then. We used to get three or four fizzy drinks.'[20]

With money so scarce, many children looked for paid work. Timber poles were carried on a horse and dray from T&C Martin's timberyard up the Liffey to Heuston Station. Barefooted Mick Comiskey was paid a shilling to walk behind them holding a red flag alerting other traffic to the dangers. The shilling went to his mother.[21] Willie Murphy Junior remembers his first job. He was 8 or 9, and smart enough to discover a way of making a little extra on the side.

We used to do newspaper rounds at six in the morning up to about eight thirty... straight home and a cup of tea and down to school and then we would do it at half four in the evening ... it was work or jail. That was for five shillings a week and whatever papers you could rob ... on the way home. You would take about an extra half a dozen papers and flog them and you got your sweet money going to school. Five shillings was exploitation so there was no harm in doing what you were doing, like getting your own back, one robber to another.

Some young workers took into their new workplaces an organising ability and sense of fairness that they had learnt from their fathers. Willie Murphy told of his sons who at 13 and 14 during the school holidays got kitchen porter work in a ship's galley. Two brothers and a friend, whose father worked for the union, laboured in the kitchen, and their demands for tea breaks were met by deaf ears and little sympathy. Knowing that this was not right and knowing what needed to be done, they went on strike, walking off the ship, to their father's approval.

School, often disliked, could not be avoided. Boys from the southside dockland areas went to City Quay National School (also known as Gloucester college because its entrance was on Gloucester Road), the Christian Brothers School (CBS) on Westland Row, and the Star of the Sea in Sandymount. Those children whose families had moved to the Cabra suburb went to Christ the King in Cabra, which was founded in 1934 as the Cabra suburb expanded or St Joseph's CBS (known as Joey's) in Marino. Some schools no longer exist, St Andrew's National School on Great Brunswick Street (now Pearse Street), founded in 1895 closed down in 1972 as families were moved from cramped inner-city tenements to new public housing estates in the suburbs of the city.[22] St Laurence O'Toole's, 'Larriers' and Rutland Street School continue to educate the children of the north inner city.

School provided food for hungry children. When the master called lunchtime, '600 boys in their bare feet ... would charge down from

Collin's House and the nuns would be there with the dinners. [We had] big tin mugs and a ton of stew and a big potato, you'd be like this slurp, slurp, more sister.'[23] Pauline Mallon, a docker's daughter remembers: 'One of the things that stands out in my mind is going to school in St. Laurence O'Tooles. The class was so full we did not get much attention off the teacher. The classes were so overcrowded.'[24]

Many Irish students of that generation, particularly of those who came from poorer families, shared these experiences of boredom and a poor standard of education.[25] In 1942 the Gardiner Street convent school crammed children into classes, the vast majority of which varied in size from more than fifty children to over eighty.[26] By 1967 there were still 108 primary schools in Dublin with classes of more than 50 pupils.[27] The docking way of life was disparaged. Dolf Brennan

Docker family outside the family home, Martins Terrace, Cardiff Lane, with the Gasometer looming in the background. Behind: Fran Dempsey. Front (from left): George Dempsey, Paddy Dempsey, Brendan Dempsey and Frank Dempsey. (Donated by Brendan Dempsey to the Dublin Dock Workers Preservation Society)

remembered how at school, if the headmaster said 'another one for the docks' in a derogatory way, he thought 'you weren't too bright'.

Dockers' children left school early, forced by the need to contribute to the household income. From 1926 until 1971, it was compulsory to attend school from aged 6 until 14.[28] A census taken in the mid-sixties, shows that the vast majority of dockers left school by the age of 14.[29] Although free secondary school education was introduced in 1967, the numbers of dockers who left school before the age of 15 remained high.[30] One docker remembered how a quarrel with the headmaster lead him to abandon his education. His mother wouldn't let him back. A child's income could be an important contribution to the household economy and extra years' schooling were often of little value.

John Walsh went to the docks at 16 and-a-half, taking his father's button as his father was too ill to use it.[31] In Chapter 2 we saw that many boys followed their fathers down to the docks, but not all fathers were pleased to see their sons working there. One docker spoke of how his father was unhappy when in the early 1950s, at 18 he left his secure job in the Post Office for dock work:

> He was reluctant … all fathers were at that stage, if they could have seen their sons work elsewhere, they would have been better satisfied.

> It was so uncertain. You were going down the docks at 18 years of age. You weren't sure of getting one day a week, you weren't sure of getting four days a week, you weren't sure of any employment at all … because you were going down as a non- buttonman.[32]

> But I think the biggest problem with a lot of fathers was that many dockers liked to socialise immediately after work and I think that was the problem. You didn't hear a lot of talk about alcoholics them days, but there were I think, a few, to put it mildly, there were.[33]

This docker's daughter explains the pressures she was under to get work, 'I had no mother and father left … my sisters, they were waiting on the money, so you had to work … It's not like nowadays, they are getting sent to college and all. You had to work.'

Willie Murphy Junior related how in the early 1950s he left school at 12 and a half:

> I should have stayed another year, I'd already gone to the last year in class. It was a matter of spending another year twiddling your thumbs. I told them that I was going to the Tech [the technical school] so I got released, from the primary to go to the Tech … I got a job as a messenger boy with McDonaghs of Moore St. It was a butcher shop in Moore St.

As with their fathers, pay packets were supposed to be handed over to their mothers to help with the household expenses. As with their fathers, something was held back. May Hanaphy, who worked in the Jacob's Biscuit Factory in the 1920s confided that as she got older 'then you didn't give it to your Mam. Oh, many a raise went into my pocket, I'll tell you that, and I wouldn't tell my Ma.'[34]

We Met at a Dance … They Had to Pay for Themselves Usually[35]

With a little extra money in their pockets, the sons and daughters of dockers went out on the town. In working-class Dublin in the early 1940s social life revolved around the ballrooms during the week, and the pictures on Sunday night. Traditionally, women would pay their own way into a dance, but would expect her cinema ticket to be bought for her. The dockers claimed that the uncertain salary of the docker precluded them from paying into the ballrooms. Willie Murphy remembers meeting his wife at one such dance.

> We met at a dance, sixpence for the gents and four pence for the ladies. They had to pay for themselves usually … We used

Dockers at a party, 1950s. Back: Cormac McDermott (missing), Johnny Kehoe, unknown, Johnny Byrne, Christy Egan and Seamus Smith. Front: Unknown, Angela O'Brien, Peggy Smith and Shamie Dillon. (Donated by Cormac McDermott to the Dublin Dock Workers Preservation Society)

to go to a little hall, up there in Sandymount and if there were four or five couples on the floor, you were hopping off one another. There was an old piano there playing and that's what you had to dance to. The Palace Ballroom was big. It was a huge place, like you were in the Phoenix Park in comparison.

After the dance, he would walk his partner for the night home. He was careful not to appear too eager 'it would be a night or two before we would make another date'. In the mid-1950s Teddy Boys came to Dublin.[36] 'There was the dance halls then, with the hops … small out houses, garages would be converted … into hops. You had the Bottle Makers Hall[37] …You had loads of them … They were great little hops and the jiving scene was the real thing … Teddy Boy suits.'[38]

In the 1960s, nightclubs opened on Dublin's Nassau Street. They were tiny places, 'a postage stamp in the corner, a café and you ordered your coffee and you put your whiskey into the coffee … it was a real

… Hernando's Hideaway'.[39] An annual dockers' dance was held in the 1960s, first in Cleary's and later in the Metropole Hotel.

The cinema has always been popular in Ireland, both with courting couples and later in married life. The Savoy, the Theatre Royal, the Regal Rooms and Lyceum Pictures (established by James Joyce and previously known as the Volta) were typical evening destinations. One type of film was known as a 'follow-oner' or 'follow-upper', that, is the films were serialised, with one on a Monday, Tuesday and a Wednesday, and a different one on a Thursday, Friday and on the Saturday matinee. There were no entrance tickets, instead the owner would hold out a bag and everyone would toss in their money. Sometimes if it was very crowded, under the cover of darkness the children would get away with throwing washers in instead. And what did they do with the money they had saved? At a shop near the cinema they could buy a cigarette for a farthing.

Once married, men and women kept separate social circles. While the pub was the docker's main venue for socialising, it would have been highly unusual to find a woman in the main bar before the 1960s. When asked if women would come into the pubs one docker exclaimed, 'Oh no way, oh Jesus we'd die… if you brought your wife into a pub in them days, she had to go into the snug, she would not be served at the bar.'[40] He continued 'it wasn't that you didn't want your wife with you beside you having a drink. It was a rule of the publicans'. They had a little snug built and that was where the women drank. Women kept a low profile, sometimes just stopping long enough to get a jug filled.

> The women would come in, a couple of women would come in and hand around a little glass of porter a glass of plain. They'd come in to have their little chat and then get their glass in the jug and go home. But some of them only just come in with the jug under their shawl, get served and go.[41]

Many dockers' daughter's avoided alcohol. One docker explained how his wife 'never drank, she hated the sight of it, because of having me and having her father'.[42]

Instead of frequenting the pub, young girls spent their free time in Melons Icecream Parlour. Annie Murphy remembered meeting her husband at the age of 17: 'I just met him at the ice cream shop at the top of the street here. I used to see him every night. Now, I wasn't going with him at the time, I just used to see him every night there … and say "goodnight" to him, and that would be it. After a while we got together.'

At 21, she married him. If married with children, social life was dependant on finding somebody to look after them. Couples would even go to different Masses, the women went to early Mass and the men attended the later services.

> We'd go early and someone would mind the babies, because there was always a baby, and they'd stay and then we'd come home and get them all ready for ten Mass and [my husband] went to eleven. He'd go to eleven because we couldn't go together and leave the children. You couldn't go anywhere to leave the children. One had to go or the other had to go.[43]

Willie Murphy remembers how, before he got married, it was a ritual in their house that they all sat down to Sunday lunch together. In the evenings, they would gather to play cards and feast on his mother's baking. She would spend all Saturday making apple tarts, jam tarts and currant bread. These would be served at the card game and who ever won the money would give the money to his mother for use in the gas meter. Once he married his wife joined in with the throng and at the end of the night his mother would give his wife a little of the leftovers to take home; 'a wrap up, a piece of jam tart, a piece of apple tart and some cake'.

Annie Murphy remembered how when her husband went off on the cattle boats he would bring her back small presents 'little souvenirs, not big things, Dutch clogs and things like that, a pair of earrings.' On summers' evenings families used to go for walks together on the Shelly Banks. On weekends the entire extended family, sisters and brothers, the gaggle of children would claim space on the beach and picnic on cake and sandwiches. Later when dockers began to be able to afford cars, couples would go for a drive to the coast. When they got a car, couples would drive to Sandymount Tower 'and we'd seen the mail boat leaving … [at] nine o'clock every night. We'd see her sailing out through the harbour and then I'd take her home. She wouldn't come in for a drink. She'd say, "you leave me home and you go in for your drink"'.

At the heart of the docker's wife's social were visits to family and friends. In particular, women would visit their sisters. One docker told how he would let his wife off to visit her sister while the children were in bed, as long as she would be back in time to let him go for a pint. Annie Murphy belonged to a choir, practising weekly with their relations, in-laws and children. A small group would stop in the pub for a drink and a singsong on the way home.

They were 'strong women' one docker proudly related 'very strong women, they managed on little or nothing'.[44] One docker felt it was the wife who ruled the roost in the house 'she wouldn't tell you what to do but she would tell you "you better curtail the drink and don't be gambling and all this carry on".'[45] Another added 'you had to do what you were told and that was that'.[46] Did they heed their wives? 'Ah no,' one docker remembered, 'you went the next day, and you got your few pints if you had the money.'[47] Angela Mc Farland, a docker's wife, sighed, 'Sure they drank more than they gave up you know … but what could you do, you had to get on with it.'[48] Some dockers were defensive of the way the women were treated. One warned that his friend's wife 'would have been the right one for to give you a lowdown on all the wrongs, but not the rights'.[49] Occasionally a woman would put her foot down. One wife tore up her husband's passport so he could no longer go to England to get work. As one docker commented 'they were powerful women'.[50]

While dockers searched for work on the waterfront, their daughters and wives grappled with equally difficult tasks. They managed the household budget. They put food on the table, they kept the house clean, their children healthy and cared for growing families. Dock work was unpredictable. When dockers were paid, they could be paid well. There were other times when work was scarce. As we've seen, in particular there was a long decline during the Second World War when many dockers were forced to emigrate to England to work in the factories, while others signed up to fight in the British Army. Willie Murphy remembers 'the hardest time of my life was 1939–1945, the war years. There was nothing here: we were lucky to survive'. Many dockers were forced to emigrate to England. He and many others were only allowed to go home once a year, 'you could take a choice of coming in the summer or coming at Christmas and of course Christmas always stood out where there was a family so I always came in the Christmas'.[51] Cissie O'Brien's father left the docks to work at sea and lost his life in 1940 when his boat was torpedoed and sank. Her two brothers were to meet the same fate in 1943.[52]

Weather conditions could cause a shortage of work. Workplace injury could also mean absence from the docks, as could other more general illnesses. Phyllis Nolan's father was alone in a yard, pulling a coal tub onto a bank of coal ready to be filled. A crane knocked the tub, trapping him against it, crushing his ribs, puncturing his lungs. His breathing was affected and he had to stop working on the docks. The tenements in particular were associated with high levels of TB. Other contagious diseases such as scarlet fever and diphtheria were also present in Dublin during the war years.[53]

Alcoholism was a frequent problem. Barney Conway, a friend of James Larkin remembered that 'the women would often come to Larkin and complain about their husbands' drinking'.[54] Emmet O'Connor, the union leader James Larkin's biographer, reported that 'more than one drunken docker went head down the steps of Liberty Hall with Larkin as the propelling force'.[55]

Strikes also brought financial insecurity. When their fathers weren't earning money, the wages of wives, daughters and sons were vital in keeping the household afloat. One daughter remembered how after years of working on the cattle boats, her father disappeared, 'so I had to take up cleaning, contract cleaning'.[56]

Before marriage, dockers' daughters took paid jobs, often in local factories. In the 1911 census, most of the women who gave an

Waterfront Mutual Benefit Society Brochure. (Michael Donnelly collection donated by Florrie Cunningham to the Dublin Dock Workers Preservation Society)

Waterfront

MUTUAL BENEFIT SOCIETY

LIBERTY HALL,
DUBLIN 1.

Tel. 42550.

EXPLANATORY BROCHURE WITH EXTRACTS
FROM RULES, ETC.

The Society is a workers' organisation, open to all workers in Dublin, clerical and manual, male and female. Its general aim is to promote the welfare of its members by encouraging thrift, by providing a medical service and affording security against sickness and accident, and by rendering financial assistance in cases of need.

1. ENTRANCE and QUARTERLY FEES.

The entrance fee to the Society is 1/-, and thereafter a quarterly fee of 1/6 is charged to help in defraying administration expenses, etc. This must be paid, and any member who falls into arrears with

I

occupation were single women in their teens and twenties. Here we find women workers in a watch factory and biscuit packers, those who described their work as book folding, book-binding and a sack-maker.

The most common occupations of dockers' wives and daughters in the 1911 census were as general domestic servants, housemaids or housekeepers. Part-time cleaning jobs enabled women to also take care of the family. Until the 1950s, domestic service was the most popular work available to working women.[57] One woman worked as a laundress. There were also some dressmakers, a tailoress and a stationary assistant. Unusually one woman, Mary Plunkett, gave her occupation as ship winch driver, aged 26. She was a visitor to Hanover Street East on the night of the census – and also perhaps that rarest of things, a female dockworker.[58] In Ringsend boatyards young women made sails and nets.[59]

During the 1930s, Irish women's employment in manufacturing increased significantly. Most female factory workers continued to be young, working in assembly or packing tasks in clothing, footwear, toiletries and confectionery plants.[60] The biscuit packers worked in Jacobs Biscuit Factory, the largest single employer of women in Dublin, with a work force which ranged from 1,300 to 3,000.[61] Kevin C. Kearns also mentions the following businesses as notable employers of Dublin women: Polikoff's Tailoring Factory, Donnelly's Bacon, Mooney's Sack Factory, Mitchell's Rosary Bead, Mount Brown Laundry, Afton Knitting, Carroll's Tobacco, Wilton's Confectionary, Winstanley Shoes, Burdon's Sewings, ammunition factory Parkgate Street. Additionally, women worked in Boland's Bakery in Ringsend and Lever Brothers Castleforbes Works on Sheriff Street. Lemons Sweet Factory in Drumcondra also employed women. During the First World War the Dublin Dockyard War Munitions Factory was based in Dublin Port. Annie Murphy worked in a sewing factory off Grafton Street for eight years, until she married her docker husband at 21. At 14 she started, cycling into Grafton Street to start work at 9. It was piece work – the more she sewed, the more money she made. She was fast, so by the end of the week she took home more pay than her sister who was working in the Glass Bottle Factory in Ringsend.

The trade union traditions of the dockers were also evident among their daughters and sisters. During the 1913 Dublin Lockout over 300 women workers in Jacobs stayed out of work throughout the entire duration of the strike[62], while the munitions workers were strongly organised in the National Federation of Women Workers.[63] In 1918, the Irish Women Workers Union had members in the Dublin Laundry

Company and Goodbody's Tobacco factory. In the same year, the union closed all hotels, restaurants and cafés on 30 August in a partially successful demand for wage increases and union recognition.[64]

Many of Dublin's street traders lived close to the city quays. While men and women might sell coal blocks in the open air, it was women exclusively who sold food. Permanent pitches required an expensive licence so fish, chicken, fruit and vegetables were hawked from moving pitches – a pram or a horse and cart. Regulations forbade the traders from selling from a stationary spot. This proved to be a 'very successful but not very profitable' way of making a living.[65]

Women's wages were low. In 1913, the average weekly wage for most of the women workers in Jacobs was between seven shillings and eight shillings. The average pay for boys and young men in the same factory was twelve shillings and two pence – considerably more than their sisters, while older men were paid more again, at twenty-eight shillings and seven pence.[66] However, despite the low levels of pay, factory work had the advantage of being regular and predictable. At times when insecurity meant no work for the docker, his wife and daughter's contributions could be vital in ensuring the household was able to maintain itself.

Many women often did not receive full pensions when they retired because their employers paid them informally. Jem Kelly spoke of how his mother was commended by the Pope for her work as a cleaner for the local priests, however 'they never stopped stamps, and she was 53 years and she never got that much at all after all those years, because she never paid stamps'. While her brother worked on the docks, Betty Dempsey was one of only five women working in Hilton Brothers mattress factory off Lombard Street, on the south side of the river. She started work there in 1933 at the age of 14, until at the age of 39, she and several other women were made redundant. In conversation with Turtle Bunbury she remembers, 'One day they just said, "We're very sorry, we haven't got enough work for you. Your cards will be ready next week. That was it. No redundancy. No nothing. After 25 years and I had never lost a day!"'[67] Chrissie McAdam, and her mother before her, both worked in Mitchell's Rosary Factory. For seventeen years, she made rosary beads for export. Her mother was over forty years on the job. Neither was given a pension.[68]

On marriage, wives usually left paid work for work in the home. In the 1911 census, few wives of dockers reported their occupation.[69] Of those who did, the older women, in their forties or fifties, often gave their occupation as widows. Others described themselves as housekeepers, charwomen or dressmakers. Jacob's Biscuit Factory forced women to leave on marriage, sending them off with a cake.[70] In Lever Brothers which made soap, a Westminister Chime Clock was both wedding and send-off gift. Only widows would return to the workplace.[71] 'We didn't stay on the way they are nowadays', a dockers wife explained: 'we left to look after the husband'. A husband described his wife as 'just an ordinary housewife'.[72] One wife emphasised that there were times when she would have liked to go out and get another job to help with the finances but it wasn't possible because there was nobody to look after the

Young men on the docks. (Donated by Billy Doyle to the Dublin Dock Workers Preservation Society)

children. Sometimes the dockers themselves stopped their wives getting paid work. One recalled his wife coming home late one evening. When he asked where she had been, she explained she had been out cleaning offices in Merrion Square. He was not at all happy with this. 'Well,' he said 'you can go out in the morning and stay right out and that was it … she was getting enough money at that time.'[73]

Dockers' wives were working women, maybe not always in paid employment, but certainly in the home. With large families, a considerable amount of time was spent by the docker's wife caring for her children.[74] For dockers' wives in the first half of the twentieth century, the tenements were difficult workplaces. Simple tasks, such as washing clothes, could take all day. Water had to be hauled in from outside, heated on an open-hearth fire before the strenuous work of wringing and rinsing could even begin. All water, for cleaning, cooking or making cups of tea, had to be carried in from the outside. In the 1940s three quarters of flats and tenements relied on shared sanitary facilities.[75] 'They were known as enamel buckets in them days and they were spotless clean so you put up your bucket of water for to do you for the next morning. There was no gas. You had your fire going, boiled your kettle and got your morning cup of tea for breakfast.'

Phyllis Nolan remembers her mother arranging towels on chairs around big baths so she and the other children could have a bath in privacy. Her father would need a bath every night to wash away the coal dust. His clothes would be stiff with the 'black stuff'. Her mother would first steep her father's 'greyback shirt' in cold water, rolled up and down, up and down in the sink. A slip was worn to keep her mother's clothes from the dust. Only then could she start washing the children with black soap. Afterwards, all the clothes from the tenements would be hung out to dry on long lines but even there, coal stored by the gas company could contaminate clothes hung beside their yards.[76] A docker's wife remembers:

'It was hard in some ways, but it was only second nature to us. We didn't know about luxuries. We didn't know about washing machines, dryers, things like that … we were just happy washing the clothes with our hands and drying them and putting them up.'

Putting food on the table was a daily duty. In the absence of fridges, ingredients were bought daily. May Malone, whose son was a docker, describe her childhood food as simple fare – stew and coddle during the weeks and cabbage and (thanks to an uncle who was a butcher) beef on Sundays.[77] Phyllis Nolan remembers her mother making her eat coddle, a traditional Dublin stew, before going to bed, saying 'that will keep the worms alive, make you go to sleep. You used to be sick eating with her … Always food, food, food'. Willie Murphy junior fondly describes watching his sister who worked in a bakery making the Christmas cake. 'She had the old gramophone', he remembered, 'and she would turn the cake on it when she was icing it. We'd all be there waiting as it would go around and they would get some of the icing.' Another wife would make grill cakes on a big iron pan on an open fire. Her daughter remembers how her father idolised them.[78] After travelling on the cattle boats to England, the dockers would come home with stories of all the new things they had experienced. On hearing of these, one mother decided she'd surprise her family.

> We were all talking about curries at sea, and we were really raving at the beauty of curries, so she says to herself, 'I'll do a curry'. Now she told none of us. So she went off and she put on a huge big pot at lunch time. We came in from the docks… we could smell the curry and we said 'What's the story?'
>
> 'Sit down' says she, and out come the big soup plates and out comes the curry.
>
> 'Oh Jesus! What's that?'
>
> 'That's curry' says she.
>
> Everyone started breaking their heart laughing and she went crying into the bedroom. She wouldn't have it. She put a big package of rice into a big pot and then boiled it, and then

threw a packet of curry powder and then boiled it. We were all breaking our heart laughing. Me Da would 'eat anything she put on the table', she said when she saw him turn his nose up at it, so [she knew] there must be something wrong. So that was the expertise of me ma.[79]

Her husband quickly added in her defence: 'other than that she was a brilliant woman in the house'.

One of the important, and often unappreciated, tasks, undertaken by the docker's wife, was the management of the household finances. Tradition held that wages were handed over to mothers and wives at the end of the week. The dockers would give a set portion of their wages, and with this they would have to manage the household's finances. Pauline Mallon, a docker's daughter from Sheriff Street remembered, 'My first job was in Abbey Street, working for a tailor. My wages were £3.50 a week. I had to bring home the wage packet unopened to my mother. She would give me £1 out of it. I used to go dancing at the weekend out of that.'[80]

One of the main problems with marrying a docker is that even when working and earning money, income was variable, as pay rates depended on the type of cargo they unloaded. Also, many dockers went to great lengths to hide the exact extent of their income from their wives. On good days, wives did not benefit from the extra money. Dockers' wages fluctuated from high to low, up and down. In contrast, many wives received either a regular amount or when no work was to be had, nothing. Women were on a 'standard rate'.[81]

When asked if all dockers gave the same to their wives, Willie Martin replied 'yes, near enough … some of them would give too much and cause problems'. He told the story of two brothers. One was a docker and managed to get his brother, a soldier, a job unloading cement. At the end of the day, both brothers came home with twenty-five shillings in their pocket. The docker gave his mother her usual amount, ten shillings, less than half. His brother, the soldier, gave twice as much, twenty shillings, keeping only five back for himself. The mother understandably was confused. How is it, she asked, that you

Ringsend Infant National School, 1924. Front row, 5th from right is Willie Payet, from Pembroke Cottages Ringsend. (Donated by Deidre Leech to the Dublin Dock Workers Preservation Society)

both are doing the same job, and you only gave me ten shillings? Placed on the spot, the docker son quickly came up with a lie, 'I don't know what happened ma, he is after getting too much, he is after getting two mans' money. He'll have to give it back to the stevedore.' The docker related that the mother fell for the lie. Whether she did or not, it would have been difficult for her to alter the tradition.

One docker remembered that his father would put the money for his mother in his top breast pocket, not to be touched. The trouble was, if he stayed late in the pub, he'd be tempted to 'dip in'. The next day when his mother saw the remainder she said with evident disgust 'that's only canboys' money'. A canboy was paid to collect water and other things on a building site. Every morning his father would leave money on the mantelpiece and ask if that was enough, and every morning his mother would respond it was not enough. His father enraged would then take the money back and he would have to go get his dinner from family and neighbours: 'I used to get me grub everywhere.'[82]

This is not to say that women were accepting of this behaviour. Another story was told of a docker family living on the top tenement in Sheriff Street. Another cement boat, another docker heading home with a pocketful of money. This docker stopped in the pub, staying until closing time. By the time he arrived home, everyone was asleep.

In the morning, he made himself a cup of tea, put money on the mantelpiece as was traditional and left the house. The sound of his leaving woke his wife up. She put on her old coat and was enraged at the meagre amount of money left for her. She ran to the balcony and roared at him, for all to hear, as he walked along the bottom of the flats. Firing the money to the ground she yelled 'Here, keep your money, you old devil, I'm not rearing your kids on that.'[83]

Phyllis Nolan also remembered her father spending as he earned. She said 'he was foolish with money. As he said, "I earned more than a bank manager and I splashed it all".' Docker Martin Mitten explained, 'We used to get paid every day of every week. That's why the divorce rate was so high – we'd get paid, go to the pub and forget to go home in the evening.'[84] Not all dockers behaved in this way. A docker from Finglas was renowned for refusing to touch the notes in his breast pocket 'not for love nor money would anybody get him to break on that, that was for the home to look after the wife and family'. His story speaks to the peer pressure in the pub to keep the celebration going by breaking into the family money. Wives who complained were called 'tarjars'. Dockers reasoned that given that their next job might pay more badly it made sense not to raise expectations, and as Willie Murphy explained 'then if they were short they would put their hand in their pockets and give them a few bob to help them out'. At another time he expressed regret that he hadn't given more to his wife, arguing that husbands often did not give enough. Yet on the other hand, they did ensure the family was provided for.

> In the final analysis, I reckon that 95 per cent of the dockers, although they done a lot of wrongs … they always went home and when they went home they had their wives wages to give to her. Now it wasn't a lot. It might not have been fair, behind it all, they always made sure that the family would be looked after, not as we should have, but …

Historian Mary Muldowney talked to women who worked in Dublin and Belfast during the Second World War. Her interviewees described how they, their fathers and brothers, handed over their unopened wages to their mothers and wives. Unlike dockers' wives and daughters, these mothers knew what the weekly wage would be and could budget accordingly.[85]

With decasualisation, dockers also were paid a weekly wage. This meant that as dockers received a fixed amount, they and their wives could objectively see exactly how much to earn. This enabled the docker to budget:

> there is this much for the Misses, this much for the housekeeping, this much for my pocket money and now I have this leftover. It was then that they started to think of 'saving' and it became obvious materially. Up until the 60's there were only bicycles, then after the 60s you saw the arrival of cars on the docks and people were now travelling in from the suburbs, and not from the surrounding neighbourhood.[86]

While some dockers preferred the casual system with its higher wages and the associated daily socialising in the pub, others recognised the advantages it brought to the docker family. One docker interviewed in the *Irish Press* in 1950 explained:

> Dockers aren't agitating for it. Times are good now. You can make more money as a casual. But a slump may come – especially if there's a war – and the misery of waiting around for a cargo and of coming back to the wife and kids with nothing in your pocket may return. Decasualisation means security. Married men with kids need security.[87]

With a permanent income, families were able to get mortgages, to buy houses. Without a steady income, it was difficult to get bank loans. There were times, particularly after the post-war boom, when dock work was plentiful, wages were high, and dockers' families did better than most. At other times, such as during the war when shipping slowed or for those without the button, wages were more unpredictable. Faced with an uncertain income women used a wide range of strategies helped to keep food on the table and the collectors from the door. The money put aside for one bill would be used to pay another. Debt was shuffled around. Here a docker explains how, in time of need, it was a normal and accepted practice to break open the gas meter:

> You put a penny in the gas, and the next minute the gas meter would be opened up and you'd take out what was there and go around and get a packet of tea … There would be nothing in the gas meter. They used to have locks on them but the locks would be broken … Then the gas man would be due every six weeks.

> Of course they would all have to get their money back. You'd be playing in the street and you'd be roared at to come down and get ten shillings in coppers from the bank to put back in the thing. The gas man … would be going on his way to another place and he'd sound the hooter to tell them he would be on his way to collect the money. He knew. The gas man used to just open it … and he'd get out the money and he'd get a refund of about one shilling and four pence and the gas man would get about eight pence out of that for himself The gas man was very well off. He knew the locks were after being opened, but he just put it back and collected it. As long as the money was there, that was all right. The gas would be opened up if they were short of a pint of milk.[88]

At the end of the day, how did they manage to find money for the gas meter? Here the pawn shop, a vital component of the docker's economy would come into play.

> You would pawn your old fella's trousers …

> Or his boots would always go in of a Monday morning and that would pay the rent and keep the stores for a couple of

weeks. You'd get eight or ten bob or something. One woman used to give a box into the pawnbroker, do you know what was in the box for years? two bricks … She'd pawn them of a Monday and get them out of a Saturday and back in of a Monday again.[89]

You had what you called a blue suit. Everyone got blue, it lasted longer, blue serge. He used to call it 'indigo blue'. In they go of a Monday to the pawn and out of a Saturday. That's the idea, everybody had a blue suit … weddings and all was the blue serge suit.

Phyllis Nolan said to her husband one day, 'Did you ever throw out them shoes, with the two big holes in them?' They were wrapped up in a parcel, safe in the pawnshop: 'they knew him well, the same parcel going in whenever he was going in'. The money wasn't for her, it was to enable him to go drinking.

The visit to the pawnshop, which was known as 'the people's bank' was for many dockers' wives part of the weekly routine. In 1870, there were seventy-six pawnshops in Dublin, with nearly fifty remaining in the 1930s.[90]

When more money was needed than the pawn could provide, sometimes the moneylender was the only option available. Charging extortionate interest, they were an unpopular lot. At collection time the moneylender stood outside the gates of the Gas Company waiting for the workers to come, forcing some to escape over the back wall. No docker could avoid meeting the moneylender forever. The longer it went on, the harder it was to pay the money back. 'If you hadn't got money you paid interest and you still owed the money', Willie Murphy explained 'that would go on, so much that a fella would pay back ten times the value of the money.'

Phyllis Nolan was widowed young. Aged only 37, she was left to care for nine children. A week after her husband's sudden death, there was a knock at the door. She recognised her caller, a big fellow with a reputation who worked for the local moneylender. She was terrified to look at him. She thought she was going to be killed. He asked for her husband by name, asked if he lived in the house. He did, she told him. 'He owes money,' he said. 'Well', she said, 'do you know where to find him? If you get a number seven shovel, go down to Deansgrange and dig him up. There's where you'll get your money. I'm left with nine orphans, and you all persecuting him to take your money … Yer man ran, he'd run away from the door when I said it to him. I was all in black when he came to the door. He ran when I said it to him. Later still another moneylender arrived, a local woman came knocking asking "Do you know who I am?" and offering a loan of a few pound. She was turned away with the excuse "I have a father in there, and he wouldn't have you coming to my door looking for money."'

An alternative was to use the local 'Jewman', who was seen to be a different class of person altogether from the crooked moneylender. Kevin Kearns reports in *Dublin Tenement* that the term 'Jewman' was not used in a derogatory manner but rather was seen as usually fair.[91] The Jewman might be fobbed off with a tall tale, but the moneylender was more likely to resort to violence: 'They were just ordinary Jewmen, nice people, ordinary people. They weren't hard enough for the people they were lending money to.'[92] 'They were good people', remembered Willie Murphy, 'they helped a lot of poor people in Dublin'. Maggie

Woman fruit sellers, Aston Quay, south of the Liffey, 1969. (Wiltshire Collection Courtesy of the National Library of Ireland, call no. WIL 58[12])

Murphy, a docker's daughter interviewed by Kevin Kearns, remembers a fruit seller who also operated as an under-the-counter moneylender. She recalls her beating up another woman who could not make her repayments. In contrast, she tells of a friend who tried to convince the 'Jewman' she was dead by putting a black wreath on her door.[93] George Parnell, a south inner-city resident interviewed in the 1980s recalled:

> The Jewman also charged what he was entitled to charge … And he wasn't going up every week. If you gave him a pound off it, well that was a pound off your bill but with other people you only paid interest and you still owed the same amount of money.[94]

Cormac O'Grada examined court reports of debt disputes from 1909–1914 to get a sense of the amount of money typically involved. The sum most frequently lent was £5.40 – though it is likely that much

W. & R. Jacob & Co. biscuit factory, Bishop Street, now the site of the Irish National Archives. (Dublin City Library & Archive)

smaller amounts were also dispensed but not pursued through the Courts. Interest rates, as with other moneylenders was high – 120 per cent of what was borrowed had to be repaid, but it was felt it was easier to delay or avoid paying than with other moneylenders. Dockers remembered their local 'Jewman'.

> There used to be Jewmen in the houses. A Jewman would lend you £5 and you paid him five bob a week, but you would be bringing it down every week. It was recognised. Everybody had a Jewman. Some of the women would renew their loan; they would take £3 off the loan and then they would renew and they would get £2 but they would owe £5 odd. Before they had done paying they would be getting what they called a renewable loan.

The 'Jewman' would also sell holy pictures of the Sacred Heart and the Blessed Virgin, which the women would buy and then pawn. It was sometimes up to the children to fob him off when he came looking for repayment 'tell him your mammy's gone into hospital'.[95]

The St Vincent's de Paul Society and the Sick and Indigent Roomkeepers' Society were seen as a place of last resort, unless they were providing for special occasions such as First Communions. One docker remembered how the dockers would get food from a soup kitchen for their dinner, 'There was a place around in the flats. It was a soup kitchen during the war … the nuns of charity run it … Me mother would send [me with] a tanner, "go over there and buy a can of stew".' Many felt ashamed at having to accept charity. 'Often times you'd see women coming across,' Willie Murphy Junior remembered, 'with it [bowls of stew] under their shawls, afraid that anyone would see them getting it.'

The work done by women in managing household money made it possible for families to survive on the variable income of dock work. Often budgeting was far from easy, and yet, if they were forced to borrow from outside, some would have to face their husband's fury, as one docker remarked 'they [the women] wouldn't let their husbands

Barefoot children watch the *Queen Elizabeth* docked at City Quay, south of the Liffey, c.1865–1914. Robert French photographer. (Image Courtesy of the National Library of Ireland, call no. L_ROY_11594)

know that they were in the Jewman and the husband would give them a lick'.[96] Women arranged among themselves a system to keep their use of a lender secret. One woman would take from her friends their debt books and repayments, and she would meet with the lender on behalf of them all.[97]

In the neighbourhood, there would also be women who acted as midwives and helped when a death occurred. Martin Mitten describes how his mother would 'wash the dead and bring the children into the world'. In the first half of the twentieth century many children were born at home. The local midwife or 'handywoman' would be called and the neighbours would gather round.[98] The husband waited in the kitchen while the babies were delivered. 'The husbands in those days were kind of pushed back,' Annie Murphy, a docker's wife, explained. 'We will let you know how she is' or 'if we want anything will you go on your bike and get us something?' Neighbours provided help and assistance.

> My husband he would take a week off the docks. He'd take his holidays to mind the rest of the children and he'd cook … and the neighbours would come up and say 'do you want anything done?' or things like that, and they would sit with you and do things for you … personal little things for you [that] you wouldn't ask your husband to do.[99]

Without doubt the most important social support came from family and friends. Dockers' families, in Dublin and in other counties, relied on networks of support, networks that would provide food and care for children, the elderly and ill at times of crisis.[100] 'We had bad times', Willie Murphy remembered. 'There were times my sister had to give me food for to feed my children. They never let one another down, you were never without a bit of grub.' The dockers would look after their own, through money collections to help the family of a docker injured at work or in sad cases where the docker died.[101] The funeral cortege of a docker would pass along the dockside as a mark of respect,[102] tools downed as one of their own passed on his final way, 'they'd look out for you on the streets… that's the bond'.[103] One docker's daughter remembered how dockers collected money for her father, week in and week out, for the six months it took for him to recover from a bad accident on the docks.[104] He had been knocked into the hull of a boat and broke his arms, his legs and his collarbone.

How much help was forthcoming could depend on how popular a man was. A collection bucket would be put outside the company office. A foreman who started life as a docker noted: 'If it was for me the barrel would be put up, the collection was good. But if was for John Doe and the barrel was put up, the collection wouldn't be so good … it depended on the kindness of the individual.'[105]

A collection to cover the immediate crisis could run short as life ground on. The dockers held a collection for Phyllis Nolan's family: 'They were good like that' and after that it was her sister-in-law and a brother-in-law, who helped as she waited months for her widow's pension of £7 a week to arrive. Although they had large families of their own they collected money and bought her the essentials she needed: bread, milk and tea. Annie Murphy's mother died when she was a year and 9 months old, and her father when she was 9. Left orphaned, she was reared by her sister. When she herself was married, she lived with her mother-in-law, while Phyllis Nolan's father lived with her.

We saw in the last chapter the strong trade union solidarity that was characteristic of dockers in Dublin. This solidarity went beyond shop-floor issues. In the 1960s, Dockers established a Mutual Benefit Society centred on a paper called *Waterfront* that was published from 1960 to 1973. As its by-line proclaimed, this was 'the paper for the port, produced for the workers by the workers'. Established in July 1960 by William (Bill) Hickey, a warehouse supervisor in B&I, the paper ran until July 1973.[106] Not only did the paper seek to present the port workers' side of the story, but the society employed three doctors, introduced a sick and medical pay scheme for all port workers, men and women, introduced Christmas savings schemes and children's scholarship schemes. It was a short-lived and ambitious example of the community organising to provide care for its members at a time when few State supports were available.

SIX

THE LEGENDARY DUBLIN DOCKER

They became supermen.[1]

Legends grow in the hazy border between cold reality and the word of imagination and myth. In this medium the Dublin docker became, alternately, an epic drinker, a give-it-all worker, a slick pilferer, good with his fists, and more, as the stories go. We start our interrogation of waterfront tales, exploits, scams, fables and craic with the legendary divide between docker clansmen, north and south.

In the Absence of an Island

Two Dublins co-existed across the Liffey, ignoring one another as much as possible. Dockers were as conscious of the divide as other Dubliners, although to a theme rather of their own. The co-existence was rather watchful among dockers as seen by the fate of efforts to found a docker social centre.

A social club of their own had been a long-time general desire. Docker family weddings and christening receptions, birthdays, dances, and other gatherings could be catered for at their own hall, avoiding both the expense of hiring halls and the repeated difficulty of searching for an available venue. As important, a private club provided alcohol consumption rights which were privately controlled. It seemed everyone

Deep-sea docker Tommy Freeman (centre) with other dockers. (Donated by David Freeman)

else had a club; and that dockers were sometimes not especially welcome. 'If you weren't known, or you were known and you were undesirable as such, well, you were told "no, you can't come in ... if you get a bit out of tune with a few drinks" at someone else's club, well, they wouldn't sign you in again.'[2] A docker's social club would solve all this. Yet, it never happened. Despite the widely felt need, and despite earnest work by active organisers who were elected to pave the way, a club site of their own remained a dream. Why? Mainly, it seems, because southsiders were disinclined to invest in a northside venue and vice versa. It seemed more acceptable to have no social club than to see it go to the rival half of the city. In practice, Christmas parties and other general events had to be alternated, north and south in turn. A docker social club foundered on, one might say, the geographical absence of a neutral island in the Liffey, the only place where a clubhouse might have been situated acceptably to both parties.[3]

Was the north/south divide significant? 'Oh, Jesus yes,' said Willie Murphy Junior. At reads, where employment itself was at stake, foremen were more likely to select gang members from their own side. One southside stevedore is reputed to have stated that, if he could not get Ringsend men to work his ships, he would, in preference to northside dockers, hire Ringsend *women*.[4]

Relations could be a little bit rough. 'A bit savage,' said northsider Tommy Bassett of the southsiders, 'but, we're savage in our own way'.[5] The rowdy reputation dockers carried, noted above in relation to access to social clubs, seems to have been acquired, not merely as a result of singular, publicised, events, but also because of the friction that sometimes erupted between dockers. 'What, a docker's dress dance? You're asking for trouble', was the attitude of many when such an event was mooted in 1961.[6] Despite rivalry, however, northside and southside dockers did not often actually fight.

Dockers married girls from their own side. Or at least dockers did this so often that the exceptions, although possibly numerous, are regarded as tales of high adventure. Southsiders gravitated toward the reads of George Bell and Carrick's, and were most likely to be selected to work the ships contracted by those agents. Northside dockers were favoured by Palgrave Murphy and certain other stevedoring companies on the same basis of traditional service. The southsiders worked on the coal ships. The northsiders were more likely to load general cargo or cattle. 'There was a barrier between them,' north and south, according to Willie Murphy Junior. He, a Ringsender from the southside married a northside woman. 'They resented us,' said his father, 'because we always thought that we were the dockers.'[7] It was felt that those on the northside avoided the shovel work[8]. A block of the southside deep-sea men customarily referred to northsiders as 'runners in'. Northsiders smelt in all this the overbearing snobbery found elsewhere on the wrong side of the Anna Livia moat. Deep-sea dockers were more likely to be southsiders. One official list of deep-sea dockers, from around 1957, provides residential address. Of those living in one of the five dockland communities mentioned in the previous chapter there was a three-to-one ratio in favour of southsiders.[9] The longer-standing tradition from which this numerical superiority derives gives rise to the southsiders view that they are '*the* dockers'.

The northside deep-sea contingent, outnumbered as it was, could hold its own. One southside docker had to cross to work with northsiders one day a week. He died on a Tuesday night in the early 1960s at a young age. His widow, Phyllis Nolan goes so far as to muse that horror of crossing northside killed him.

> He used to have to work over in the northside of a Wednesday.
> And he used to hate the thoughts. I think he must have died,
> it was Wednesday the next morning, and he died 'cause he
> dreaded going over … You know, I mean, he used to dread
> the northside. He wasn't a bully you know, he was very gentle.

One source of dread was the animal gang who inspired fear in the hearts of southsiders. 'Animal gang' was a popular term for fight-minded street gangs during 1930s through to 1950s Dublin, but everyone knew which was *the* animal gang. The core of Dublin's archetypal animal gang were dockers, mainly from around the Corporation Street and Foley Street area: northsiders.[10] Foley Street was called 'the valley of the giants' because the local dockers were so tall.[11] And they sometimes targeted southside dockers.

'They'd always come over looking for trouble,' said Phyllis Nolan, 'if they caught you looking sideways, you'd get it, you know.' The trademark weapon of the animal gang during one phase was raw potatoes. Rumour had it that razor blades were embedded inside. One animal gang attack on a southside workingmen's sports club was carried forth by an army including women and children!

These gangs also played a Robin Hood role. During one port strike they stole two hanging cows from butcher's hooks, sliced them up, and delivered meat to the Monto area community north of Talbot Street.[12] These gangs appear also to have been involved in the shipboard and embarkation point 'riots' among seagoing cattlemen at the same period. SS *Hagno* could not weigh anchor on 1 August 1951 because 'some cattlemen disliked each other and refused to sail'. Dockers, seamen and bullockmen, probably members of rival gangs, battled one another both at sea and in front of embarkation points in contests over cattle-tending assignments.[13] Shoving and scuffling among dockers broke out not only in the Pond,[14] but on Custom House Quay over cattle matters. Perhaps because of the advantageous conditions of the assignments, cattle loading situations and cattle tending issues seemed to raise docker temperatures most easily.

The rivalry existed in various areas, work and recreation being most prominent. In pubs the battle was joined with song.[15] Forces of northside baritones, tenors and basses marshalled against their southside vocal battalions. Performance was judged to alternate by south/north allegiance. Judging the contest was apparently done without bias, the biggest cheer at the end of it all determining the outcome. O'Connor's on the North Wall, especially of a Friday morning, was a prime place to hear the dockers in the battle of lungs.

Singsongs also erupted inside the hatches; wonderfully eerie to hear as it floated alongside a ship. At least one docker songster, Bill Preston, became well known on stage. Preston, was the author of 'The Docker's Song' lament of the non-buttonman. He appeared at the Queens, the Royal, the Olympia, the Gaiety and the Rotunda theatres.

As they worked often in public urban spaces close to the city centre, a celebrity might appear in their purview, as Judy Garland once did. A little girl encountered the actress on the street at quayside, and, having just seen her film in the Palace, asked her to sing 'Meet Me in St. Louis'. 'I will sing,' said Garland to her entourage, 'for this little girl on her own.' Not quite on her own. Dockers floating on their coalboat below gazed up in blackened-faced thrall during the performance.[16]

The public houses in which the song battles took place, were also used, as described in the opening chapter, as pay office when a ship finished, and for further ends.

Decorating the Mahogany and Papering the Ceiling

Silvery glints brightened the interior of many of the port pubs. The gleaming came from the number seven and other docker shovels, which were often stored in the nearby public houses. One way or another, dockers used the licenced premises a lot. The classic use was the 'beero'.

Coalies. (Donated by Cormac McDermott to the Dublin Dock Workers Preservation Society)

The beero was the docker's teabreak: in the strictest sense the coalie's teabreak. The morning break was at half past ten. The first two-plus hours of the day were, if a ship had commenced that day, just enough 'for sinking to berth', as described in Chapter 2. The coincidence that the work time before the morning break was about right for sinking to berth, gave the docker a feeling of satisfaction as he left the ship for the beero. Refreshment, rather than self-reward or rest, is how the break was individually experienced. The thirst was upon you, and the dryness keenly felt. Sucking the lump of coal had been a poor stopgap. 'Imagine working in a hold with 200 tons of coal from eight in the morning to four in the afternoon', Willie Murphy remembered, 'and it's easy to see why we needed to slake our thirst. With that sort of work you're not playing around – the sweat we lost had to be replaced somehow.'

A workgroup took the beero together, each man, as was traditional in Irish culture, buying his round. Coalies would often have enjoyed four pints as eleven o'clock arrived to end the break. Some observers, themselves presumably drinking orange lemonade, claim to have witnessed a regular docker five-pint morning beero: specifically at O'Connor's on the north quays. Dockers working Spencer Dock drank the beero at Macken's on the corner of Guild Street.

Lack of lavatory facilities was a notorious gap in working conditions on the wharfs. Public houses provided this, and were used all the more by dockworkers accordingly.

Pubs and ships faced one another broadside, within the distance of a couple of gangways during most of the history of the Dublin docker. Most of the overall loading and discharge took place on the quays and in the inner city interior docks. The bayward northside dock extensions were later historical worksites. Pubs were everywhere facing the worksite. On the southern quay front on the city side of Ringsend, Sir John Rogerson's Quay, was The Lighthouse Bar. Joe Kelly's, stood nearest the wide Grand Canal Docks gap in the south quays. Kathleen Bergin's pub came next, beyond the site of the Marine School for children, then Walsh's public house, then the pub re-named The Dockers, then Macmanus, and, we could stop the count, although artificial a halt it is indeed, at Butt Bridge: Kennedy's stood at Tara Street. Groceries which doubled as bars were called shops, rather than pubs by deep-sea dockers. The record of Sir John Rogerson's Quay for alcohol-dispensing waterfront commercial sites was almost dramatic. In addition to the line-up already listed, there are also the following facts. The first building ever erected on Sir John Rogerson's Quay was the Fountain Tavern of 1718. When the quay's post office was closed in the mid-nineteenth century, it became The Old Post pub.[17] The Marine School for children rather dominated the line of buildings, at least in size, until it burned down in 1876, after which its ruins gaped among the public houses.

Watering holes were *there*: extremely present, and were used for everything. Traditions developed which involved the pubs in further ways, for example when a bonus, or 'sub' was paid for certain collier discharges. Part or all of that particular bonus was regarded as 'for socialising … [to] wash down the coal dust.'[18] If not coal dust, it might be the sting of copper ammonia or the stench of guano to be washed away. Then, after work you had to go in for a jar with your mates. Avoiding that gesture of social convention might scarcely be understood by others. You could then also leave your shovel there for the next day.

Some seem to have turned to the pubs to drown the disappointment when unsuccessful at the read. In Chapter 1 we quoted part of a poem by a docker condemning the read system. The poem continues on to blame that system for docker alcoholism.

Down at the reads by eight o'clock,
And then again at ten,
A visit to the bru,
And back down again by two,
The read it was a bad place,
The system a disgrace,
A good man could be left there,
If they didn't like his face.
Stand by all day, without any pay

Discharging bags. (Donated by Dublin Stevedores to the Dublin Dock Workers Preservation Society)

The system diabolic
Is it any wonder
You became an alcoholic?[19]

Public houses in the port had permission to open at 7 a.m., and had earlier legal opening hours during some periods since such exemptions began in the late nineteenth century. The rationale for dawn licencing was to allow fair refreshment to working people who toiled unusual hours in their 'lawful trade or calling', for example hospital staff. While the sea tide still controlled ship movement, dockers might have to work at any hour. If a ship finished in the early morning hours, should not the exhausted workers be permitted revitalisation of choice at 7 a.m. or thereabouts? Conveniently, cash payoffs were in hand upon ship finish and sacking. Dockers were a significant Dublin early clientele, judging from the number of city public houses whose formal application justified early opening 'for the accommodation of a number of persons their lawful trades and calling as dockers, in the vicinity of the applicant's premises'.[20]

The sand bar in the bay was scoured, defeating the determining force of the tide. Early opening remained, although part of the logic for early opening was gone. Early bars were used as 'the seven o'clock shop' for news of ship arrivals, as we saw in Chapter 1. Only a small proportion of dockers took a drink before the first morning read, although there have been those who regarded a pint before work as normal, and others who customarily downed several before 8 a.m. Oft-used, or not, the right to have one in the early hours was a privilege jealously guarded: a status symbol for the profession. The normally conservative port workers' organ *Waterfront* defended early opening in positively militant terms in 1962, claiming no knowledge of patron misuse of the early privilege.[21] The publicans, for their part, appreciated the volume of docker trade. The proprietor of Mulligan's in City Quay, a long-time docker watering place, was overheard responding to a customer, out of the nearby *Irish Press* plant, who had remarked on the extraordinary dirt of the coalies at the bar. 'What's wrong with those men,' retorted the publican, pointing to Tommy Freeney and another especially grimy coalie at the counter. 'Clean dirt. Them men give you ready money … I could paper the ceiling with the cheques I got off them, see. I built the shop with them. They pay ready cash.'[22]

Some publicans however, in lieu of cash, extended credit. And if it was needed, many publicans could be called on to help out with the expense of a funeral, often giving a loan that would be repaid over time.

Dockers could be eloquent and articulate. Both dockers and stevedores referred to their ability to argue their point of view on weighty matters. Political and trade union issues were often up for discussion.[23] Arguments honed in the pub could be repeated on the dockside, giving challenge to a perceived injustice – challenges that were often won.

Brendan Behan, famous both in literature and drinking capacity, exchanged rounds with deep-sea dockers in city-centre pubs. Both parties, Behan and the dockers, tended, however, to strong opinion, and the sessions ended often enough in argument. 'The Pope is afraid to die,' Behan once declaimed to dockers in a pub. The inflammatory statement was not left unanswered by a Catholic docker who met fighting words with fighting words until Behan was forced to withdraw, no doubt, to another quieter drinking hole.[24] Despite, or perhaps because, of the arguments, Behan, whose brother worked as a docker, was well liked. On another occasion a quiet pint in Flynns of Fleet Street was disturbed by the fierce swearing of Behan. Refused a drink he called the barman 'a red-necked country … He called him everything'. In the midst of the furious outburst Behan turned and recognised a deep-sea docker nursing his pint. Hand out, Behan strode over and addressing Willie Murphy by name he said, 'You've done me a lot of good turns … where did we meet.' Turning back to the bar man he roared, 'You're not serving me? Well I don't want to go back to jail again, the police station is too close to me.' Pearse Street police station was within spitting distance. Pointing to his docker acquaintance Behan said, 'Will you serve that gentleman sitting over there?' The barman agreed that he would, at which point Behan ordered a glass of whiskey and a glass of stout, throwing the money at the barman and strode out in search of a more agreeable hostelry.

Smuggling was part of an earlier tradition of round-the-clock drinking in the docklands.[25] Black Lion Alehouse, again on Rogerson's Quay, was one of those establishments which kept illegal hours, tempted to do so by the availability of smuggled wines and brandies which could be sold cheaply.[26] If something was wanted, in certain pubs an order could be placed which would be filled the following day.

If a gang became thirsty down in the hold, rescue was possible right there on the quay. Billy the Hogger carried out a small trade, carting two buckets at a time of beer from a pub to the hatch, to lower down to the waiting inside men.

Did dockers drink too much? 'He'd pawn his shoes for a drink,' said Phyllis Nolan of her husband. She spoke literally: he frequently took a shoebox to the pawn. 'Thirteen Pints' was a docker, by nickname. Dockers were barred from certain pubs on occasion. Excessive bad language was most likely to be the publican's objection. Such barrings were for a stipulated period of only a couple of weeks.[27] And, they were announced extraordinarily gently by the proprietor. Barmen did not risk such action without considerate, reasonable explanation. Dockers were respected and were valued customers.

Some dockers never used alcohol. The most difficult part of abstention was finding a way to absorb the brunt of their own violation of social convention in not joining their mates at the pub after leaving the ship in the evening. At the other extreme, 'fellas down there would sell their souls to the devil for a pint', claimed an observer with negative judgement: 'they'd do anything for a few jars'.[28] 'They worked hard for it, do you know that kind of way,' the same critic adds. Was this entirely self-reward on the docker's part? Many people, swayed in part by the slogan 'Guinness is good for you', once regarded stout or porter as nourishing liquid food. Perhaps Glass-of-X McGowan earned his nickname in pursuit of good health. Whisky Murray, Guzzler Smith, and Ball-o'-Malt Byrne were other deep-sea dockers. Were there alcoholics among the ranks of the traditional deep-sea dockers? 'To put it mildly,' said a lifelong docker, 'there were.' A few men even lost the desire or ability to work and joined the ranks of the hoggers we observed on the quayside in Chapter 3. Former dockers could actually be found making up the bulk of a particular group of hoggers. One hogger foreman – yes, hoggers had a foreman overseeing pouring and other procedures – was ex-docker Uncle Bob.[29]

What happened when individuals became less than functional on the job from too much drink taken – especially given the dangers, described in Chapter 2, involved in the work? Other gang members took up the slack and covered for a drunken mate. This support system was so strong and reliable that employers did not reckon it worth the bother to punish men who might be seen to be inebriated. The decline of the era of legendary drinking began when daily, or end-of-job, payout ended in the 1960s, in favour of a weekly payday. Before then 'every night was Saturday night', states Martin Mitten. Suddenly, ready money was now largely gone. Many dockers resented it because they felt their holidays were ended. It took away the freedom of the daily pay from them that they enjoyed. It took away an awful lot of their independence. They got paid on Friday; and Wednesday and Thursday they had to look for a pint on the slate.[30] Deep-sea dockers subsequently demanded, unsuccessfully, a return to daily pay.[31]

As the port extended baywards, the public houses were literally receding

Cattle ship. Joseph Foley is second from left at the back. (Donated by John Foley to the Dublin Dock Workers Preservation Society)

into the distance. Mulligan's, Kennedy's and the other quayside pubs, and even the Wharf Tavern on East Wall Road, were left stranded further and further in the town side. Thirsty or not, dockers no longer faced a Black Lion.

The Liffey Perpetual Challenge, Pugilists, and Toss

While in the imagination of many Dubliners the docker was legendary only for an ability to drink, docking communities took pride in other skills. Many docker families, whether turning out great singers or famous pintsmen, or not, produced fine soccer players. Football and boxing were the main athletic pursuits of the Dublin docker. At the centre of the athletic tradition of the docklands were the legendary Liffey Wanderers. In 1885 no less or later, saw the, initially modest, founding of the Wanderers. They called it a 'shamier', the ragbag football of the nineteenth-century waterfront.

Slamming around the shamier when the morning read, one 1885 morning, had brought disappointment, some dockworkers had an idea. They founded a soccer club. Liffey Wanderers, an amateur club, where originally nearly all dockers reached an early peak of competitive success in 1904–7, led by star goalie Danny Conway. The innumerable Mittens who were both dockers and footballers were already playing then.[32] Liffey's was a City Quay club, it must be noted, and thus rather nearer the hearts of the southside deep-sea dockers than northsiders. The northside animal gangs, which included dockers, were known to attack Wanderers' clubhouse. Westland Rovers was another team of the era numbering many dockers, such as Sailor Kiernan, a tipper.

By the 1920s and 1930s, dockers were playing semi-professionally for Dublin's Shamrock Rovers and Shelbourne, and were serving on the administrative boards of the same clubs. Bob Fulham was a coalie who played for Shamrocks. It is said that, on Saturdays at two o'clock, Bob would emerge from the coal boat, get out to Milltown, or whichever ground at which the team was playing, shower there, and be on the pitch for kick off at three o'clock. Ben Hannigan was the most internationally successful football player who also had a career as a Dublin docker. Hannigan had stints with both Fortuna Köln and Wrexham. Legend has it that he trained on the docks with sixteen stone bags of sugar.[33]

Recruitment circulated both ways between the docks and the football clubs. One of the Carricks became chairman of Shelbourne. When he discovered good prospects, he would 'sign' them for soccer by offering singing-out jobs on the ship gangs, thus recruiting into docking from off the pitch.

Waterfront competitions were formed, featuring checker teams and clerical teams ranged against each other and against a variety of docker squads. One team was drawn from a single deep-sea work gang, Paddy Nolan's.[34] Exclusively deep-sea docker-manned teams crossed the Irish Sea annually to play English counterparts in Liverpool and Manchester in the 1960s. These all-docker tournaments were hosted alternately in the three ports. At stake was the Liffey Perpetual Challenge Cup. The cup was of Irish origin. It was sponsored by the Dublin Master Stevedores' Association and presented to the annual winner by the secretary of the association. The Dubliners won most often.

Boxing was the number two Dublin docker sport. Kick Casey was a singer-out for stevedore Kevin Kelly, and a boxer. He is also the nephew of playwright Sean O'Casey. Boxer Elliott was another accomplished boxer who carried his nickname along the gangplanks and into the hold with his dockside workmates. The boxing docker remembered by his nickname Buckets O' Blood, seems to have got the name from the amount of his own spilled when he fought, given his lack of success in the ring. Boxer Hanlon, a Ringsend man, was presumably a pugilist. Peter Glennon left the docks to attain considerable success boxing in America.

Rowing, another muscular sport, was popular among Ringsend dockers. Included in the docker members of successful rowing teams were John Hawkins, and 'King Billy' Murphy.

Toss schools and cards were further games of contest enjoyed by dockers. Brag, scoop, and poker were played between reads by those still waiting for work. The wide Custom House steps were good for card games. Toss school was a more serious matter, and might even mean leaving dockland in order to try one's luck. The final set of lock gates on the Grand Canal just before it reached the Grand Canal Docks was a frequent site; but, being illegal, the schools sometimes had to alter venue daily. In toss, one gambled on whether the tossed ha'penny would match the previously tossed coin, or on the results of two simultaneously tossed coins. In a third variation, the nearest coin to the wall won. If not called at the read one might yet claim some income on the day in toss school winnings, or lose one's beero money. Morning play began at ten o'clock. Bookies also worked the quays, taking illegal bets from dockworkers. Sometimes you could get a bet down without the cash, and pay, if you lost, on payday.

The fame of the footballers and boxers who were dockers tended to be somewhat local. Such also tended to be the fate of the docker heroes of the Irish insurrections and wars of independence.

Docker Heroes

Dockers, who had taken the oath of allegiance to the republican movement, made up, at the time, Q Company of the Irish resistance. Q Company had its origin in the 1913 Lockout. At the height of the 1913 Lockout Dublin Metropolitan Police (DMP) and Royal Irish Constabulary (RIC) attacked the docklands, breaking into houses, beating the occupants and breaking their possessions. In this context, dockers and seamen began to import arms and ammunitions for the Irish Citizen Army and the Irish Volunteers. After the defeat in the 1916 Rising, all the arms dumps were empty and they renewed their focus, until early in 1919 when Q Company was formally established. Q Company consisted of about forty dockers, coincidentally (or not) about the size of two work gangs and almost sixty sailors based on over twenty-one boats covering both the cross-channel and continental routes. Dockers had the extremely dangerous task of secreting arms out of ships in which they were being smuggled. Sometimes Q Company members got munitions off onto the quays in hoists with other cargo. Often, they carried guns or ammunition out on their person. Sometimes they made night forays into the hatches to bring off arms under cover of dark.[35] Stevedores, checkers and storemen turned a blind eye. The captain of the company, John P. Kennedy reported: 'I had to have my quay men on duty the twenty-four hours of the day as time, tide and the bad weather plays all sorts of tricks with the arrival of ships. Some would arrive before time, and over and over again be hours late. We … never had a seizure or capture of consignment of stuff.' He concludes his account of their activity: 'We beat the combined forces of the BPD, of Europe and the British Empire. Capture meant certain death, as the Tans had instructions to shoot members of our unit on the spot without trial or jury.'[36]

Sailor and dockers saw things that others didn't. Photographer and critic Allan Sekula noted that:

> Sailors and dockers are in a position to see the global patterns of intrigue hidden in the mundane details of commerce. Sometimes the evidence is in fact bizarrely close at hand: Weapons for the Iraqis in the forward hold. Weapons for the Iranians in the aft hold. Spanish dockers in Barcelona laugh at the irony of loading cargo with antagonistic destinations.[37]

Irish dockers were well placed to acquire guns destined for the British Army or the United States. In one instance, guns destined for transport by the USS Defiance were re-routed by dockers.[38] Tasked with loading the ship with wooden boxes, the dockers' curiosity was awakened by the sight of guards posted on the deck and in the hold and by unusual security arrangements which required the dockers to have a permit to go on and off the ship. A look in the hold confirmed it was full of guns and ammunition. The final tally was fifty- six .45 revolvers, 2,000 rounds of ammunition, 5,000 rounds of Springfield ammunition and a number of pistols. Getting the booty smuggled on shore was another matter. The rifles were too large to hide on the person and reluctantly were left behind. Over several days with great care not to be observed, the ammunition and revolvers were secreted ashore.[39]

Michael Donnelly was a Dublin docker from North Wall who fought with the Citizen Army in 1916. He survived 1916, and was again active in the 1920 War of Independence.[40] His nickname was 'The Bishop' because

> when advocating socialist theories as against the present day
> capitalist system he always quoted scripture, his strong line
> on most occasions being the Sermon on the Mount where it
> is said it is harder for a rich man to get into heaven than it is
> for a camel to get through the eye of a needle.[41]

One morning, walking along the North Wall Extension he saw a ship unloading weapons for the British Army. This led him to argue that no docker should handle military goods. What began as a local action holding up that first ship, grew to become the Munitions of War Strike, in which dockers and railwaymen refused to unload munitions ships during the Anglo-Irish War of 1920 and 1921. Unloading was halted in Dublin and Dún Laoghaire, as well as in Cobh, Cork and the other Irish ports.[42]

Daniel Courtney, a casual grain labourer, also joined the Citizens Army. He was one of the last prisoners to be released from English jails following the Rising and on returning to Dublin he found himself black-listed and unable to find work on the docks.[43]

Hobblers also played their part. When, in 1919, Éamon de Valera escaped from Lincoln gaol, he risked crossing to Ireland on a B&I ferry bound for Dublin. Hobblers named Donoghue and Byrne employed at-sea hobbling skills to spirit the fugitive swiftly off the ferry before docking, and possible capture.

In the 1940s a different type of docker hero emerged, William 'Billy' Dean. One November he was working the winch in the hatch of a US coal boat berthed on John Rogerson's Quay. At four o'clock a shout went up that gas was escaping from the hold. William, along with the other dockers and sailors, raced to the hatch and peering down saw the body of Captain John Munro. Grain from a previous journey had got into the ballast tank and fermented. On opening the tank the Captain Munro was immediately overcome and collapsed. Later he reported that on opening it he smelt a strong gas and from then remembered nothing until he woke on the deck some time later. The engineer and boson followed the captain down to help him but were also rendered unconscious. The ship's mate attempted to rescue them but was repelled by the gas, as were the efforts of another crew member. Billy Dean called for help but fearful of the noxious fumes the sailors and dockers withdrew to a safe distance.

Without aid, Billy tied a handkerchief around his mouth, and made his way down a 14-metre iron ladder deep into the ship. He first came upon the boson comatose on the ground. He dragged him to the ladder tying a rope around him so he could be hauled to safety. He then descended again to the hold, this time to rescue the engineer, and then a third time to bring back the captain. By the end, he was weak and exhausted, his elbows sore from banging against the steel girders of the hold. In honour of his bravery he was awarded a bronze medal by

Waiting for the pub to open. (Donated by Tom Boland to the Dublin Dock Workers Preservation Society)

the Lord Mayor of Dublin. Correspondence between the Lord Mayor and Billy Dean indicates that delivery of the medal was delayed as pressure of work and staff shortages had prevented the supply of die for the medal.[44] Before heading back to sea, the ship's captain presented him with a hamper of food, cigarettes and sweets and £5 in recognition of his bravery.

While docker communities told stories of heroism, strength and skills, in the city at large dockers had a shadier reputation, a reputation that some dockers were happy to uphold, a reputation that had its basis both in fact and in embellishment.

Bunkering up and the Cabbage Bank

A port inspector charged with controlling pilfering, on seeing a large group of dockers, said 'Y's are like the Ali Babas in the one act.'[45] In contrast, another employer did not consider theft by dockers a serious issue, 'It went on, but, it was not a major problem … The cargoes weren't very attractive stuff: fertilisers, coal, well coal you can't steal.'[46] But with the wider public and the shipping companies, theft was something to be worried about. A reputation for pilferage by dockworkers was far from unusual internationally. Deep-sea shippers, agents, stevedores, importers, supervisors, in Dublin or elsewhere, disliked it, to say the least. Yet, at the same time, pilferage was generally accepted as a fact of the business. One scholar, studying Newfoundland docks, suggests that pilferage was 'part of an understood indulgence pattern'.[47]

Did the dockers steal or were they simply equivalently notorious without justification? Some of the stories of docker pilfering and scams are no doubt embellished in the telling, dockers taking to heart Mark Twain's advice that the truth should not get in the way of a good story. It was told that brand-new shoes adorned the feet of remarkably many dockers' children on a single morning. A Polish vessel carrying a cargo of shoes had tied up the previous day. As we look further into pilfering we encounter both interesting facts and indictable legend.

Small-scale theft seemed common enough. Apples, lemons, tea and sugar were little things, which when slipped into the pocket would save the docker from having to buy them on the way home. Fruit cargoes brought children right up to shipside, to beg oranges from discharging dockers. The children could be lucky and have oranges tossed directly to them.

Loose coal was perhaps the commodity most widely handed out to passers-by near the ship, or carried off the docks. Time was that a few good lumps of coal was a nice gift. Some men made a regular practice of bringing some coal home for the hearth. If you stopped in the pub for a jar 'you could go in and leave your bike outside with a couple of stone of coal that you were after picking up. Well you'd have to say you picked it up you were after robbing it, do you see?'.[48] At least one docker made a special nightly trip back the short distance to the docks for his family's next day fire. Complications arose for a certain docker when it came time to give away his daughter in marriage. His wife insisted on him going to confession for the occasion. He went up to Gardiner Street church and entered the confessional box:

> He said 'I'm away from confession for nine years and I also stole some coal' … The Father said that 'you need [to make] restitution'. 'I know that Father', says he, 'once I have the money I'm going to pay off a few bob'. 'You'll have to give the coal back,' says he: 'I couldn't give it back.' 'What do you mean you couldn't give it back?' 'I'd want a tipper to bring it back!'[49]

Spillage did occur purely accidentally, leading to the understandable wish to avoid wastage. 'Sure, if you are walking on things: tea that would be bursted. You would be up to your knees, or up to your ankles in tea, right? So, why not put it in a bag and bring it home? It would only be thrown out.'[50] The parish priest however insisted that, unfortunately, this still counted as stealing. 'Tea Leaves' was in fact a one-time docker label for dockers who pilfered. Some commodities were apparently routinely sampled: Jacob's Biscuits, Morney's chocolate, cakes by Gateaux, sultanas, grapes, apples, oranges, demerara, Irish whisky. Cargos could also spill on purpose.[51] When the banana boat came, 'My father would go out on the docks maybe eight stones,' a docker's son commented, 'he would come back maybe fourteen stones.'[52] Siphoning a barrel of porter by boring the wood with a gimlet was an old Dublin custom, of which dockers were neither ignorant nor unskilled.

Bits of most commodities disappeared one time or another. Guano was singled out for the comment, we saw in Chapter 2, that 'no one robbed it'.[53] The implication to be drawn was that anything short of stinking bird droppings could be stolen. A parallel comment occurred after the success of the first catered docker dress dance. There were no fights, the proud deep-sea docker organiser said, 'and', equally significantly, 'there wasn't a spoon missing'.[54] Some dockers carried on legitimate side businesses. Scrap metal and wire are examples (leading to nicknames Metaller and Wire-Head). It was necessary for these docker businessmen to assert the legitimacy of their sources of supply, sharply and regularly, to their customers, the dockers' reputation being what it was.

The product of the brewmaster's art tempted at least one work gang, according to this story:

> There was another ship ... loading beer of Nigeria: crates of beer and cartons of beer ... A carton of beer went down the hold and there was no one coming out of it ... The foreman was blowing his top, at the top of the hatch ... This fella staggered out ... He [the foreman] says this was 'the worst gang' I'd 'ever seen'. Your man was locked from the beer, and he says: 'we may be the worst gang, but we are the happiest.'[55]

During World War Two, one deep-sea docker intercepted a barrel of the light casings used for sausages, emptied it, and hawked the much-wanted skins around Dublin's butcher shops. To achieve this, he bunkered up.[56] That is, he stitched himself a bunker pocket. A bunker pocket was a half sack sewn inside the coat, replacing the normal pocket. A few departures with a full bunker pocket, the remaining casings being hidden meanwhile, and the heist was complete. The same approach was used for tea. Another strategy was to wear two pairs of trousers and two coats. A northsider remembers his father coming from work and telling his mother to 'get the newspaper'.

> I remember him putting the newspaper on the floor. He had two pairs of trousers on him. He had a piece of twine around one pair and he pulled the twine and all the tea rolled down his trousers. The same with the sleeves. We had plenty of tea for a long time. That was part of living on the docks. Some people that got tea would make it up in little packages and sell it around the neighbourhood.[57]

Free food was so available on the north quays at one time that one quay acquired an appropriate sobriquet locally. Opposite New Wapping Street, a section near the centre of North Wall Quay, was known as the Cabbage Bank: a 'market' of free vegetables, which, in the folk memory, fed the community well.[58]

Two combine harvesters – at the other extreme in size from cabbages – were stolen in 1964,[59] 100 barrels of nickel each weighing 254 kg in 1970.[60] One close observer wrote of 'the frightening value of goods missing from the docks'.[61] In the early 1960s 2,200 rounds of .22 ammunition were taken from a warehouse on North Wall.[62] Lead ingots, liquid mercury, eighty-one rolls of wallpaper, fifteen suits, twenty-five lamb carcasses, eleven hindquaters of beef, anything it seems, was stolen one time or another on the docks.

Having said this much, it must be emphasised that some dockers decidedly never took anything whatever. 'You couldn't make them; they wouldn't take a matchstick.' One stevedore generalised this more widely, stating: 'the majority never got involved [in pilfering]; they had a code.'[63] There were even some in-hatch enforcers. 'If you were a bold boy and put something in your pocket, and if there was a squealer in the hatch, you didn't get any more work.'[64] Some dockers would warn others off saying: 'don't forget you are eating your buttons here'.[65] Others saw little harm in the practice, which was more public service than actual theft 'sure we were walking on it anyway and sooner than

Unloading bags. (Curtis Collection, donated by Joe Mooney to the Dublin Dock Workers Preservation Society)

let it go to waste we'd take it home'.[66] Were the various entrepreneurs, consciously, indirectly paying in this fashion for the tremendous benefit to them, in a port such as Dublin, of a casual labour force, ready when needed, but unpaid while waiting to work? Some Irish businessmen saw it that way.

Theft was nevertheless often punished. A guilty dockworker might be suspended for a first offence, and prosecuted and/or permanently sacked for repeated offences.[67] The dockers negotiated that suspension, rather than sacking was an appropriate punishment in the first instance – an outcome they felt was unprecedented in workers' relations. The Dublin Master Stevedores Association wrote to the newspapers stating in no uncertain terms that their policy was not to employ men convicted of pilfering.[68] The association followed newspaper reports of court cases involving dockers, carefully noting the names and addresses of those involved, and from there the accused union number. Such cases took up to two years to be held and the final result was recorded.[69] If found guilty, and if it was shown that the goods were taken from the docks, those convicted were barred from seeking work on the docks again.

In 1972, the problem of theft was described as 'petty and widespread' by dockland authorities, though it should be noted, that many of these authorities depended on shipping companies for their livelihoods so it was in their interests to downplay the problem.[70] Yet it did not involve organised rings.

The Irish Institute of Marine Underwriters represented the biggest insurance companies operating in the docklands.[71] At their annual general meeting they reported each year on the challenges facing their industry. Theft was not often mentioned. In 1958, they were faced with the costs of goods remaining in transit sheds during labour disputes. The Liberty Ships of the 1940s and 1950s, 'built for a short life and a gay one', grew older and were increasingly expensive to repair. Later they were concerned with increased costs associated with personal accidents.[72] Of criminal losses they noted obliquely 'there had not been any decided change at the reports in regard to theft and pilfering'.[73] In the 1960s, their concern was for the increased numbers of ships lost at sea. While there was always room for improvement, Dublin, unlike other ports, was felt to have escaped the serious problem caused by theft elsewhere.[74]

Some measures were taken from time to time. In the mid-1960s, a Garda motorcycle patrol was formed to police the north dock area.[75] 'By the early 1970s, the Harbour Police encompassed thirty-eight constables, five sergeants and one superintendent and were using the pages of the *Sunday Independent* to argue that they were 'grossly understaffed'.[76] In 1970 there was increased concern about the rate of theft, with Dublin City Chamber of Commerce commissioning a report that suggested changes in the documentation of cargo.[77] The underwriters blamed the 'general decline in moral standards and the lack of respect for property' for claims made to them for both theft and damage.'[78]

Toy merchant Hector Grey was wont to recommend his goods to customers by suggesting that they could check on the quality of any of his goods with the dockers. 'Ask the dockers. They know first; they sample everything. Ask the dockers, they were genuine, they are the first to sample it.'[79] Grey, as we saw in Chapter 2, went out of his way to employ dockers privately. Grey no doubt knew that dockside losses were not to be laid primarily at the feet of dockers. There was no effective way to know whether thefts were occurring at the port or elsewhere.[80] Some theft occurred as trucks left the dockside and travelled through the streets of Dublin. Coal trucks shed their loads as they spun around corners. A truck stopped at a traffic light could be descended on by gangs of young men, grabbing what they could before the light changed and the treasure went on its way.[81] Other losses occurred as cargo had reached its destination, for example, crates of whiskey were stolen from a bonded warehouse.[82] Too much of the docksides were unguarded after cargo was unloaded but before cartage. Access for organised or random theft was too easy.[83]

Dockers themselves had, however, other scams. Sailors bringing tea on the long voyage halfway around the world from Ceylon on 'India tea boats' were the inspiration for many a trick by dockers. The sailors were Indian or Sinhalese, and avid for any Western products which could be got in their port of call. They did not, however, reckon on the Dublin deep-sea docker. At one point forged £10 notes were passed to the Indian sailors, from whom dockers could buy whiskey. This backfired on one docker, who was stuck with one of the bogus notes in change from a sailor of a £20 note. The Indians were also lumbered with sweepstakes

Bales of hay in a ship's hold. (Donated by Robbie Cox to the Dublin Dock Workers Preservation Society)

tickets that they were told were banknotes. And the sailors of one ship bought bicycles.[84] Michael Donnelly remembers

> One Indian tea boat, *The City of Calcutta*, where the crew were buying bicycles for £4 a go. In those days to own a bicycle in India was the sign of wealth. Anyway, all the bicycles left unchained outside the pubs on the North Wall started a new life in the streets of New Delhi.

> Business was booming with bikes until a foreman was seen struggling on the deck with a [sailor] holding on for dear life to the handlebars of the bike he'd bought from two of the dockers. And the foreman hanging on to the back wheel of

On a timber boat. Front from left: Paddy Daly, 'Gandhi' Savage and Strannie Fitzsimons. (Donated by Christy Fitzsimons to the Dublin Dock Workers Preservation Society) the bike, shouting it was his and he had not given anyone permission to sell it. Anyway the gang from Store Street Garda station was sent for and they had to bring a lorry down to take away the stolen bicycles.

Elaborate schemes were mounted at one period for signing on at the Labour Exchange for unemployment benefit, while actually working on the days in question.[85] Dockers hid shipside from visiting Department of Social Welfare inspectors, whom they seemed to be able to easily identify. Little work was done during such an inspection by men not legally present. The scam was far from foolproof, however, and some men had to refund monies to the Exchequer.

There were limits. According to the story which went around about a *Sunday World* reporter during the streaker craze of the 1960s, a reporter approached a stevedore, asking about the chances of getting a docker to do a streak for £50. 'Unlikely,' responded the stevedore, 'I'm paying them £60 a day, and can't even get a docker to take his coat off.'[86]

If the docklands had a reputation for scams and dodgy dealings, dockers equally had a reputation for wit and humour. 'The whole day was a wind-up,' explained deep-sea docker John Walsh, 'even though you were working. It was a great way of getting through heavy and hard work. Just keep laughing all the time.'[87]

Lousy-Shoulders O'Shea and The Rat Whelan could scarcely have felt to have been labelled estimably. Ass-Jaw Mckeevers, Dogfish Clarke, Muddler McDonnell, Joe-the-Goat Behan, Weasel Tobin, Whinger Behan, the Beak Birrall, Shiter Kennedy, Sow Byrne and Flea Lawless probably felt the same. All of these were Ringsend monikers. Lights Out, Hairy-Eye and Spit in Pint were other deep-sea dockers. Distinguished-sounding and laudatory nicknames were plentiful, to be sure: Lightheart, Doctor, Stevedore, Swift, Tiger, Bishop, Professor. One is sure that most, possibly all, of these were, however, ironic, meant to mock rather than praise. 'Fingers' was a man who only had three. The ironic intent of so many nicknames corresponds to the dockers' daily joy: mocking, goading and baiting one another.

Timber and poles at the North Wall Extension, 1947. (Donated by Jimmy McCarthy to the Dublin Dock Workers Preservation Society)

Nicknames have appeared liberally in previous chapters: the reader may recall Bulletproof Power or Heave-Ho Daly, among others. Almost everyone had such a title. Martin Mitten was able to write out for us six pages of deep-sea docker nicknames, numbering 118, of which only a few had ever been slapped on more than one recipient.[88] Name origins could be simple sometimes. 'The Shakins' was the kind of docker who always scraped for the last bits in a sack, or the last bits of anything. Whispering Grass Floridy tended to converse close to your ear, ever so secretively. Eat-the-Baby got his nickname from an expression which 'Eat' used too often. 'Hearse-Man' Flynn was sombre-looking. 'Wiggie' Nolan wore one. All were dockers, as was Nicky Knack, that relentless deviser of methods whom we met in Chapter 2. The hobbler Green Splashers Dunne sneezed with unfortunate display – once! Nickname assignment was often part of a tormenting form of humour dockers directed at one another. A fictional Dubliner captures part of the idea this way: 'the insult was a truly intimate term of endearment in which you graced your friends with mock expressions of contempt'.[89] The docker had to be not just physically hard, but well-armoured mentally too, for derision was raised to an art form. 'You would be surprised what they would come up with. There was no prisoners taken if they started jeering.'[90]

The majority of docker appellatives, in contrast to those just mentioned, are actually of unknown origin. Surprisingly, it is quite typical that no one can recall where most nicknames came from – including, very often, its possessor. Generations of Abber Doyles could pass the blue button from father to son, but could not pass on a notion how they acquired their shared nickname.[91] When the hobbler German Lawless died, it was realised that no one then living knew why he was called German.[92] Why is Docker Montgomery the unique possessor of an occupational title? When one of the authors circulated a list of more than 400 dockland nicknames in the docker cafeteria in Alexandra Basin, not a single origin could be identified by the old-time dockers then at the tables.

The richness of these nicknames is impressive. So many have already been recorded in these pages, yet the opportunity to list some more of them cannot be bypassed. From among the hundreds of further Dublin dockers' monikers, here is a handful more, alphabetised not by surname but by operative handle:

> The Bleeder Walsh
> Da Gaines
> Deviler Nolan
> Deviler O'Connor
> Facey Kiernan
> Find the Lady Duffy
> Funnier Dardis
> Gagger Hynes

Giggie Andrews
Greasy Meat Murphy
Icer Mooney
La-La Smith
Lil-La Montgomery
Lips Finn
Little Pal Byrne
Monkey Blood Nolan
Nuggy Bar Connolly
Pump Your Bike Reilly
Salt Box O'Connor
Shagger Doyle
Snowey Farrell
Stale Loaf Cummins
Tart Eye Dardis
Tear the Herring Allen
Uncle Mullen
Wiffler Farrell

Almost every conceivable kind of label was worn by someone. It is notable that, although jokes were made about 'Irish rheumatism', none among the many hundreds of nicknames attributes shiftlessness or even weakness. This is consistent with our general finding that hard work was not optional, it was requisite. Men worked despite injuries and illness. Some worked on with injuries which were in fact their proximate cause of death: in a sense experiencing their own death day-by-day on the job. They needed to maintain their source of income, but were also attached to and committed to work. Dockers were known to have died while on a working gang. Heroism of a rather different form is exhibited by other Dublin dockers who laboured rather heroically in this demanding work quite late in life. No few worked on until seventy, and some well beyond that.

Old Joe couldn't read nor write, so he come in here; Dolf and me were filling out the form. 'When were you born?'

'1886'. And he was still working on the docks: nearly 80 years of age and he still working on the singing out. I often gave him a job in Nicholl's, that's where he worked.[93]

Singing-out was the usual speciality of the older docker.

Stories of drinking, singing, sport, smuggling, of wit and lyricism or off fighting with the Citizens Army don't get to the heart of the docker. Their legendary status was grounded in the hard work they did, work that was dangerous, work that left some battered and broken, work that was hard on the old. For all of this, it was also work that was varied and interesting, work that built friendships and communities, the memory of which persists long after the job itself has disappeared.

CUSTOM HOUSE DUBLIN 4825. W.L.

SEVEN

THE ESSENCE OF A TRADITION

Dockers don't see it as an occupation,
they see it as a way of life.[1]

The Dublin docker carries a defining quality. That quality generates his contribution to the city's unique culture. Let us look at the facets of the docker way of life, building towards a description of the ultimate essence of the docker.

Writers used the dockers' spirit to frame many lasting characters in Irish literature. In James Joyce's *Dubliners* the story 'An Encounter' describes the quays as the two boys travel across the ferry, mitching from school to spend the day by the Pigeon House.[2] James Plunkett's *Strumpet City* describes the times around the 1913 Lockout and one of his short stories centres around a dockers' dispute and Liffey Wanderers, the football club is fondly recalled often in his writings.[3] For the docker has perennially been at the centre of Dublin life. His daily worksite lapped boldly straight through mid-city for most of Dublin's history. The River Liffey is of course this site, where important wharfs relocated gradually seaward from Wood Quay. In Joyce's days, ships and quayworkers were the dominant aspect of Carlisle Bridge itself.

Ships' cargo on the quays at the Custom House, c.1880–1900. Robert French photographer. Image Courtesy of the National Library of Ireland, call no. L_ROY_04825)

Dublin is a port city. As a small island nation on the edge of Europe, Ireland is dependent on shipment by sea. Some 4,500 shipping containers arrive at Dublin port every day but their contents are hidden in steel boxes.[4] Cargo only reaches the newspapers if it is illegal. Drugs, smuggled ammunition and counterfeit goods make the columns, everything else flows into the port, through the city and to the rest of the country without comment. It was not always this way. Newspapers used to take note of the goods arriving at port. In 1946, as shipping returned after the war, *The Irish Times* announced that 30,000 seville oranges were due to arrive on a boat from Brazil, while from Belgium there were grapes – the first since 1939. Irish smokers must have eagerly awaited the delivery of 200 tons of tobacco from the United States.[5] A short paragraph from 1950 declares the arrival of two steamers from Rotterdam, one containing grapes, pears, onions, textiles, the other 'general cargo'.[6] Lists of expected ships were printed in the 1960s, each giving the name, origin, cargo and expected date of arrival.[7] 'How,' asked a stevedore 'did 1000s of tons of cargo go to houses? Imported bricks built the houses, each house heated by imported coal.'[8] Dockers were at the heart of economic life.

Through dockers' hands goods poured into the city. Many hands they have been, too, for much of history. Recall the 150-odd men who would be discharging a single ship. This labour intensiveness showed a different aspect of economic salience: dockworking occupied a significant portion of the Dublin workforce in the prime years of dockwork.

Quay worker and docker communities were planted close to the city's watery belt. They shared the community life of Sheriff Street, City Quay, Ringsend, East Wall, and the more far-flung communities in which they lived, and brought there the patterns of the dockers' way of life. They forged the mighty Liffey Wanderers. Docker-frequented pubs, where the beero might be in session, or where a glistening number seven shovel might be resting, were in the city's very heart. They appeared with faces black from dust off coal boats, in The Wharf, Mulligans, Kennedys, Walshs and Kellys, and other pubs, dragged weary through local lanes after a night-time ship discharge, and splashed money when they had it. They brought the flavour of their way of life, a way of life where each ship was a new unknown. The docker was one of the essential Dubliners.

Yet docking was not seen as respectable work. Astrid Wonneberger interviewed dockland dwellers who spoke of being discriminated against when they applied for jobs on the basis of their dockland address.[9] In the words of *Waterfront*, 'he is looked upon as a sort of social outcast in polite society', he is 'the maligned Dublin docker'.[10]

Irish newspaper reports mention dockers in three main capacities; injury and death due to workplace accidents, strikes and work-stoppages, and drunken fights or thefts in which the accused is identified as a docker. Although there were considerably fewer reports of theft, dockers throughout the world had a reputation for

The CIÉ container yard with the old Gasometer in the background. (Donated by Florrie Cunningham from Michael Donnelly's collection to the Dublin Dock Workers Preservation Society)

John Hawkins Senior.
(Donated by John Hawkins to the Dublin Dock Workers Preservation Society)

light fingers. Pilfering had become, we saw in Chapter 5, a trait of legendary proportions in the tale of the Dublin docker. His ultimate employers, the importers, often watched (or looked the other way) with some amusement, if not appreciation. Losses from a docker pilfering was a relatively small trade-off, during most of the history of the port, for the advantageous industrial relations position of the employer over the docker.

Stevedores and tradesmen, the carpenters or the brickies, were seen as a higher class and would drink apart from the dockers.[11] Membership of a known work gang increased the chances of being picked at the read. Drinking with the gang was part and parcel of getting acceptance. When dockers were paid daily, as Martin Mitten proclaimed 'every night was a Saturday night', and with this dockers gained a reputation. A docker could face difficulties getting into Dublin's clubs 'if you were known and were undesirable as well, you were told you can't come in, end of the story or you had go get someone to sign you in and then if you got a bit out of turn with a few drinks they wouldn't sign you in again.'[12] This led to an attempt in the 1960s to set up a social club for dockers, so they could have their own parties, somewhere for families, for wedding and birthdays.

Part of the view of the docker as disreputable may be linked to the fact that dock work broke many of the work norms of society. Dockers could choose not to work if they wanted to, though of course often, inactivity was often forced upon them. When waiting for the read or the next ship, they would play poker or brag on the Custom House steps, or gamble illegally in toss schools ('pitch and toss') occasionally having to run from police raids. Some days would unfold in a leisurely way 'home at lunchtime and have a wash and change and then go off rambling around town'.[13]

The historian E.P. Thompson noted that as working time became regular and predictable, those whose working hours varied and who retained a measure of control over when they did or didn't work were characterised as outside respectable society. The Mexican mineworker who worked irregularly was considered 'indolent and childlike', the Bombay cotton workers were backward and the Irish peasant was lazy.[14] Like them, dock work was unpredictable and the docker was reckoned as a breed apart. Their manner of payment, cash in hand, every day, was perhaps also seen as suspect. Moreover, this made it difficult for dockers and their families to plan for the future and perhaps this further set them apart.

In response, perhaps, the dockers' magazine *Waterfront*, produced in the 1960s, devoted some of its pages to highlighting the respectability of dockworkers, carrying articles on the churches and famous families in the docklands, families that could trace their contribution to docking over three or four generations. When reporting on their annual dinner dance they said: 'A feature of the dance was the very large number of young people present, who thoroughly enjoyed themselves; and their general conduct was of the very highest standard … The Metropole management have stated more than once that the Waterfront Annual Dance is the most orderly and well-conducted function of the year.'[15] This account can be seen both as a nod to and refutation of the slurs heaped on dockers by wider society.

What then were the true features in the Dublin docker tradition? Discharging each ship was a work of manual design. Creating the hoist, donnaging, levering the cargo into position for moving: these and other techniques were highly developed skills. Pride in performance drove the discharging and stowing docker arts: as men in

PORT OF DUBLIN

EXPECTED

Louis S (D. J. Twohig) (Copenhagen), Mar., seed; Ellinis (MacKenzie and Co.) (Gdansk), do., coal. Yesterday—Menje (Gruno Shipping) (Antwerp), sand; Barreras Puente (R. A. Burke) (Malaga), general. To-day — Valbella (British and Irish Steam Packet Co.) (Rouen), general; Stadland (P. Donnelly and Sons) (Hamburg), fertilizer; Lenie (P. Donnelly and Sons) (Rotterdam), fertiliser; Auriga G (Geo. Bell and Co.) (Zandvoorde), fertilizer; Frank Danz (D. J. Twohig) (Aalborg via Waterford), seed; Belgian (The Wexford Steamships Co.) (Hamburg), to load. To-morrow—North Devon (R. A. Burke) (Freemantle), general; Laverock (Palgrave Murphy) (Casablanca/Cadiz/Oporto), general.

March 25th — Trito (Palgrave Murphy) (Rotterdam), general; Lingedijk (Palgrave Murphy) (Rotterdam), general; Crane (Palgrave Murphy) (Bordeaux), general; Lisa (Geo. Bell and Co.) (Hamburg), machinery. 26th — Duquessa (Geo. Bell and Co.) (Buenos Aires), general; American Veteran (Geo. Bell and Co.) (New York via Liverpool), general. 26-27th—Gretchen Muller (P. B. Killen and Co.) (Hamburg), potash. 27th—City of Cork (Palgrave Murphy) (Bremen/Hamburg), general. 28th —Thallo (Palgrave Murphy) (Rotterdam), general; Bel Mare (The Wexford Steamships Co.) (Bahrain via Avonmouth), oil. 29th — Monbatsa (Geo. Bell and Co.) (Pacific), general. 30th—City of Dublin (Palgrave Murphy) (Antwerp), general; Torr Head (Palgrave Murphy) (Baltimore/Norfolk), general; Theano (Palgrave Murphy) (Amsterdam/Rotterdam), general. 31st—Runa (Geo. Bell and Co.) (Gothenburg), general.

April 1st — Clan McGillervray (Geo. Bell and Co.) (Far East), general. 3rd —Suderau (Palgrave Murphy) (Bremen/Hamburg), general. 4th—Thalio (Palgrave Murphy) (Rotterdam), general. 8th—Trito (Palgrave Murphy) (Amsterdam/Rotterdam), general. 9th — City of Dublin (Palgrave Murphy) (Antwerp), general. 10th—City of Cork (Palgrave Murphy) (Bremen/Hamburg), general. 11th—Thalio (Palgrave Murphy) (Rotterdam), general. 16th—Theano (Palgrave Murphy) (Amsterdam/Rotterdam), general; Suderau (Palgrave Murphy) (Bremen/Hamburg), general. 18th — City of Dublin (Palgrave Murphy) (Antwerp), general; Peleus (Palgrave Murphy) (Far East), general.

Listing of ship arrivals and cargo into Dublin Port. (*Irish Times*, 23 March 1963)

gangs all pulled, for example, to fill tubs or pack hoists which were only momentarily hovering, demanding attention. Virtually everybody pulled his weight, whether or not he carried a nickname such as Beat-the-Dark Geoghan or One-More-Bucket Ellis.

No two days were the same, so many different goods were arriving and departing. Today's ship was likely to be carrying a different commodity to those of yesterday or last week. 'You could go up seven days a week,' Martin Mitten remembered fondly, 'and get seven different jobs.' That variety made the working life attractive to those who followed it. Masted sailing ships, moreover, alternated with steamships for more than a century after about 1820, adding to the range of workplaces. Even the size of the floating workplace altered with some regularity. Generally ships became larger; yet, late-nineteenth-century clipper ships were smaller than their predecessors. All this change was loved by deep-sea dockers – they were never bored.

Docking was an exclusively male pursuit. Sons followed their fathers, younger men learned from the old. Men working together, men drinking together, long hours spent in the company of men: 'Dockers, they worked and drank, worked and drank.'[16] The cost of hard physical labour could be seen on the men's bodies. Danger surrounded the occupation. Yet the Dublin docker experienced neither thrill nor bravado from danger. We have seen that he did not dwell on the risks, putting it to the back of his mind, hoping that he would not be the unlucky one.

Dock work brought status to family men as the main breadwinner: 'I reared my family off the docks.'[17] For some this absolved them of responsibility for running the home and family. The pub was refuge from overcrowded homes, from grief, from the indignity of the read and the depression that accompanied unemployment: 'They were millionaires when they were working … that night, but they may be paupers for the rest of the week.'[18]

Solidarity was also part of the docker's story. Among dockers it thrived in the many kinds of mutual support described in this book. Community was built through voluntary effort. Mutual aid began with the family but spread through the wider community. Traditions

of financial support in times of sickness or death were strong. There was also a significant tradition of voluntary organisation that arranged picnics for orphans, dinner dances, a social club for retired dockers and the erection of the Realt Na Mara statue on the Bull Wall promenade. This tradition persists to the present day with the remembrance work of the Dublin Dockworkers Preservation Society.

Militancy too has appeared in all of its forms: as wildcat stoppages, extended strike action, and as trade union activism. It would be wrong to see union organisation as uncomplicated. We have seen destructive sectarian battles between unions and within unions. The pages of *Waterfront* in the early 1960s, a decade that was to see a remarkable improvement in working conditions, bemoaned the apathy of dockers to their own situation and the non-attendance at union branch meetings.[19]

Dockers were also in competition with each other, competing for work. Gang reliants versus floaters, sons of dockers versus those less well connected, front row at the read versus back row, non-button versus button, old versus young, regulars to the particular read versus opportunists, yesterday's gang versus yesterday's unsuccessful, and more. Yet despite these considerable difficulties, docker workers deserved their reputation as strong trade unionists.

It is perhaps this aspect of the docker's life that is of most relevance to today's workforce, for casualisation is back. From zero hour contracts to the tech casualisation of Uber and Deliveroo, once more employees do not know how many hours they will work this week, whether they will receive a wage the next. They lack sick pay or pensions. The grim consequences of insecurity are similar as are its negative impact on mind and body, on families and communities, and on society as a whole.

This new generation cannot draw on traditions of organisation handed down from father to son. They do not share the same bonds of friendship and community as were evident among dockworkers. They live in a different world, yet the history of the Dublin docker does show that exploitative work practices can be challenged. Despite their vulnerability in the face of their employers, despite being in competition with each other for their work, dock workers showed a remarkable capacity to organise together in defence of their individual interests, both within their local gangs and within their unions. They drew on and maintained a tradition of self-organisation and solidarity. Rate of pay and hours of work were frequently renegotiated to the dockers' advantage.

Changes in hiring practices were more resistant to change. Willie Murphy started his working life at 14, hoping that his father's name would give him an advantage at the morning's read. During World War Two he was forced to emigrate to find work. By the time he was 48, he had won the right to be a buttonman, with the poor guarantee that if there was work available he would be among the first chosen. At 58, he had fought for and obtained a guaranteed weekly wage and permanent employment. Change came, too slowly perhaps, following too much struggle, but it came. In the lives of Dublin dockers we can see warning of how persistent exploitative employment practices could be. Yet despite this persistence we also see that improvement was possible.

What was different about the Dublin docker? What was at the essence of dock work? The defining quality of dock work was freedom. Freedom, for the Dublin deep-sea docker, exceeded militancy, matching and surpassing even solidarity. This is his theme and the essence of his tradition. What thrilled him most was not pride, solidarity, danger, camaraderie or money – but freedom. Each of the qualities mentioned in this chapter is intrinsic to the Dublin docker. They, with their work, their contribution to the economy, their customs, history, nicknames, communities, and more, were the substance of the tradition. Each quality was enriched, despite the painful stab of uncertainty. For indeed it took an amount of spirit and resilience to put up with all they faced, as freedom without economic security is hollow. Willie Murphy looking back on his inherited career remembered: 'I tried all my life, all my young life, to get a permanent job.' Uncertainty about work, about income, had been the docker's shadow companion.

Yet, not an entirely loathsome one, involving one's own decision, one's own gamble. Which read to attend? You make the decision; you take the gamble. You felt that loss if you were without a ship, but you felt the freedom either way. They could choose a read site, choose the commodity to work, stop work to bargain, better their own high standards, or, indeed, go to work or not. They felt they could act in their own interests more independently than other workers. This gave them satisfaction, as they left behind the ship that has been their latest conquest, and strode back across the wharves into the city. That freedom was their defining characteristic. We leave the final word to Martin Mitten, who, in old age, avowed: 'If I was to come back, I'd still go to work as a docker.'

AFTERWORD

by Declan P. Byrne
No More on the Dockside:
The Dublin Dock Workers Preservation Society

The Dublin Dock Workers Preservation Society was set up in early 2011. The group is made up of ex-dock workers and people interested in preserving the industrial history of Dublin Docks and the rich history of the dockland communities. We started by collecting old photographs and are delighted to report that our collection has broken through the 4,000 mark. Every photo or document we receive is scanned and given back and credited to the person who has made the donation. Most of our photos can be found on our FaceBook page, 'Dublin Dockers', and a web page: www.bluemelon.com/alanmartin. The Society is currently working on a new web page: www.dublindockworkers.com.

In 1973, I made the short journey from Ballybough to a job on Dublin's docks. I was a son of a builder's labourer and though the distance was short in miles, it was a whole new world: a world I inhabited until December 2000 when I received the 'lump' (redundancy pay). I worked as a junior clerk and early on when I joined the Marine Port and General Workers Union (MP&GWU), an act of treachery according to my employer who then informed me that no matter how long I worked in the docks I would always remain a junior clerk. I hadn't done well in school (Joey's Fairview). If I had I would have secured a good civil service job and would have missed out on the excitement, the craic, the struggles, the victories, the bad times and the losses that I experienced over a twenty-year period.

ommy Carthy, founding member of the Dublin Dock Workers Preservation Society, holding a bag hook, a short ool with rounded spines that were used for grabbing bags. Other names for it were 'cargo hook', 'sugar hook' r 'catspaw'. (Photographer Jeannette Lowe)

Not coming from a dockland family, I was completely ignorant of the rich traditions that existed back to the 1870s. For me a button was something that you used to hold up your trousers. Decasualisation came in 1972 and when I started it was a period of rapid change and constant conflict. I worked in the deep-sea section in Dublin Port, which over a short period of time was to experience the number employed fall from around 1,000 to only a handful.

A Joyous Journey

I was having a cup of coffee with my wife Margaret in a coffee shop in Coolock village when I was approached by a retired docker, Jimmy Carthy, who said there was something small he wanted me to do. Always ask before you agree to do something!

He wanted my help in setting up a group that would preserve the history of Dublin Docks and which would fight for the building of a docklands museum. I now refer to him as the Buddha of East Wall because he predicted that to start with our efforts would bear small fruit and if it was meant to happen it would take off. This is the story of a positive journey, which just keeps getting better and better.

Both of us knew that an ex-checker, Alan Martin, who was a keen photographer, had taken photographs of strikes, retirements and Christmas parties. We decided to invite Alan and anyone else we thought might be interested to a meeting in Kilbarrack. We discovered that Alan had started a collection numbering 600 (made up of his own photos plus a donation of photos from a company called Dublin Stevedores). His efforts to collect more had met with little success but he was enthusiastic to give it another go. We strived to keep our group open to anyone who worked in any section of the docks or anyone interested in preserving the history of the docks. The numbers that attended were small but our collection began to grow. Michael Corcoran (ex-union official) donated a docker's button and a number of publications. John 'Miley' Walsh (ex-docker) collected cargo hooks and photos and Michael Foran (ex-haulier) also donated photos. Alan set up a Facebook page Dublin Dockers and the *Northside*

People featured our appeal for photographs. I remember one of the first photographs donated was from Anna Wickham, which showed five dockers, including her grandfather Paddy 'Tucker' Dennis. The trickle of photographs then became a stream. John Hawkins (ex-docker) then came on board and our meetings shifted to St Patrick's Rowing Club in Ringsend (most appropriate as the meeting room overlooks the docks).

Smiley Bolger looks at the Dublin Dock Workers Preservation Society exhibition in Liberty Hall, May 2017. (Photograph by Aileen O'Carroll)

When our photo collection broke through the 1,000 mark we decided to approach the Dublin Port Company for help. We set up a meeting with Charlie Murphy (Community Liaison Manager) and were joined by Eamon O'Reilly (Chief Executive Officer). Both were interested in our idea of holding a photo exhibition, which would then tour the dockland communities. They instantly agreed to pay for forty pictures to be framed and to cover the costs of the launch in the Port Centre.

We decided to choose our photos from the period 1940 to 1990, picking those that we thought had family significance. The rooms picked were excellent and the Port Company informed us that the space could only cater for 200 people. Our invitation system was mostly by word of mouth. I was a nervous wreck leading up to 23 March 2012. What if 300 turned up or worse still if no one turned up (that would certainly put paid to our argument that people were interested and that there was a need for a docklands museum). The exhibition was taking place in the Port Centre, the headquarters of the Dublin Port Company, the very building that we thought about occupying in the 1992 lockout/strike, which had lasted for eight months.

The night was a night of pride. A large contingent of dockers, dockworkers and their families turned up. It was a night when dockers and their way of life were commemorated. An odd tear of joy and remembrance was shed that night. In the following week the exhibition was transferred to the lobby of the Port Centre, where a further 100 people turned up. In addition to the framed photos the Port Company downloaded around 1,000 photos onto a memory stick and these were projected onto an overhead screen.

Thus the roller coaster ride began. It was around this time that Padraig Yeates from the Irish Labour History Society and Joe Mooney from the East Wall History Group joined our gang. We were then approached by Roisin Lonergan (Five Lamps Arts Festival) to put on our exhibition in Connolly House, North Strand, using the same format as the Port Centre. The launch was planned for 18 April 2012. Maureen O'Sullivan TD opened it by talking about her own connections to the docks and she was joined by Noel Gregory (brother of Tony), who talked about his father working in the Tea Sheds for the Dublin Port and Docks Board.

After the Port Centre event we received an additional 200 photos. On the night Mrs Terri McDermott became transfixed when a particular photo came on the screen. It showed her father and grandfather working together in the hatch of the ship. It was a photograph of Alan Martin's father working as a docker in the B+I but we did not know the identities of the others in the photo. Terri had brought to the exhibition a publication on B+I and her father's cattle dockers passport, which now forms part of our collection.

In early May 2012, SIPTU asked to host the exhibition in Liberty Hall. On the day I got a phone call asking if three of us could be in Liberty Hall within an hour because RTÉ wanted to interview us in front of the photos. Jimmy Carthy, Alan Martin and I made the mad dash and it was well worth it. That night our efforts were featured on the *Six One News*. Just under 200 people turned up on the night to see Jack O'Connor (President of SIPTU) launch the exhibition and then to our amazement 600 people turned up in the following week. A big 'thank you' for this is due to Scott Millar and all our supporters in SIPTU.

A few weeks later the exhibition moved to Ringsend. The Minister for European Affairs Lucinda Creighton TD was surprised by the guard of honour she received from the members of St Patrick's Rowing Club, who held their oars for her to walk under. This honour is normally preserved for club members who are getting married or for their funerals. In her speech she said she was already married and a wag in the audience said it was an early funeral. Lilly McDermott donated a fantastic photograph the 'House Gang' on the night. The warmth and joy were there to be seen both on the night and the days that followed with 200 people turning up to enjoy the memories.

In July the exhibition was in the East Wall Community Centre. Again it was a unique experience. Don Bennett, a sociologist, gave a talk on Dublin Docks pre-1972. In his talk he spoke about how coal dockers attempted to keep coal dust out of their lungs by sucking on a lump of coal while working in the hatch. I could hear someone muttering what 'a load of crap'. We then held an open microphone session where people from the audience talked about the nicknames, the stories from their families and then I saw 'Bronco' Dennis (from Kilbarrack) take the microphone. He told the audience about the hardship, the dangers and the earnings of working coal and yes he sucked a lump of coal every time in the hatch.

The exhibition then went to Cabra the weekend before the Tall Ships Festival 2012. For the Tall Ships Festival, we were given a room in the CHQ Building and a more appropriate place you could not imagine. Over the three and a half days we featured guest speakers Don Bennett, Padraig Yeates, Sarah Lundberg and Joe Mooney. We even had a singsong lead by Paul O'Brien (singer/songwriter). At one stage the organisers said that we couldn't sing but through good times and bad times we have always sung.

During the Festival over 2,000 people attended our exhibition and talks. On the last day Tom Boland (retired docker) came in with a great big bag of photos, books and magazines. The group and I can honestly say that we have not worked as hard in the past forty years! At the end of it we were totally exhausted. But it was greatly worthwhile because we knew that we had brought a 'bit of joy' into people's lives and the craic that we had with old and new friends will be remembered for some time.

Since then Brendan Dempsey has presented us with a great collection of photographs and Florrie Cunningham has donated Michael 'Mika' Donnelly's collection. Mika was President of the Marine Port and General Workers Union and a lifelong docker. The collection of photographs and documents will take us months to get through, but already we have found some great gems, including the 1946 and 1957 deep-sea dockers registers.

We would like to acknowledge the support we have recieved from Dublin City Council, the National Heritage Council, the Dublin Port Company, SIPTU, International Transport Workers' Federation and the CHQ Building. We have also received incredible support from the Dockland communities including the Ringsend Irishtown Community Centre, St Patricks Rowing Club (Ringsend), St Andrews Resource

Centre, Sean O' Casey Community Centre, East Wall History Group, the North Docks Peoples Project, Sheriff Youth Club F.C. It has also been a pleasure to have been involved in the Dublin's Culture Connects initiative and each year with the Five Lamps Arts Festival. Our journey has also brought us in contact with some great historians such as Don Bennett, Ann Matthews, Padraig Yeates, Hugo McGuinness and Joe Mooney. In the Dockers tradition of having a singsong after a few pints it has been great to work with the singer-songwriter Paul O'Brien.

The Buddha from East Wall was spot on – if the time is right your efforts will be rewarded and even if we never achieve our goal of a docklands museum we have shown that there is great interest in the history of Dublin Docks and that it is worth preserving. Everyone has their own story – no more so than those who worked in the docks. One of our founders who was our inspiration was Jimmy Carthy who passed away on 28 February 2017. He said, 'Do not lose hope and keep fighting on until we realise our dream.' Many people have donated photographs, documents, magazines, cargo hooks, coal shovels and Dockers' buttons – we urgently need a heritage centre to display our collection and to make sure that our history is not lost. The struggle continues – the unique history of Dublin Docks needs to be told and preserved.

APPENDIX 1

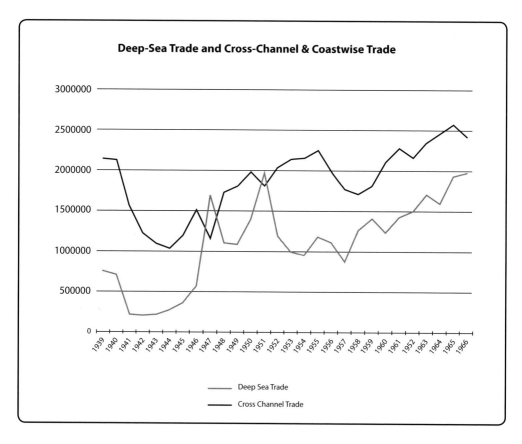

Graph 1: Trade (imports and exports) on Dublin Docks. Deep Sea Vs Cross Channel & Coastwise trade

Source: 'Employment structure in course of change', *The Irish Times,* 31 October 1967, p. iv.

APPENDIX 2

TABLE 1: Variations in the numbers of dockers registered at Dublin Employment Exchanges at the end of each week

	1947	1947	1948	1948
	Lowest weekly number	Highest weekly number	Lowest weekly number	Highest weekly number
	235	811	438	689
January	585	667	438	571
February	618	663	566	595
March	658	771	493	585
April	776	811	591	684
May	748	789	570	684
June	466	671	587	683
July	322	460	579	671
August	276	318	604	636
September	310	339	596	651

Source: Labour Court Report, Department of the Taoiseach, S14752a, 28 September 1951, National Archives of Ireland, Dublin.

TABLE 2: Variations of Trade of Port of Dublin Import and Export Combined, Peak and trough months, 1947 and 1948

Trade	Peak Months	Peak Months	Trough Months	Trough Months
	1947	**1948**	**1947**	**1948**
Coastwise	October	October	April	August
Foreign	December	March	February	July
Coal	October	July	March	May
Cattle	December	November	March	June

Source: Labour Court Report, Department of the Taoiseach, S14752a, 28 September 1951, National Archives of Ireland, Dublin.

TABLE 3: Dublin Docks: Imports and Exports (tonnes), 1939–71

Year	Total Imports (tonnes)	Total Exports (tonnes)
1939	2,606,440	294,320
1940	2,502,166	334,762
1941	1,437,358	324,569
1942	1,225,000	201,714
1943	1,153,776	162,841
1944	1,122,412	189,393
1945	1,304,261	254,265
1946	1,779,726	302,751
1947	2,562,083	292,782
1948	2,504,121	331,917
1949	2,515,867	381,373
1950	2,967,235	413,095
1951	3,354,105	427,910
1952	2,795,284	433,001
1953	2,667,042	475,765
1954	2,644,586	465,669
1955	2,962,031	472,540

1956	2,633,600	465,228
1957	2,187,503	460,641
1958	2,471,487	506,733
1959	2,710,370	508,102
1960	2,784,648	563,595
1961	3,037,838	669,230
1962	3,063,347	599,447
1963	3,391,134	661,403
1964	3,395,980	665,036
1965	3,817,865	687,959
1966	3,750,796	649,121
1967	4,036,255	506,733
1968	4,372,555	746,938
1969	4,778,366	916,256
1971	5,040,217	1,040,839

Source: 'Employment structure in course of change' *The Irish Times*, 31 October 1967, p. iv; *Thom's Directory*, 1939–1972.

TABLE 4: Average annual strike frequency per employee by sector, 1922–7

	Average annual strike frequency per 100,000 employees				
	1922–41	**1942–61**	**1962–81**	**1982–92**	**1993–97**
Manufacturing	21	21	17	17	3
Agriculture, Forestry & Fishing	n/d	1	0.6	0.6	0.6
Building & Construction	52	30	3	3	0.8
Transport & Communications	22	18	2	2	6
Electricity, Gas & Water	26	24	29	29	1
Mining, Turf, Etc	163	98	30	30	-

Source: T. Brannick, F. Devine and A. Kelly, 'Social Statistics for Labour Historians: Strike Statistics, 1922–99', *Saothar*, 25 (2000), pp. 118.

TABLE 5: Fluctuations in Earnings of Dockers, September 1948

	Week ending 2nd	Week ending 9th	Week ending 16th
	Number of dockers	Number of dockers	Number of dockers
11 pounds and over	2	4	13
Over 10 pounds and under 11	6	3	5
Over 9 pounds and under 10	32	4	15
Over 8 pounds and under 9	11	50	18
Over 7 pounds and under 8	71	122	117
Over 6 pounds and under 7	140	52	144
Over 5 pounds and under 6	98	55	66
Over 3 pounds and under 5	91	141	75
Over 1 pound and under 3	26	50	34
Total number of dockers	477	481	487

554 dockers on the register. Labour Court Report, Department of the Taoiseach, S14752a, 28 September 1951, National Archives of Ireland, Dublin.

TABLE 6: Interviewee Information

Interviewee name or code	Year of interview	Occupation	Year started on the docks	Other family working on docks
Annie Murphy	1995	Factory worker, home duties	Married a deep-sea docker in 1942	Father
Herby Doyle	1995	Coal docker (southside)	Late 1940s	Grandfather, Father, Uncles, Brothers
Jem [Metaller] Kelly	1995	Deep-sea docker (southside)	1922	Father
Martin Mitten	1995	Deep-sea docker (southside)	1934	Father, Grandfather, Brothers
Michael Donnelly	1998	Deep sea docker, MP&GWU President		Uncles, though not father
Phyllis Nolan	1998	Factory worker, home duties	Married a cross-channel docker in the early 1950s	Grandfather was a stevedore, father a docker
Willie Murphy	1995	Deep-sea docker (southside)	1927	Hobbler family (father and four uncles were hobblers), uncle was a stevedore, son also worked on the docks
Willie Murphy Jr	1995	Deep-sea docker (southside)	1952	Father, grandfather, great-uncles
Interviewee 4	1995	Shipping company executive	Late 1940s	
Interviewee 7	1995	Coal docker (southside)	Early 1940s	Uncles, Brothers, Nephews, Brother-in-law. Not Father
Interviewee 10	1995	Dock Superintendent	Early 1960s	Father was not associated with the docks
Interviewee 11	1997	Stevedore	Late 1950s	
Interviewee 12	1997	Stevedore	Late 1960s	Grandfather, Father

Interviewee 14	1998	Stevedore	1950s	Father and other family members
Interviewee 15	1995	Coalie (northside)	Early 1950s	None
Interviewee 17	1995	Deep-sea docker (northside)	Early 1950s	Father
Interviewee 18	1995	Stevedore	Early 1960s	
Interviewee 20	1995	Deep-sea docker (southside)	Late 1950s	Father

The identities of living interviewees have been anonymised.

ENDNOTES

Introduction

1   F. Lane, 'Envisaging Labour History: Some Reflections on Irish Historiography and the Working Class' in F. Devine, F. Lane, N. Puirseil (eds), *Essays in Irish Labour History* (Dublin: Irish Academic Press, 2008), p. 9.

2   For occupational culture see P. McCaffery, 'Jacob's women during the 1913 Lockout', *Saothar*, 16 (2013), pp. 1–12; M. Muldowney, 'A world of its own: recollections of women workers in Guinness's brewery in the 1940s', *Saothar*, 23 (1998), pp. 103–117; D. Cowman 'Life and Labour in Three Irish Mining Communities circa 1840', *Saothar*, 9 (1983), pp. 10–19.

3   See Lane, 'Envisaging Labour History', pp. 9–25.

4   J. Gray, *Spinning the Threads of Uneven Development: Gender and Industrialization during the Long Eighteenth Century* (Oxford: Lexington Books, 2005); B. Messenger, *Picking Up The Linen Threads: Life in Ulster's Mills* (Austin: University of Texas Press, 1978).

5   Miriam Nyhan, 'Narration and Memory: The Experiences of the Workforce of a Ford Plant', *Irish Economic and Social History*, 33 (2006), pp. 18–34; M. Muldowney, *The Second World War and Irish Women: An Oral History* (Dublin:

Irish Academic Press, 2007); C. Clear, *Women of the House: Women's Household Work in Ireland, 1926–1961 – Discourses, Experiences, Memories* (Dublin: Irish Academic Press, 2000).

6   M. Silverman, *An Irish Working Class: Explorations in Political Economy and Hegemony, 1800–1950* (Toronto: University of Toronto Press, 2006) page ref?; C. Eipper, *The Ruling Trinity: a Community Study of Church, State and Business in Ireland* (London: Gower, 1986).

7   Peter Turnbull, 'Dock strikes and the demise of the dockers' "occupational culture",' *The Sociological Review*, 40 (1992), 294–318; Peter Turnbull and Victoria Wass, 'The Greatest Game, no more-Redundant Dockers and the Demise of Dock Work', *Work, Employment & Society*, 8 (1994), pp. 487–506; J. Hamark, 'Strikingly indifferent: the myth of militancy on the docks prior to World War II', *Labor History*, 54 (2013), pp. 271–85; A. Parnaby, *Citizen Docker: Making a New Deal on the Vancouver Waterfront, 1919–1939* (Toronto: University of Toronto Press, Sam Davies, C.J.D., David de van Voss, Lidewij Hesselink, and Klaus Weinhauer, *Dock Workers: International Explorations in Comparative*

Labour History, 1790–1970 (Aldershot: Ashgate, 2000; W. Kenefick, *Rebellious and Contrary: The Glasgow Dockers, 1853–1932* (East Linton: Tuckwell Press, 2000) p. 112, 115.

8 J. Lovell, *Stevedores and Dockers* (London: Macmillan, 1969) p. 57–8, p. 81; M. Leonard, 'Learning the Ropes: The Politics of Dockland' in S. Wallman (ed.), *Social Anthropology of Work* (London: Academic Press, 1979), p. 83; (Colin J Davis, 'New York City and London Dockworkers: A Comparative Perspective of Rank-and-file Movements in the Post-Second World War Era', *Labour History Review*, 65 (2000), p .4.

9 Lane, 'Envisaging Labour History', p. 22.

10 Patrick Sweeney, 'On the Waterfront, Some Aspects of the Dispute', 13 January 1958, p. 5.

11 See Table Three in the Appendix.

12 Dockers earned twenty-four shillings for a seventy-hours week, while a labourer earned twenty. P. Berresford Ellis, *A History of the Irish Working Class* (London: Pluto Press, 1985), p. 184.

13 Our Industrial Correspondent, 'Brighter Trade Outlook With End Of Container Dispute', *Irish Times*, 1 Dec. 1961, p. 11; Michael Finlan, 'Deep-Sea Dockers Decasaulise: Force will reduce to 550', *The Irish Times*, 8 March 1971, p. 1.

14 For the impact of containers on docking communities see A. O'Carroll, 'Work Organisation, Technology, Community and Change: the Story of the Dublin Docker', *Saothar*, 31 (2006), pp. 45–53.

15 Report to the Minister of Industry and Commerce from the Labour Court Under Section 24 of the Industrial Relations Act, 1946.

16 In 1951, the Labour Court reported figures for men who had unemployment books in the Dublin Employment Exchange who were classified under the Industrial Trade Group RF (docks, harbours, piers and lighthouses, including the loading and discharging of vessels etc.). See Table One in the Appendix which shows variations in the numbers of dockers etc. registered at Dublin Employment Exchanges at the end of each week. Report to the Minister of Industry and Commerce from the Labour Court Under Section 24 of the Industrial Relations Act, 1946, National Archives of Ireland.

17 See Table Two in the Appendix which shows the peak and trough months for 1947 and 1948.

18 'Serious Labour Unrest in Ireland: Truce Broken at Cork, Dublin, Holyhead Steamers Stopped Weekly', *The Irish Times*, 4 February 1922, p. 2.

19 Report to the Minister of Industry and Commerce from the Labour Court Under Section 24 of the Industrial Relations Act, 1946, National Archives of Ireland.

20 'The Port Workers', *The Irish Times*, 28 June 1957, p. iv.

21 B. Fokkinga and E.D.J. Kruijtbosch, *Studies In The Long Term Development of*

the Port of Dublin (Dublin: Dublin Port and Docks Board, 1973), p. 5.

22 A. Wonneberger, *Waterfront, Culture and Community in Transition* (Hamburg: Universitat Hamburg, 2010), p. 7.

23 See Appendix for more detailed information on the interviewees.

24 Martin Mitten.

25 Andy Medhurst, 'If anywhere: class identification and cultural studies academics' in Sally Munt (ed.), *Cultural Studies and the Working Class: Subject to Change* (London: Cassell, 2000), p. 20.

One

1 Willie Murphy.

2 In New York, USA and New Brunswick, Canada this method of selection is known as 'the shape up', in the UK as the 'call'; Bonnie Hustings and Michael Boudreau, *Irresponsibility, Obligation, and the "Manly Modern": Tensions in Workingclass Masculinities in Postwar Saint John* (New Brunswick: 2016), p. 10; P. Turnbull (ed. W.K. Talley), *Port labor* (2012), p. 518; Peter Turnbull and David Sapsford, 'Why did Devlin fail? Casualism and conflict on the docks', *British Journal of Industrial Relations* 29 (1991), p. 256.

3 *Waterfront*, June 1961, p. 1.

4 The Seal McGuinness, Oko Sweeney, Salt Box O'Connor, Big Bob McCann, The Wire Robinson and Appler Farrell were Ringsend deep-sea dockers.

Nicknames and their sources are fully explored in Chapter 6.

5 Stevedoring is discussed further in Chapter 3.

6 Interviewee 11. The Appendix lists our own project interviewees and dates of interview. All quotations in the text are from our own project interviews, unless otherwise cited.

7 The names are those of employing companies or foremen.

8 Interviewee 17.

9 Martin Mitten.

10 Interviewee 17.

11 Interviewee 14.

12 Interviewee 14.

13 Interviewee 14.

14 See Chapter 3.

15 Isolating the best job was an ongoing science: 'Following discussions with the Union over the confusion and difficulties of reading the Best Job, the Union have now agreed that "the Best Job is the best possible earnings, between 8.00 a.m. and 5.00 p.m. on tonnage; delay hours, ships' hours, tonnage hours, dirty money and hardship money not to count." Therefore … ignore any reference to tonnage "In the hatch".' In Paragraph 1 of 24 February l967, manuscript 'Agreements and Rules Register', 24 May 1967, UCDA P 299 Records of the Association of Dublin Stevedores, UCD Archives, Dublin.

16 Martin Mitten.

17 From K. Connolly and A.M. Kennedy (eds), *Along the Quays and Cobblestones.*

Folklore of the South Docks Community (Dublin: St Andrews Heritage Group, 1992), p. 53.

18   Interviewee 17.

19   'Reads', *Waterfront*, July 1960, p. 1.

20   Jem Kiernan interviewed in 1994 (Interview K), North Inner City Folklore Project Archives, Dublin.

21   Interviewee 12.

22   Interviewee 20.

23   Interviewee 15.

24   Handwritten manuscript, North Inner City Folklore Project archives; thanks to Mick Rushe and Terry Fagan.

25   Interviewee 10.

26   Interviewee 17.

27   Martin Mitten.

28   Interviewee 20.

29   Interviewee 14.

30   *Waterfront*, March 1962, p. 1.

31   Interviewee 11.

32   The term 'ganger', used elsewhere for such gang leaders, was seldom employed in Dublin.

33   Yarra Duffy, docker, in R. Sheehan and B. Walsh, *The Heart of the City* (Dingle: Brandon, 1988), p. 48.

34   Willie Murphy Junior.

35   Bill 'Wilo' Nelson, National Folklore Archive interview, transcript folio no. UFP0043, pp. 76–8. Payout in public houses originated centuries earlier in the British Isles. Before 1819, in Manchester, 'it was general practice to pay a lump sum to one of the workpeople, who took it to the public-house where there were regular pay-tollers.' Those being paid 'were expected to drink' to compensate the publican, J.L. and Barbara Hammond, *The Town Labourer, 1765–1832* (London: Longmans, 1920), pp. 50–1.

36   Yarra Duffy, *The Heart of the City*, p. 48.

37   Willie Murphy.

38   'Dockology and Codology', *Waterfront*, August 1960, p. 2.

39   Willie Murphy Junior.

40   Between 100,000 and 150,000 people emigrated during the war years, and a further estimated 50–70,000 joined the British armed forces. Most emigrants were unskilled, men under 30. Dublin had the second highest emigration level after Mayo. D. Ó Drisceoil, 'Whose Emergency Is It? Wartime Politics and the Irish Working Class, 1939–45' in F. Lane and D. Ó Drisceoil (eds), *Politics and the Irish Working Class, 1830–1945* (Basingstoke: Palgrave Macmillan, 2005).

41   'Preference of employment to be given to "button" men wearing Union buttons prominently displayed' is stated in the 'Agreement between Marine Port & General Workers' Union, Irish Transport & General Workers' Union, Workers Union of Ireland, and The Society of Dublin Coal Importers' (1962), p. 1. See also J.B. Smethurst and F. Devine, 'Trade Union Badges, Mere Emblems or Means of Membership Control', *Saothar, Irish Journal of Labour History*, 7 (1981), pp. 85–6.

42   D. Greaves, *The Irish Transport and General Workers Union: The Formative*

Years 1909–1923 (Dublin: Gill and Macmillan, 1982), p. 21.

43 Smethurst, John B. & Devine, Frances (1981) *Trade Union Badges, Mere Emblems or Means of Membership Control. Saothar, Irish Journal of Labour History*, 7, pp. 85–6.

44 Ibid. pp. 86–8.

45 Jem Kiernan interviewed in 1994 (Interview K), North Inner City Folklore Project Archives, Dublin.

46 Minute no. 283, Claims Committee, 31 May 1962, UCDA P299 Records of the Association of Dublin Stevedores, UCD Archives, Dublin.

47 Claims Committee, 9 April 1964, UCDA P299 Records of the Association of Dublin Stevedores, UCD Archives, Dublin. Capitalisation as in the original.

48 A stevedore.

49 See Chapter 2 on singing-out.

50 Written about 1948. Reproduced here from *Dublin Opinion* (Winter 1988), p. 13. Bill Preston was a well-known singer, as well as being a docker. Thus he likely would have been singing on the ship as he claims in this lament. We return to singing as part of the story of the docker in Chapter 6.

51 The deep-sea section worked mainly without the middle-range red buttons, which were worn principally by cross-channel dockers.

52 Interviewee 17.

53 Willie Murphy.

54 Willie Murphy Junior.

Two

1 Michael Donnelly.

2 Interviewee 14.

3 A derrick is a lifting machine with a long arm that is used to move heavy loads.

4 Interviewee 14.

5 Martin Mitten in K.C. Kearns, *Dublin Voices: An Oral Folk History* (Dublin: Gill & Macmillan, 1998), p. 89

6 Willie Murphy.

7 Martin Mitten.

8 Michael Gill, in K.C. Kearns, *Dublin Pub Life and Lore: An Oral History* (Dublin: Gill & Macmillan, 1996), p. 222.

9 Interviewee 14.

10 Martin Mitten.

11 The importance of the tides to the port of Dublin is explained in Chapter 3.

12 Martin Mitten, *Dublin Voices*.

13 James Plunkett, 'The Plain People', *Collected Short Stories* (Dublin: Poolbeg Press, 1977), p. 273.

14 Some commentators (e.g. H.A. Gilligan, *A History of the Port of Dublin* (Dublin: Gill & Macmillan, 1988), p. 148) state that vessels could 'berth and sail at all stages of the tide' on the south quays, all the way to Butt Bridge, from 1913. This does not seem to be the effective reality, according to our research and docker testimony. See further discussion of conditions in the port in Chapter 3.

15 Interviewee 17.

16 Willie Murphy.

17 'Those Were The Days', *Waterfront*, November 1960, p. 9.

18 Confidential Minutes of Claims Committee, 16 April 1964, records of the Dublin Master Stevedore Association.

19 Willie Murphy.

20 'Those Were The Days', *Waterfront*, November 1960, p. 9.

21 Ibid.

22 Willie Murphy.

23 Martin Mitten.

24 H.A. Gilligan, *A History of the Port of Dublin* (Dublin: Gill & Macmillan, 1988) p. 197.

25 Willie Murphy.

26 Ibid.

27 'Dublin Harbour Notes, Nature's Sense of Humour, Seven Years at Sea', *The Irish Times*, January 1931, p. 4.

28 Willie Murphy.

29 Interviewee 11.

30 Tommy Bassett, interviewed in 1989 (Interview B16), North Inner City Folklore Project Archives, Dublin.

31 Trouble over cattle assignments reappears when we discuss industrial relations in Chapter 4.

32 Michael Donnelly.

33 Tommy Bassett, ibid.

34 See Graph 1 in the Appendix which compares trade on the deep-sea section with that on cross-channel.

35 Letter and enclosure, Joint Managing Director, Palgrave Murphy to Dublin Master Stevedores' Association, 10 March 1964.

36 Manuscript, 'Claims and Reports: Index 1', 1975–77, UCDA P299 Records of

the Association of Dublin Stevedores, UCD Archives, Dublin.

37 Martin Mitten.

38 'The Cross-Channel Docker Fifty Years Ago', *Waterfront*, December 1960, p. 7.

39 Ibid.

40 Ibid.

41 'Absentees: If a man left his job and did not return, he did not get his book back until the job was finished, no freight was to be paid to him that day, and if he was not replaced the Union got the freight.' Agreements and Rules Register, 2/3/1960, unpublished manuscript.

42 Paddy Robinson, North Inner City Folklore Project Archives, Dublin. UCDA P299 Records of the Association of Dublin Stevedores, UCD Archives, Dublin.

43 C.B. Barnes, *The Longshoremen* (New York: Russell Sage Foundation, 1915), pp. 39 & 53 emphasise the 'peculiar skill' required of the hooker-on.

44 T.S. Simey (ed.), *The Dockworker* (Liverpool: Liverpool University Press, 1956), p. 64. See also J. Lovell, *Stevedores and Dockers* (London: Macmillan, 1969), p. 53.

45 Nicknames and their sources are especially treated in Chapter 6.

46 John Brown, Branch Secretary, No. 2 Branch Office, letter of 9 February 1970 to L.F. McGinn.

47 Agreement made between the Association of Dublin Stevedores Ltd. and the Marine Port & General Workers Union, No. 2 Branch, Dockers' Section,

January 1982, UCDA P299 Records of the Association of Dublin Stevedores, UCD Archives, Dublin.

48 'Those Were the Days', *Waterfront*, November 1960, p. 9. The first 'forklifters', as this docker terms them, actually appeared in the port as early as the end of the 1940s. The first fork-lift trucks in Ireland were part of a six-truck order placed by Dublin Port and Dock Board in 1946 (Gilligan, p. 174). In the same year, new electric cranes were ordered to replace old cranes.

49 Martin Mitten.

50 *Deep Sea News*, Oct. 1975, pp. 4–5.

51 Martin Mitten.

52 Michael Donnelly.

53 Yarra Duffy, *The Heart of the City*, p. 49.

54 Martin Mitten.

55 Interviewee 12.

56 'Overtime snag in quick turn around time for ships', *The Irish Times*, 24 September 1964, p. 5.

57 Michael Donnelly.

Three

1 Jem Kiernan interviewed in 1994 (Interview K), North Inner City Folklore Project Archives, Dublin.

2 There is some controversy as to the size and importance of the settlement prior to the arrival of the Vikings, with some arguing that there is evidence of a stable population engaged in maritime trade prior to the Vikings, see George A. Little, *Dublin Before the Vikings* (Dublin: M.H. Gill and Son Ltd, 1957).

3 D. Moore, 'The Port of Dublin', *Dublin Historical Record*, XVI, 4 (1961), pp. 132, 344, 380–1, 424–5; J.W. De Courcy, *The Liffey in Dublin* (Dublin: Gill and Macmillan, 1996), p. 272; G. Little, *Dublin Before the Vikings* (Dublin: Gill, 1952).

4 D. Ó Cróinín, *Early Medieval Ireland* (Harlow: Longman, 1995), p. 270.

5 S. Conlin and J.W. De Courcy, *Anna Liffey, The River of Dublin* (Dublin: The O'Brien Press, 1988).

6 'The Continental/Irish trade remains largely unquantifiable' for the fourteenth and fifteenth centuries, 'except for the Bordeaux wine trade, and the balance of English and Continental trade in any one Irish port, let alone overall, is unknown', W. Childs, 'Ireland's Trade with England in the Later Middle Ages', *Irish Economic and Social History*, IX, 2 (1982), p. 33. See also J. Bernard, 'The Maritime intercourse between Bordeaux and Ireland c.1450–l520', *Irish Economic & Social History*, VII (1960), p. 14–16 and M. Lyons, 'Maritime Relations between Ireland and France c.1400–l630', *Irish Economic and Social History*, XXVIII (2000), pp. 1–24.

7 J.W. De Courcy, *The Liffey in Dublin* (Dublin: Gill & Macmillan, 1996), p. 272.

8 In 1716, the Ballast Office reported that it was 'about to can'y the bank of Kishes

up towards Moumey's Dock', ibid. p. 273.

9   Anthony Marmion, *The Ancient and Modern History of the Maritime Port of Ireland* (London: privately printed, 1860), pp. 243–4.

10 Ibid.

11 De Courcy, *The Liffey in Dublin*, p. 199; Joseph W. Hammond, 'George's Quay and Rogerson's Quay in the Eighteenth Century', *Dublin Historical Record*, V (1942–43), p. 47–8.

12 A. Halpin (ed.), *The Port of Medieval Dublin* (Dublin: Four Courts Press, 2000), p. 24.

13 A roadstead is a nautical term for a sheltered body of water where a ship can safely wait.

14 J.T. Gilbert, *Calendar of ancient records of Dublin, in the possession of the municipal corporation of that city* (Dublin: J.W. Allen, 1913), p.118.

15 Gerard Boate, 'A Natural History of Ireland' (1652) quoted in B.P. Bowen, 'The North Strand', *Dublin Historical Record*, XI (1950), p. 51.

16 De Courcy, *The Liffey in Dublin*, p. 243.

17 Andrew Yarranton quoted in C.Haliday & J.P. Prendergast, *The Scandinavian Kingdom of Dublin* (Dublin: M.H. Gill & son, 1884), p. 242.

18 C. Smith, *Dalkey: Society and Economy in a Small Medieval Irish Town* (Dublin: Irish Academic Press, 1996), pp. 50–3.

19 G.T. Gilbert, *Calendar of Ancient Records of Dublin, in the possession of the*

municipal corporation of that city Vol 1 (Dublin: John Dollard, 1889), p. 19.

20 Bill 'Wilo' Nelson, National Folklore Archive interview, transcript folio no. 1951, pp. 49–50.

21 Paddy 'Lyrics' Murphy, National Folklore Archive interview, transcript folio no. 1951, pp. 136–7. Archie Murphy, Lyric's father, teamed as a hobbler with George Gough.

22 'Famous Families of the Port. No. 1. The Murphy's', *Waterfront*, August 1960, p. 6.

23 Ibid.

24 'Hobbler's End', *A Social and Cultural History of Sandymount, Irishtown and Ringsend* (Dublin: Sandymount Community Services, 1993), p. 110.

25 John Jenkins in E. Malone, *In the Mind's Eye – memories of Dun Laoghaire* (Dublin: Dun Laoghaire Borough Heritage Society, 1991), p. 14.

26 Paddy 'Lyrics' Murphy, National Folklore Archive interview, transcript folio no. 1951, p. 134.

27 John Jenkins, in 'Malone, Emer' (1991) *In the Mind's Eye - memories of Dun Laoghaire*, Dún Laoghaire Borough Heritage Society, Dublin, p. 15.

28 Paddy 'Lyrics' Murphy, National Folklore Archive, p. 137; Wilo Nelson, National Folklore Archive, p. 52; 'Famous Families of the Port. No. 1. The Murphy', *Waterfront*, August 1960, p. 6.

29 Willie Murphy Junior, also Michael Donnelly.

30 For example, by James Connolly in 'Ireland Sober is Ireland Free?', *The Workers' Republic*, 15 July 1900, reprinted in O.D. Edwards and B. Ransom (eds), *James Connolly: Selected Political Writings* (New York: Grove Press, 1973), pp. 366–8.

31 Willie Murphy.

32 'One scarcely envies the job,' writes the anonymous author of Dublin Harbour Notes 'of the mate whose duty it is to engage the crew. His discriminating eyes wander over the miscellaneous crowd which stand before him. He notes the old men pathetically holding themselves as upright as possible in order to appear younger; he sees the glances of sailors, almost imploring, who are hoping to be able to rush home to their wives with the glorious news.' 'I've got a ship!'; 'Dublin Harbour Notes', *The Irish Times*, 18 February 1931, p. 4.

33 Interviewee 17.

34 The first known use of the word stevedore was in the *Massachusetts Spy* on 10 July 1788: 'stevedore, n.'. *OED Online* (Oxford: Oxford University Press, 2015), Web, 27 March 2015.

35 In some ports stowing and trimming, the usual work of a stevedore, carried more prestige than does discharge. Dublin port culture does not make such a rating.

36 Interviewee 14.

37 Ibid.

38 Interviewee 10.

39 J. Connell, 'Ireland Sober is Ireland Free?', *Workers' Republic*, p. 368.

40 Ibid. p. 367.

41 D. Greaves, *The Irish Transport and General Workers Union: The Formative Years 1909–1923* (Dublin: Gill and Macmillan, 1982), p. 79.

42 Interviewee 14.

43 Further information on the Carricks, in addition to our interviews, in 'Famous Families of the Port. No. 12. The Carricks', *Waterfront* January 1961, p. 4.

44 Census of Ireland, 1901, Irish National Archive; 'Famous Families of the Port. No. 3. The Goughs', *Waterfront*, Sept. 1960, p. 8, and 'Famous Families of the Port. No. 7. The Darcys', November 1960, p. 8.

45 Interviewee 11.

46 'Screwy Phrases and Nicknames', *Waterfront*, October 1960, p. 4.

47 Interviewee 10.

48 Willie Murphy.

49 Interviewee 17.

50 Martin Mitten.

51 Ibid.

52 Willie Murphy Junior.

53 Jem Kiernan interviewed in 1994 (Interview K), North Inner City Folklore Project Archives, Dublin.

54 'Famous Families of the Port. No. 16. The Shaws', *Waterfront*, May 1961 p. 9.

55 Interviewee 17.

56 Ibid.

57 Ibid.

58 Willie Murphy Junior.

59 Martin Mitten.

60 Willie Murphy Junior.

61 Herby Doyle.

62 Martin Mitten.

63 D. O'Carroll and S. Fitzpatrick, 'Hoggers, Lords and Railwaymen – A History of the Custom House Docks, Dublin', Custom House Docks Heritage Project (1996). See also Paddy Robinson, stevedore, in K.C. Kearns *Dublin Voices: An Oral Folk History* (Dublin: Gill & Macmillan, 1998).

64 Michael Donnelly, manuscript, 'Times Gone By', n.d.

65 'Ships From 14 Countries With Cargoes for Dublin', *The Irish Times*, 12 October 1946, p. 8.

66 Martin Mitten.

Four

1   Willie Murphy in K.C. Kearns, *Dublin Voices: An Oral Folk History* (Dublin: Gill & Macmillan, 1998), p. 119.

2   Des Geraghty, 'Beauty and Vitality', *The Irish Times*, 18 May 1976, p. vi.

3   A. Boyd, *The Rise of Irish Trade Unions* (Dublin: Anvil Books, 1985).

4   Willie Murphy Junior.

5   C.D. Greaves, *The Irish Transport And General Workers' Union: The Formative Years, 1909–1923* (Dublin: Gill & Macmillan, 1982), p. 21.

6   Ibid. p. 55.

7   Ibid. p. 153.

8   Ibid. p. 250.

9   Devine describes this as an attempt to set up a company union in competition with the ITGWU. Devine, RFS, *Historical Directory of Trade Unions: Volume 6* (Farnham: Ashgate, 2013), p. 169.

10 In 2007, the ATGWU merged with British union Amicus to become Unite.

11 S. Ward-Perkins, *Select Guide to Trade Union Records in Dublin: With Details of Unions Operating in Ireland to 1970* (Dublin: Irish Manuscripts Commission, 1996).

12 Martin Mitten.

13 Ibid.

14 Tom Byrne in M. Rush, *North of the Liffey, Reminiscences* (Dublin: North Inner City Folklore Project, 1999).

15 'Prompt Deliveries of coal: attack on transport workers', *The Irish Times*, 4 September 1925 p. 5; E. O'Connor, *A Labour History of Ireland 1825–1960* (Dublin: Gill & Macmillan, 1992) p. 140.

16 'Unity', *Waterfront*, September 1961, p. 2.

17 'Seamen's Strike Drags on', *The Irish Times*, 5 July 1933, p. 7.

18 'History of the Dispute. The Issue At Stake', *The Irish Times*, 14 July 1933, p. 7; P. Carter and J.B. Smethurst, *Historical Directory of Trade Unions: Volume 6* (Farnham: Ashgate, 2013), p. 184. The docker had established a short-lived union, the Dockers and Carters' Union, which then merged with the seamen in the IS&PWU. Ibid. p. 273.

19 F. Devine, *Organising History: A Century of SIPTU, 1909–2009* (Dublin: Gill & Macmillan, 2009), p. 272.

20 'Seamen and Port workers: Annual Meeting of New Union', *The Irish Times*, 14 August 1933, p. 5.

21 Quoted in Devine (2009), p. 273.

22 Ibid.

23 Ibid.

24 Commission on Vocational Organisation, *Report* (Dublin: Stationery Office, 1945), pp. 237–248.

25 'Shipping Dispute', *The Irish Times*, 27 January 1958, p. 3.

26 Carter and Smethurst, *Historical Directory of Trade Unions: Volume 6*, p. 184. 'At Work Again', *The Irish Times*, 24 February 1958, p. 5.

27 'Dublin Docker and Crews Go Back to Work', *The Irish Times*, 24 February 1958, p. 1.

28 Patrick Sweeney, 'On the Waterfront', *The Irish Times*, 13 January 1958, p. 6.

29 Carter and Smethurst, *Historical Directory of Trade Unions: Volume 6*, p. 186.

30 Interview with Des Brannigan by Conor McCabe, 22 January 2010. https://www.youtube.com/watch?v=OAFTLB0roBM. Accessed 23 January 2010.

31 Michael Donnelly (former president of the Marine Port & General Workers Union).

32 Patrick Sweeney, 'On the Waterfront', *The Irish Times*, 13 January 1958, p. 5. Trade union divisions were definitively buried when in 1990 the ITGWU merged with the Federated Workers of Ireland to form SIPTU. The MP&GWU merged with SIPTU in 1998.

33 Greaves, *The Irish Transport And General Workers' Union*, pp. 109, 272, 320.

34 L.F. Cain, 'The Irish Labour Movement Under the Free State and the Republic', Ph.D thesis, The Catholic University of America (1967), p. 153.

35 'Wage Increases', *Irish Independent*, 27 January 1966, p. 8.

36 'Union calls for Government Action in Port Dispute', *The Irish Times* 16 September 1963, p. 9.

37 'Docks strike ends after five weeks', *The Irish Times*, 7 February 1966.

38 Patrick Nolan, 'State of the Unions 1965: VI Problem of the Docks', *The Irish Times*, 10 November 1965, p. 10.

39 'Attitudes out of the past still inhibit mechanisation', *The Irish Times*, 22 September 1964.

40 'New Canteen At Port of Dublin', *Irish Press*, 30 September 1966, p. 7.

41 Lord Devlin, 'Final report of the committee of inquiry under the Rt. Hon. Lord Devlin into certain matters concerning the port transport industry'. Cmnd. 2734. (London: HMSO, 1965), p. 106.

42 Interviewee 17.

43 Ibid.

44 'Brighter Trade Outlook With End of Container Dispute', *The Irish Times*, 8 December 1961, p. 11; Des Geraghty, 'Labour Relations in the Port', *Irish Times*, 23 Aug. 1972, p. 5.

45 'Dublin Dock Strike Now affects 1000', *Irish Times*, 29 June 1946, p. 1.

46 Ibid.

47   Ceisteanna – Questions. Oral Answers. Dockers and Holidays (Employees) Act, Wednesday 25 October 1950.

48   Conditions of Employment Bill, 1944 – Second Stage. Wednesday, 1 March 1944.

49   'Dublin Docker's offer', *The Irish Times*, 8 July 1946, p. 1; 'Food and Produce Markets: Dublin', *The Irish Times*, 11 July 1946, p. 6.

50   'Uniform Wages for Workers Urged', *The Irish Times*, 11 July 1946, p. 6.

51   'Dock Strike End Now in Sight?', *The Irish Times*, 13 July 1946, p. 13.

52   'Liffey Strike Ended, Mr Lemass Thanked By Dockers', *The Irish Times*, 3 August 1946 p. 1.

53   One of the difficulties faced with resolving the strike was that as casual workers, the number of annual hours worked varied. Under a 1944 agreement cross-channel dockers were entitled to three, four, five or six days holidays a year, depending on how many hours they worked annually. Following the strike, this was increased by three days, so that they now were entitled to six, seven, eight or nine days a year. A particular sticking point was the situation of those known as 'casuals',very short-hours workers. The agreement stated that provided that a 'casual' worked more than 1,000 hours a year, he would be eligible for three days' holidays. Ibid.

54   'A harbour authority may either alone or in co-operation with any other body or bodies, take such steps as they think proper to improve conditions of employment of casual workers at their harbour and, in particular, may institute a system of registration of such workers and of confinement of employment to registered workers, but the harbour authority shall not exercise any of their powers under this section where such workers and their employers have themselves instituted any such system.' Harbour Act, 1946.

55   Interview with Michael Donnelly, former President of the Marine Port and General Workers Union.

56   Tommy Bassett, interviewed in 1989 (Interview B16), North Inner City Folklore Project Archives, Dublin.

57   Willie Murphy.

58   Kearns, *Dublin Voices: An Oral Folk History*, p. 192.

59   Report to the Minister of Industry and Commerce from the Labour Court Under Section 24 of the Industrial Relations Act, 1946, National Archives of Ireland.

60   'Unity', *Waterfront*, September 1961, p. 2.

61   M. Leonard, 'Learning the Ropes: The Politics of Dockland' in S. Wallman (ed.), *Social Anthropology of Work* (London: Academic Press, 1979), p. 44; Peter Turnbull, 'Dock strikes and the demise of the dockers occupational culture', *The Sociological Review*, 40 (1992), p. 294–318.

62   'The Docker and The Press', *Waterfront*, April 1961, p. 1.

63 Des Geraghty, 'Beauty and vitality', *The Irish Times*, 18 May 1976, p. vi.

64 Patrick Nolan, 'State of the Unions 1965: VI Problem of the Docks', *The Irish Times*, 10 November 1965, p. 10.

65 Turnbull, 'Dock Strikes and the Demise of the Dockers' "Occupational Culture",' p. 295

66 J. Hamark, 'Strikingly indifferent: the myth of militancy on the docks prior to World War II', *Labor History*, 54 (2013), pp. 271–85.

67 A workday is a multiple of days lost and number of workers involved. For example, if a strike only lasted one day, to be included in the statistics, at least ten people must have been out of work.

68 T. Brannick and A. Kelly, 'The Reliability and Validity of Irish Strike. Data and Statistics', *The Economic and Social Review*, 14, 4 (1983), pp. 249–58.

69 T. Brannick, F. Devine and A. Kelly, 'Social Statistics for Labour Historians: Strike Statistics, 1922–99', *Saothar*, 25 (2000), pp. 114–120. See Table Four in the Appendix.

70 Dock workers can be found in the Transport and Communications group. This is a broad group which also includes CIE the Irish public sector rail organisation. This employer was particularly strike prone in the period 1963–77 which means that the Transport and Communications group has a higher strike frequency which is caused by one particular group of workers, see D. Sapsford, 'Strike Activity in Ireland: An Economic Analysis of a Particular Aspect of Irish Industrial Relations', *Journal of the statistical and Social Inquiry Society of Ireland*, Vol. XXIV, Part 11 (1979/1980), pp. 29–68.

71 *Irish Press*, 28 January 1966.

72 Interview with Des Brannigan by Conor McCabe 22 January 2010. https://www.youtube.com/watch?v=OAFTLB0roBM 37.12 minutes. Accessed 23 January 2010.

73 'Unofficial Stoppages in the London Docks: Report of a Committee of Inquiry, Ministry of Labour and National Service' (London: HMSO, 1951), p. 7 quoted in C.J. Davis, *Waterfront Revolts: New York and London Dockworkers, 1946–61* (Urbana and Chicago: University of Illinois Press, 2003), p. 308.

74 *Irish Independent*, 5 September 1973.

75 Willie Murphy.

76 Interview with Willie Murphy. Such action is much more difficult to undertake these days as the 1990 Industrial Relations Act prohibits unions from taking part in these types of solidarity actions with other unions. http://www.irishstatutebook.ie/eli/1990/act/19/section/12/enacted/en/html#sec12. Accessed 23 January 2016.

77 Nellie Cassidy in K.C. Kearns, *Dublin Tenement Life* (Dublin: Gill & Macmillan Ltd, 2006), p. 88.

78 F. Devine, *Organising History: A Century of SIPTU, 1909–2009* (Dublin: Gill & Macmillan, 2009), p. 272.

79 E. O'Connor, *Reds and the Green: Ireland, Russia, and the Communist Internationals, 1919–43* (Dublin: UCD Press, 2005), p. 107.

80 Martin Mitten in K.C. Kearns, *Dublin Voices: An Oral Folk History* (Dublin: Gill & Macmillan, 1998), p. 23.

81 Interviewee 20.

82 'Bomb Thrown Into Dublin Coalyard', *The Irish Times*, 28 September 1925, p. 1.

83 Kearns, *Dublin Voices: An Oral Folk History*.

84 Ibid. p. 199.

85 Ibid.

86 Nellie Mc Cann in Kearns, *Dublin Voices: An Oral Folk History*, p. 413.

87 Tommy Bassett, *Dublin Streetlife and Lore*, Kindle Edition Loc 1495

88 Kearns, *Dublin Voices: An Oral Folk History*, p. 192.

89 Interview with Michael Foran. https://www.youtube.com/watch?v=7F3FwU8Xv6U. Accessed 20 January 2017.

90 C.J. Davis, *Waterfront Revolts: New York and London Dockworkers, 1946–61* (Urbana and Chicago: University of Illinois Press, 2003), p. 308; G. Brown, *Sabotage: a study in industrial conflict* (Nottingham: Spokesman, 1977).

91 'Beauty and vitality', *The Irish Times*, p. vi. 1976.

92 Interview with Patrick Bradley, Traffic Inspector with Dublin Port and Docks Board, conducted by Anita Ní Nualláin and Louise Tobin as part of their group thesis for the MLIS in UCD. https://www.youtube.com/watch?v=Fqmb1LR7lY0&list=PL-5jN0VjmpUowC7tC5wk50u-lYiSb6Z3i&index=5. Accessed 18 January 2017.

93 Willie Murphy.

94 A bob is slang for a shilling.

95 Interviewee 14.

96 Michael Donnelly.

97 Arthur Kelly, interviewed in 1992 (Interview K9), North Inner City Folklore Project Archives, Dublin.

98 James Plunkett, 'Plain People' in *Collected Short Stories* (Dublin: Poolbeg, 1977), p. 269.

99 Arthur Kelly, interviewed in 1992 (Interview K9), North Inner City Folklore Project Archives, Dublin.

100 Member of parliament.

101 Mr Barry Desmond, Labour Party Committee on Finance. - Vote 39: Labour (Resumed). Thursday, 6 November 1969. http://oireachtasdebates.oireachtas.ie/debates%20authoring/debateswebpack.nsf/takes/dail1969110600005. Accessed 17 January 2017.

102 Original letter and press clipping in UCDA P299 Records of the Association of Dublin Stevedores, UCD Archives, Dublin.

103 Tommy Bassett interviewed in 1989 (Interview B16), North Inner City Folklore Project Archives, Dublin.

104 Labour Court Report, Department of the Taoiseach, S14752a, 28 September 1951, National Archives of Ireland, Dublin.

105 On 16 May 1966, an agreement was reached between the Dublin Master Stevedore Association and the unions that Foremen/Checkers would receive a basic wage of £25 per week. Overtime on Monday to Friday to be paid at a rate of 18.9d an hour. Agreement and Rules Register, UCDA P299 Records of the Association of Dublin Stevedores, UCD Archives, Dublin.

106 Tommy Bassett interviewed in 1989 (Interview B16), North Inner City Folklore Project Archives, Dublin.

107 Manufacturing figures calculated for 1966 from Year Book of Statistics 1970, Geneva, International Labour Office see Table 19 Wages in manufacturing A. All Industries p. 565 and Table 13 hours of work in manufacturing A. All Industries p. 470; Docker's daily pay of £3. 6. shillings 7d led to a weekly basic pay of £15. 15 shillings and 5d, reported in *The Irish Times*, 'Dock strike ends after five weeks', 7 February 1966, p. 1.

108 See Table Five in the Appendix.

109 Agreement between Marine Port & General Worker's Union, Irish Transport Union and General Worker's Union, Worker Union of Ireland and The Society of Dublin Coal Importers, UCDA P299 Records of the Association of Dublin Stevedores, UCD Archives, Dublin.

110 Manuscript claims book, 14 August 1963, p. Unnumbered, UCDA P299 Records of the Association of Dublin Stevedores, UCD Archives, Dublin.

111 Interviewee 10.

112 Ibid.

113 Martin Mitten.

114 C. Eipper, *The Ruling Trinity: A Community Study of Church, State and Business in Ireland* (Aldershot: Gower Publishing Company, 1986). p. 21.

115 Legation of Netherlands to Department of External Affairs, Department of the Taoiseach, SII825, 1 March 1954, National Archives of Ireland, Dublin.

116 P. Nolan, 'They Melt Away', *The Irish Times*, 15 November 1966, p. 12.

117 This was agreed in 1969. Agreement and Rules Register, Records of the Association of Dublin Stevedores Ltd.

118 Dublin Port and Docks Board (1978) *Report on Stevedoring*, December, unpublished manuscript, UCDA P299 Records of the Association of Dublin Stevedores, UCD Archives, Dublin.

119 The practice of specialising in particular commodities was also common on London docks. John Lovell, *Stevedore & Dockers, A Study of Trade Unionism in the Port of London 1870–1914* (London: Palgrave Macmillian, 1969), p. 35.

120 The introduction of the Button system in 1946 and 1947 has been described in Chapter 1.

121 Arthur Kelly interviewed in 1992 (Interview K9), North Inner City Folklore Project Archives, Dublin.

Five

1   Willie Murphy.

2   5,000 tenement houses were home to 118,000 Dubliners. Michael Pierse, *Writing Ireland's Working Class: Dublin After O'Casey* (Basingstoke: Palgrave Macmillan, 2010), p. 13.

3   A. Wonneberger, *Waterfront, Culture and Community in Transition: Urban Regeneration of the Dublin Dockland* (Hamburg: University of Hamburg, 2010), p. 60.

4   1957 Dockers Register, partial document which lists 518 names from those beginning with A to those beginning with R and their associated address. On this list most parts of the city are represented, including the growing suburbs of Ballyfermot, Cabra, Crumlin, Donnycarney, Inchicore, Finglas, Rialto and Marino.

5   Ruth McManus, *Dublin, 1910–1940* (Dublin: Four Courts Press, 2002), p. 176.

6   Eoin O'Mahoney, 'The spatial distribution of municipal housing in Dublin city', Working Paper, Dublin (2016).

7   D. Fallon, 'The tenement crisis in Dublin, 1963', 26 August 2013. http://comeheretome.com/2013/08/26/the-tenement-crisis-in-dublin-1963/ Accessed 9 July 2014. Two children were also killed in 1936 following the collapse of a building on Asylum Yard off Pearse Street. 'City Children Killed', *The Irish Times*, 3 August 1936, p. 2.

8   'I wanna go home [*sic*] He longs for a home on City Quay', *Waterfront*, December 1962.

9   Willie Murphy.

10 Willie Murphy Junior.

11 A. Davin, 'Working or Helping? London Working-Class Children in the Domestic Economy' in J. Smith, I. Wallerstein and H. Evers (eds) *Households in the World-Economy* (London: Sage, 1984), p. 217.

12 Phyllis Nolan.

13 Martin Mitten.

14 For an explanation of the rules see Eilis Brady, *All in! All in!: a selection of Dublin children's traditional street-games with rhymes and music* (Michigan: University of Michigan, 1975), p. 153.

15 Interviewee 4.

16 *Comhairle le Leas Óige, Souvenir and Programme of Youth Week* (Dublin: CLLO 1944), p. 5; see also C. Holohan, 'A Powerful Antidote? Catholic Youth Clubs in the Sixties' in C. Cox and S. Riordan (eds), *Adolescence in Modern Irish History* (Basingstoke: Palgrave Macmillan, 2015), pp. 176–98.

17 Jimmy Kelly in T. Fagan and D.G. Hiney, *Larrier's personal recollections of more than a century of education at St. Laurence O'Toole's schools in Dublin's north inner city*, North Innercity Folklore Project, Dublin (1996), p. 27.

18 Fagan and Hiney, *Larrier's personal recollections*, p. 32.

19 T. Fagan and B. Savage, *Down by the dockside, Reminiscences from Sheriff Street*

(Dublin: North Inner City Folklore Project, 1995), p. 19.

20 Interviewee 20.

21 As told by Ellen Comiskey in Fagan and Hiney, *Larrier's personal recollections*, p. 4.

22 Wonneberger, *Waterfront, Culture and Community in Transition*, p. 70.

23 Interview 15.

24 Fagan and Savage, *Down by the dockside, Reminiscences from Sheriff Street*, p. 19.

25 Jane Gray, and Aileen O'Carroll, 'Education and Class Formation in the 20th Century: A retrospective qualitative longitudinal analysis', *Sociology*, 46 (2012), pp. 696–711.

26 General Mulcany, Committee of Finance, Vote 46 Primary Education, Tuesday, 2 June 1926. http://oireachtasdebates.oireachtas. ie/Debates%20Authoring/ DebatesWebPack.nsf/takes/ dail1942060200022?l Accessed 7 November 2016.

27 Dáil Debate, Ceisteanna – Questions – Oral Answers. Dublin Primary School Classes, Mr O'Malley. http:// oireachtasdebates.oireachtas.ie/ debates%20authoring/DebatesWebPack. nsf/takes/dail1967061300022. Accessed 7 November 2016.

28 In 1972 the age of compulsory attendance was raised to 15.

29 In the 1966 Irish census it is recorded that of 4,027 men who have their occupation as dock labourers, 199 left school before 14; 3,367 (83 per cent) at the age of 14. Available at

http://www.cso.ie/en/media/csoie/ census/census1966results/volume7/ C,1966,VOL,7,T16ab.pdf. Accessed 18 September 2013.

30 In the 1971 Irish census it is recorded that 3,068 men gave their occupations as dock labourers, 2,578 (84 per cent) had left school before the age of 15. Available at http://www.cso.ie/en/media/csoie/ census/census1971results/volume12/ C,1971,V12,T18ab.pdf. Accessed 18 September 2013.

31 Interview with deep-sea docker, John Walsh. http://tinyurl.com/octcfgl. Accessed 17 July 2015.

32 Interviewee 17.

33 Ibid.

34 May Hanaphy in K.C. Kearns, *Dublin Voices: An Oral Folk History* (Dublin: Gill and Macmillan, 1998), p. 91.

35 Willie Murphy.

36 Teddy Boy was a working-class youth subculture which first originated in England in the 1950s. For more on Teddy Boys in Ireland, see D. Fallon, 'Eccentrically dressed and jitterbugging away: Dublin's Teddy Boys in the 1950s', *Come Here To Me: Dublin Life and Culture*, 2013. https://comeheretome. com/2013/09/16/eccentrically-dressed- and-jitterbugging-away-dublins-teddy- boys-in-the-1950s/. Accessed 4 July 2016.

37 This was in Ringsend and was a social club for workers from the nearby Irish Glass Bottle factory. The hall ceased to be used in the 1960s and the factory closed in 2002.

38   Willie Murphy Junior.

39   Willie Murphy Junior. The tango 'Hernandos Hideaway', from the musical *Pajama Game*, was a hit tune in 1955.

40   Herby Doyle.

41   Willie Murphy.

42   Interviewee 7.

43   Annie Murphy.

44   Interviewee 20.

45   Interviewee 7.

46   Herby Doyle.

47   Interviewee 7.

48   'Angela McFarland remembers her early married life', Lifescapes: Mapping Dublin Lives, Item #236. http://bridge-it.tchpc.tcd.ie/items/show/236. Accessed 30 November 2016.

49   Willie Murphy.

50   Interviewee 15.

51   Willie Murphy.

52   Fagan and Hiney, *Larrier's personal recollections*, p. 31.

53   Muldowney *The Second World War and Irish Women: An Oral History* (Dublin: Irish Academic Press, 2007), p. 150.

54   J. Kok, *Rebellious Families: Household Strategies and Collective Action in the 19th and 20th Centuries* (Oxford: Berghahn Books, 2002), p. 117.

55   Emmet Larkin, *James Larkin: Irish Labour Leader, 1876–1947* (London: Routledge and Kegan, 1965), p. 163. See Chapter 6 for further discussion of alcohol.

56   North Dublin Inner City Folk Project, interview with Mrs Doody, 16 August 1997.

57   Maria Luddy, 'Working Women, Trade Unionism and Politics in Ireland 1830–1945' in F. Lane and D. O'Drisceoil (eds) *Politics and the Irish Working Class, 1830–1945* (Basingstoke: Palgrave Macmillan, 2005), pp. 44–61.

58   Though it is more likely that this is a clerical error.

59   Joe Murphy, shipwright, in Kearns *Dublin Voices: An Oral Folk History*, p. 84

60   M.E. Daly, *Industrial Development and Irish National Identity, 1922–39* (Syracuse, New York: Syracuse University Press, 1992), p. 123.

61   K.C. Kearns, *Dublin's Lost Heroines, Mammies and Grannies in a Vanished City* (Dublin: Macmillan, 2004), p. 70.

62   Patricia Cafferkey, 'Jacob's Women Workers during the 1913 Lockout', *Saothar*, 16 (1991), pp. 118–29. Fourteen per cent of the women workers in Jacob's Biscuit Factory stayed on strike during the 1913 Lockout.

63   Luddy, *Working Women, Trade Unionism and Politics in Ireland*, p. 52. For more information about the women munition workers see 'Did your Granny make bombs in World War One? The story of the Dublin Dockyard War Munitions Factory' by the East Wall History Group, 9 May 2016 at http://eastwallforall.ie/?p=2841. Accessed 26 August 2016.

64   Luddy, *Working Women, Trade Unionism and Politics in Ireland 1830–1945*, p. 52.

65   D. Bennett, 'Maggie Feathers and Missie Reilly: hawking life in Dublin's City

Quay', in C. Curtin, M. Kelly and L. O'Dowd (eds), *Culture and Ideology in Ireland* (Galway: Galway University Press, 1984), p. 146.

66   P. McCaffery, 'Jacob's women during the 1913 Lockout', *Saothar*, 16 (2013), pp. 1–12.

67   Interview with Betty Dempsey conducted by Turtle Bunbury, available at http://www.turtlebunbury. com/interviews/interviews_ireland/ vanishing_3/interviews_ireland_betty_ dempsey.html. Accessed 18 July 2013.

68   Kearns, *Dublin Voices: An Oral Folk History*, p. 255.

69   Data from a sample of the 1911 census for the South Dock, Trinity Ward or Pembroke East DED area. Occupations given for wives, daughters or sisters of males who gave their occupations as dockers, quay labourers, labourer on docks, labourer on quays, electric crane drivers, steam crane man, winch driver, labourer/hobbler or stevedores. In 1926 only 5.6 per cent of married women were in paid employment in the Irish Free State. M.E. Daly, *Women and Work in Ireland* (Dundalk: Dundalgan Press, 1997), p. 41.

70   May Hanaphy in Kearns, *Dublin Voices: An Oral Folk History*, p. 236.

71   Maureen Boyd in Kearns, *Dublin Voices: An Oral Folk History*, p. 248.

72   Interviewee 7.

73   Ibid.

74   Historian Mary Daly reports 'in 1955 … 28 per cent of children born to unskilled labourers in Dublin were the sixth or subsequent child'. M.E. Daly, 'Marriage, Fertility and Women's Lives in Twentieth-Century Ireland (c.1900–1970)', *Women's History Review*, 15 (2006), p. 579.

75   Muldowney *The Second World War and Irish Women: An Oral History*, p. 134.

76   Interview with Betty Dempsey whose brothers worked on the docks, conducted by Turtle Bunbury, available at http://www.turtlebunbury. com/interviews/interviews_ireland/ vanishing_3/interviews_ireland_betty_ dempsey.html. Accessed 18 July 2013.

77   Interview with May Malone conducted by Turtle Bunbury, available at http:// www.turtlebunbury.com/interviews/ interviews_ireland/interviews_ireland_ may_malone.html. Accessed 18 July 2013.

78   Phyllis Nolan.

79   Willie Martin Junior.

80   Fagan and Savage, *Down by the Dockside, Reminiscences from Sheriff Street.* p. 19.

81   Willie Murphy, also interviewee 17.

82   Jem Kelly.

83   Martin Mitten.

84   The interviewee is referring to marital break-up as up to 1995 it was not legally possible to obtain a divorce in Ireland.

85   Muldowney, *The Second World War and Irish Women: An Oral History*, p. 58.

86   Interviewee 17.

87   Rex Mac Gall, 'All along the Waterfront, Steady Work for Dockers', *The Irish Press*, 23 October 1950, p. 2.

88 Martin Mitten.

89 Ibid.

90 K.C. Kearns, *Dublin Tenement Life* (Dublin: Gill & Macmillian, 1995), p. 31.

91 Kearns, *Dublin's Lost Heroines, Mammies and Grannies in a Vanished City*, p. 30.

92 Phyllis Nolan.

93 Kearns, *Dublin Tenement Life*, p. 63.

94 See also Cormac Ó Gráda, *Jewish Ireland in the Age of Joyce: A Socioeconomic History* (Princeton: Princeton University Press, 2006), pp. 63 and 223.

95 Interview with Phyllis Nolan.

96 Martin Mitten.

97 Kearns, *Dublin Tenement Life*, p. 136.

98 See also discussion of working-class midwifes in Muldowney *The Second World War and Irish Women: An Oral History*, p. 159. The Midwives Act, passed in 1917 and, strengthened by similar acts in 1931 and 1934, made it illegal for an untrained person to assist at birth if a trained person was available. Handywomen additionally helped out in the house and with care of the other children.

99 Annie Murphy.

100 Anna Davin reported on similar networks in London: 'The family-based household economy in the late nineteenth-century London working class was based on a pooling of resources by all members. Most important was labour, cash and kind.' Davin, 'Working or Helping? London Working-class

101 Reported by our interviews, and by Wonneberger, *Waterfront, Culture and Community in Transition*, p. 146.

102 Reported by many of our interviewees and by Kearns, *Dublin Voices: An Oral Folk History*, p. 81.

103 Interviewee 12.

104 Interviewee 19.

105 Interviewee 17.

106 Thanks to Declan P. Byrne for information on *Waterfront*.

Six

1   Martin Mitten.

2   Willie Murphy.

3   Strictly speaking, the Liffey does have some islands in its course through the capital, at the Islandbridge stretch, but they are considered to be on the southside.

4   Larry Pullen, 'Ringsend Boatbuilding', *News Four* (Summer 1998), p. 20.

5   Tommy Bassett, interviewed in 1989 (Interview B16), North Inner City Folklore Project Archives, Dublin.

6   *Waterfront*, October 1961, p. 7. Among the deep-sea social organisers of the period were Brendan Brophy, Christy Byrne, Jack Hawkins, Willie Hickey, Martin Mitten, Willie Murphy and Dick O'Reilly.

7   Willie Murphy.

8   See interview with Martin Mitten in Kearns, *Dublin Voices: An Oral Folk*

children in the Domestic Economy', p. 229.

History. A number of our interviewees also referred to dockers' capacity for argument and debate.

9 Typescript records of the Dublin Master Stevedore's Association, n.d. UCDA P299 Records of the Association of Dublin Stevedores, UCD Archives, Dublin.

10 May Corbally in Kearns, *Dublin Tenement Life*, p. 67.

11 According to local ethnographer Terry Fagan, North Inner City Folklore Project.

12 Docker Tommy 'Duckegg' Kirwan from Kearns, *Dublin Tenement Life*, p. 67. Robin Hood actions in the docklands occurred in the past too. In the eighteenth century, ship cargoes might be looted and distributed by bands of unknown locals. J. Hammond, 'George's Quay and Rogerson's Quay in the Eighteenth Century', *Dublin Historical Record*, 5, 2 (1943), p. 48.

13 Department of Industry and Commerce Memo for Government, Appendices. Department of the Taoiseach, S11825, 15 March 1952, National Archives of Ireland, Dublin.

14 Dockers referred to Alexandra Basin as 'The Pond'.

15 Michael Donnelly (Interview D15), North Inner City Folklore Project Archives, Dublin. A number of our interviewees also referred to dockers singing while at work.

16 Sadie Fitzsimons of Ringsend was the little girl; St Andrews Heritage Project & FÁS, *Along the Quays and Cobblestones* (Dublin: St Andrews Heritage Group, 1992), p. 43.

17 Hammond, 'George's Quay', p. 41. Other pub names occurring along the same quays were The Sugar Loaf, Tobin's, Dooley's and the Ferryman.

18 Interviewee 17.

19 Handwritten manuscript, North Inner City Folklore Project archives.

20 From the manuscript application of Daniel Anthony Morony, 81–82 Pearse Street, District Court Licensing Office, Four Courts. Regulations are in Liquor Licensing Laws of Ireland, pp. 139–41. Thanks to Eamon Casey and Kevin McCormick for some of this information.

21 *Waterfront*, May 1962, p. 3.

22 As overheard by Martin Mitten. From the early 1960s, Dockers were paid by cheque.

23 See interview with Tom Byrnes in Kearns *Dublin Voices: An Oral Folk History*, p. 80.

24 Martin Mitten.

25 Intervewee in Wonneberger *Waterfront Culture and Community in Transition*, p. 147.

26 Hammond, 'George's Quay', p. 47.

27 Some sources state that such barrings of dockers were rare; others (e.g. Larry Pullen, 'The Cabin', *News Four* (Summer 1998), p. 13) indicate that they were frequent.

28 James O'Toole (nicknames: Sonny, Nutsy) interviewed in 1990 (Interview

03), North Inner City Folklore Project Archives, Dublin.

29 Martin Mitten; Willie Murphy.

30 Martin Mitten.

31 Jim Brennan, 'Dockers want to be paid daily', *Sunday Independent*, 19 June 1966, p. 5.

32 'Liffey Wanderers: Centenary Year, 1885–1985' (privately printed, 1985).

33 Michael Donnelly, 'Dublin Dockers Sporting Superstars', papers of Michael Donnelly, archives of the Dublin Dockworkers Preservation Society.

34 Captained by the ubiquitous Martin Mitten; *Waterfront*, May 1961, p. 3. Deep-sea and cross-channel section dockers organised separate competing teams.

35 'Unsung Heroes of Dockland', *Waterfront*, January 1961, p. 7.

36 RO/611 'Record of "Q" Coy, G.H.Q./ A.S.U', Irish Military Archives, Dublin.

37 A. Selula, *Fish Story* (Dusseldorf: Richter Verlag, 2002).

38 McKenna, J. 2011. *Guerrilla Warfare in the Irish War of Independence, 1919–1921*. Jefferson: McFarland, p. 59; http://comeheretome.com/2013/06/17/raiding-the-defiance/. Accessed 20 July 2015.

39 Ibid.

40 Greaves, *Irish Transport and General Workers' Union*, p. 272.

41 Bureau of Military History, 1913–21. Statement by Witness, Document No. W.S. 585. Statement by Frank Robbins. Matthew 19:24, Irish Military Archives, Dublin.

42 Greaves, *Irish Transport and General Workers' Union*, p. 272 and 293; E. O'Connor, *Syndicalism in Ireland* (Cork: Cork University Press, 1988), p. 87.

43 H. Mc Guinness, *Daniel Courtney, The Grandfather of the Irish Citizen Army* (2015). http://eastwallforall.ie/?p=2001. Accessed 20 July 2015.

44 Police Report, 'Re./Rescue of three men who were gassed on S.S. *Amasa Delano* at Dublin Port on 12 November 1947.' Dublin Dockworker Society Collection. http://www.bluemelon.com/ alanmartin/williambillydeans#page-0/ photo-5188115 Accessed 17 July 2015.

45 As overheard by Martin Mitten.

46 Interviewee 4.

47 G. Mars, 'Dock Pilferage', in P. Rock and M. McIntosh (eds) *Deviance and Social Control* (London: Tavistock, 1974), p. 96.

48 James O'Toole interviewed in 1990 (Interview 03).

49 Interviewee 15.

50 Willie Murphy.

51 According to oral history interviews with residents of Dublin Dockland Communities in Wonneberger, *Waterfront Culture and Community in Transition*, p. 147.

52 Ibid.

53 Martin Mitten.

54 Ibid.

55 Ibid.

56 The origins of this Dublin slang may be related to the more common meaning of the term. To bunker is to refuel a ship's

fuel tanks or to store fuel for a ship. The phrase originates from when coal for steamships was stored in bunkers.

57 Interview quoted in Wonneberger, *Waterfront Culture and Community in Transition*, p. 147.

58 Margaret Kenny of Abercorn Road and New Wapping Street, National Folklore Archive interview, manuscript no. 1991, pp. 163–7.

59 'Stolen Combines freed for Harvest', *The Irish Times*, 28 August 1964, p.8. A machinery salesman from Kildare was charged with the theft and the combine harvesters were released by the court to the original purchaser, a Wexford farmer. The *Sunday Independent* also reported on the theft of combine harvesters in 1969 from Alexandra Basin on a Sunday morning, but no detail is given in the article and there are no other reports of this theft so the accuracy of this report is unclear. Michael Brophy, 'Great Port Robbery, what can be done?', *Sunday Independent*, 21 May 1972, p. 8.

60 'Nickel disappears from warehouse', *The Irish Times*, 31 July 1970, p. 4.

61 Berkeley Vincent [Director, George Bell Ltd.], 'Opinion', *Deepsea News*, Oct, 1975, p. 8.

62 'Ammunition stolen at Dublin Docks', *The Irish Times*, 10 May 1962, p. 4.

63 Interviewee 12.

64 Interviewee 15.

65 Overheard by Willie Murphy.

66 Willie Murphy.

67 For example, a District Court conviction of a docker on a pilfering-related charge for being in possession of six tins of fruit cocktail to the value of ten shillings resulted in a sentence of five months' imprisonment. 'Jail Sentence for Receiving', *The Irish Times*, 17 September 1964, p. 8.

68 'Pilfering at Dublin Docks', *Evening Herald*, 19 June 1967, p. 2.

69 UCDA P299 Records of the Association of Dublin Stevedores, UCD Archives, Dublin.

70 'Pilfering at Dublin Docks', *Evening Herald*. 19 June 1967, p. 2.

71 Ibid.

72 'General fall in marine premiums', *The Irish Times*, 13 March 1957, p. 4.

73 'Goods still in transit after docks dispute', *The Irish Times*, 26 March 1958, p. 4.

74 'Record Year for losses at sea', *The Irish Times*, 9 June 1964, p. 1.

75 'New patrol for docks', *Irish Press*, 19 May 1965, p. 4.

76 'Pilfering in Dublin Dockland', *Sunday Independent*, 22 Aug. 1971, p. 5.

77 This report was drawn up by a committee made up of the Dublin Master Stevedores Association, Dublin Port Area Association, Dublin Port and Docks board, The Irish and British Traffic Association and the Irish Institute of Marine Underwriters.

78 Chairman of the Irish Institute of Marine Underwriters, report in 'Pilferage at Port', *Irish Independent*, 18 June 1970, p. 9.

79 Martin Mitten.

80 Chairman of the Irish Institute of Marine Underwriters, 'Pilferage at Port'.

81 Report on contents of a dossier on theft prepared by the Dublin Crime Prevention Branch. Michael Brophy, 'Great Port Robbery, what can be done?', *Sunday Independent*, 21 May 1972, p. 8.

82 'Whiskey crates in court room, dockers on theft charge', *Irish Press*, 25 June 1968, p. 4.

83 For commodities stolen see Michael Brophy, 'Great Port Robbery: What Can Be Done?'. On the porousness of the docks see the editorial page, 'Dock Thieves', *The Irish Times*, 19 April 1921, p. 4.

84 These stories and the following told by Michael Donnelly in T. Fagan, B. Savage and North Inner City Folklore Project, *Down by the Dockside: Reminiscences from Sheriff Street* (Dublin: North Inner City Folklore Project, 1995), p. 6.

85 'Big Probe of Docks Racket, Men at work got dole?', *Evening Press*, 27 June 1971, p. 1.

86 As told by docker Michael Donnelly in Fagan, Savage and North Inner City Folklore Project *Down by the Dockside: Reminiscences from Sheriff Street*, p. 6.

87 Interview with deep-sea docker John Walsh conducted by Neasa McHale and Ann Wade as part of their group thesis for the MLIS in UCD, http://tinyurl.com/octcfgl. Accessed 17 July 2015.

88 Thanks also to Norman Byrne, deep-sea docker, for supplying a copy of an anonymous manuscript list of Ringsend nicknames, most believed to be those of dockers. Some of these appear with asterisks here. Many other informants have also provided docker nicknames for us. 'Screwy Phrases and Nicknames', by 'Professor McCarthy', *Waterfront*, October 1960, p. 4, has further nickname information, as does Margaret Biggs, 'Dedicated to the Late Lyrics Murphy', *News Four*, Summer 1998, p. 4. The North Inner City Folklore Archives were also helpful. We have drawn on all sources for nicknames throughout, most of them known to be deep-sea docker titles.

89 H. Hamilton, *Headbanger* (London: Vintage, 1977), p. 94.

90 Michael Donnelly.

91 The current generation, including the present holder of the Abber title, have a theory that the name stemmed from a mispronunciation by the original Abber.

92 Sandymount Community Services, *Social and Natural History of Sandymount, Irishtown, and Ringsend* (Dublin: Sandymount Community Services, 1993), pp. 110–12.

93 Interviewee 7.

Seven

1 Michael Donnelly.

2 James Joyce, 'An Encounter', *Dubliners* (Hertfordshire: Wordsworth Classics, 1993), pp. 9–16.

3   James Plunkett, *Strumpet City* (London: Arrow Books, 1978); Plunkett, 'The Plain People', p. 273.

4   In 2016, 663,732 Lo/Lo (Lift on, Lift off) units arrived in Dublin and 944,531 Ro/Ro (Roll on/ Roll off) units, which includes containers shipped on mafi trailers, cassettes or slave trailers. Dublin Port Company, *Dublin Port 2016 Full Year and Q4 Throughput Statistics* (2016).

5   'Orange, Grapes For Dublin', *The Irish Times*, 3 April 1946, p. 13.

6   'Ships Due Tomorrow', *The Irish Times*, 5 January 1950, p. 4.

7   'Dublin Shipping Movements', *The Irish Times*, 4 March 1960, p. 12.

8   Interviewee 11.

9   'It was put out to us that we were inferior. When we would apply for jobs, our address would be against us. And if you went out into the outer life then, you would be wondering, am I carrying a stigma from where I come from? That was there, let's not kid ourselves. You could feel it. This was very unfortunate.' (C81c.). Wonneberger, *Waterfront,*

    Culture and Community in Transition, 2010 p. 157.

10 'Portrait of Docker', *Waterfront*, November 1961 p. 2; 'Tale of A Tomato, by Tarps', *Waterfront*, August 1961, p. 8.

11 Tommy Bassett in K.C. Kearns, *Dublin Pub Life and Lore: An Oral History* (Dublin: Gill & Macmillan Ltd, 1996), p. 80.

12 Willie Murphy.

13 Willie Murphy Junior.

14 E.P. Thompson, 'Time and Work Discipline', *Customs in Common* (Middlesex: Penguin, 1991), p. 396.

15 'The Next Function', *Waterfront*, October 1966, p. 9.

16 Tommy Bassett in K.C. Kearns *Dublin Street Life and Lore: An Oral History* (Dublin: Glendale, 1991), p. 80.

17 Interviewee 20.

18 Tommy Bassett in Kearns, (1991) *Dublin Street Life and Lore: An Oral History*, p. 85.

19 'The Branch Committee', *Waterfront*, April 1961, p. 5.

INDEX

Hannigan, Ben 200–1
Harbour Act (1946) 123
Harbour Police 211
hardship money 134
hatchway man 66, 70
Hawkins, John 69, 201, 233
Hawkins, John, Snr **224**
health hazards 71–2; asbestos and 72; dust and
    71–2; phosphorus and 71; sulphur ammonia
    and 146
Heitons 14, 66, **116–17**, 132
heroism 204–6, 217–18
Hickey, William (Bill) 186
hides 56, 78, 82
Hilton Brothers mattress factory 171
hobblers 9, 86–7, 89, 92, 95, 204
hobbling 9, 77, 87–8, 89, 92, 97
Hogg, Martin 103
hoggers 106, 199
Holidays (Employees) Act (1939) 121
hooker on 50, 65, 66
horses 56–7; carts and **28–9**
'hot money' 143
housing: public housing projects 153–4; relocation,
    dockers and 155; *see also* tenements
hoveller 87
Howth Pipe Band 120
Hughes, John 89

idleness 111, 126
importers' personnel 106
Indian sailors 212–13
industrial action 111, 133, 140; *see also* strikes
industrial unrest 118; docklands and 124; English
    ports and 125–6; strike breakers and 129–30
'inside men' 8, 60, 65
interlopers 28
intra-union conflict 115, 116, 118, 130–1, 227
Ireland's Eye 83
Irish Citizen Army 202, 204, 218
Irish Dockers and Workers Union 113
Irish Independent 119
Irish Institute of Marine Underwriters 211

Irish Journal of Labour History 3
Irish Labour History Society 234
Irish Military Archives 7
Irish Press 137, 178, 197
'Irish rheumatism' 73, 217
Irish Sea 84
Irish Seamen's and Port Workers' Union (ISPWU)
    30, 58, 115–16, **132**, **136**, **139**
Irish Seamen's Union 115, 116, 118
Irish Shipping Limited 118
Irish Shipping Owners Association 116, 118
Irish Times 6, 118, 126, 222; dockers' strike (1966)
    119–20; 'Dublin Harbour Notes' 56; ISPWU
    115, 116; ship arrivals (1963) 225
Irish Trade Union Congress 122–3
Irish Transport and General Workers' Union
    (ITGWU) 30, 113, **115**, 118, 120; WUI and
    115, 130–1
Irish Volunteers 202
Irish Women Workers Union 170–1

Jacob's Biscuit Factory 163, 170, 172, **182**
Jealous of Me (skiff) 89, 97
Jewmen 181–2, 183, 184
job satisfaction 73–4, 98
Joyce, James 165, 221

Kearns, Kevin C. 7, 170, 181
Kelly, Arthur 136, 137, 147
Kelly, Jem 27, 171
Kelly, Patsy 38
Kennedy, John P. 203
Kennedy's pub 195, 200, 222
kickbacks 8, 25–6, 28, 35, 96
Kiernan, Jem 100–1, **153**
Kiernan, Sailor 90, 200
Kinch family 89

Labour Court 137–8; report 6, 124
Labour Exchange 214
Lambay 83
Lane, Fintan 3, 4
Larkin, James (Jim) 95, 112, 113–14, 115, 168